MULTICULTURAL EDUCATION SERIES

James A. Banks, Series Editor

(continued)

Creating a Home in Schools

Sustaining Identities for Black, Indigenous, and Teachers of Color

FRANCISCO RIOS
A LONGORIA

TEACHERS COLLEGE PRESS

TEACHERS COLLEGE | COLUMBIA UNIVERSITY

NEW YORK AND LONDON

Published by Teachers College Press,® 1234 Amsterdam Avenue, New York, NY 10027

Library of Congress Cataloging-in-Publication Data

Names: Rios, Francisco, 1956– author. | Longoria, A., author.
Title: Creating a home in school : sustaining identities for black,
  indigenous, and teachers of color / Francisco Rios, A. Longoria.
Description: New York, NY : Teachers College Press, [2021] | Series:
  Multicultural education series | Includes bibliographical references and
  indx.
Identifiers: LCCN 2020055863 (print) | LCCN 2020055864 (ebook) | ISBN
  9780807765272 (hardcover) | ISBN 9780807765265 (paperback) | ISBN
  9780807779521 (ebook)
Subjects: LCSH: Minority teachers—United States. | Teaching—Vocational
  guidance—United States. | Culturally relevant pedagogy—United States.
  | Multicultural education—United States. | Identity (Psychology)
Classification: LCC LB2844.1.M56 R56 2021 (print) | LCC LB2844.1.M56
  (ebook) | DDC 371.10089—dc23
LC record available at https://lccn.loc.gov/2020055863
LC ebook record available at https://lccn.loc.gov/2020055864

ISBN 978-0-8077-6526-5 (paper)
ISBN 978-0-8077-6527-2 (hardcover)
ISBN 978-0-8077-7952-1 (ebook)

Printed on acid-free paper
Manufactured in the United States of America

You are not fifteen, or twelve, or seventeen—
You are a hundred wild centuries

And fifteen, bringing with you
In every breath and in every step

Everyone who has come before you,
All the yous that you have been,

The mothers of your mother,
The fathers of your father.

If someone in your family tree was trouble,
A hundred were not:

The bad do not win—not finally,
No matter how loud they are.

We simply would not be here
If that were so.

You are made, fundamentally, from the good.
With this knowledge, you never march alone.

You are the breaking news of the century.
You are the good who has come forward

Through it all, even if so many days
Feel otherwise. But think:

When you as a child learned to speak,
It's not that you didn't know words—

It's that, from the centuries, you knew so many,
And it's hard to choose the words that will be your own.

From those centuries we human beings bring with us
The simple solutions and songs,

The river bridges and star charts and song harmonies
All in service to a simple idea:

That we can make a house called tomorrow.
What we bring, finally, into the new day, every day,

Is ourselves. And that's all we need
To start. That's everything we require to keep going.

Look back only for as long as you must,
Then go forward into the history you will make.

Be good, then better. Write books. Cure disease.
Make us proud. Make yourself proud.

And those who came before you? When you hear thunder,
Hear it as their applause.

—"A House Called Tomorrow," *Alberto Rios*

Contents

Series Foreword

Francisco Rios and A Longoria, the authors of this innovative, interesting, and compassionate book, believe that Black, Indigenous, and Teachers of Color (BI-TOCs), because of the distinctive cultural characteristics and insights acquired during their socialization in marginalized communities, can play an essential and critical role in the transformation of schools to make them caring and intellectually enriching spaces for students. Although Rios and Longoria believe that BITOCs can help to transform schools, they perceptively point out that teachers alone cannot change schools in substantial ways. In addition to BITOCs, deep structural changes must be made in schools in order to substantially change them in ways that will make them culturally sustaining and affirming for students from diverse racial, ethnic, cultural, and linguistic groups. The major aim of this book, which is creatively constructed using the metaphor of the rooms of a house, is to enable Teachers of Color to become effective culturally responsive and affirming instructors. Rios and Longoria make the important point that Teachers of Color are needed not only to enhance the academic achievement of students of color, but also to help mainstream White students attain a liberating and pluralistic education, which is indispensable for survival in a diverse, changing, and complex world.

Rios and Longoria contend that one of the reasons they wrote this book and designed it for Black, Indigenous, and Teachers of Color is because most teacher education textbooks, as well as teacher education programs and curricula, focus on the needs and aspirations of White mainstream middle-class or middle-class–aspiring teacher education candidates. The authors also believe that the content, concepts, and personal reflections included in this book will help BITOC teacher education candidates attain knowledge, attitudes, and skills that will enable them to become effective teachers who can build upon their ethnic and racial experiences and characteristics to make their classrooms culturally responsive and sustaining. The authors, who grew up in a Mexican American family (Rios) and a mixed Mexican American/Chinese family (Longoria), insert their cultural experiences into the text using "testimonies" (*testimonios*) to enrich it and to illustrate how readers can use their ethnic and cultural experiences to enhance their teaching. Rios and Longoria view testimonies as "counter narratives," which are important components of Critical Race Theory.

It is important to increase the percentage of Teachers of Color in U.S. class-rooms and to have targeted goals for their training because of the wide gap between the racial and ethnic characteristics of teachers and students. Most of the nation's teachers are White; the majority of students now attending American schools are students of color. During the 2015–2016 school year, 81% of the teachers in U.S. traditional public schools were White; 71% in public charter schools were White (National Center for Education Statistics, 2019). The percentage of students of color, immigrant-origin students, and students who speak a first language other than English is growing significantly within the nation's public schools, which should make increasing the percentage of Teachers of Color in U.S. schools a high priority.

American classrooms are experiencing the largest influx of immigrant students since the beginning of the 20th century. Approximately 12.6 million new immigrants—documented and undocumented—settled in the United States in the years from 2000 to 2016 (Zong et al., 2018). Less than 10% came from nations in Europe. Most came from Mexico and from nations in South Asia, East Asia, Latin America, the Caribbean, and Central America. Although African immigrants make up a small part of the U.S. immigrant population (over 2 million in 2015), they increased by 41% from 2000 to 2013 (Anderson, 2017). In 2018, the largest number of U.S. immigrants came from China (149,000 people), India (129,000), Mexico (120,000), and the Philippines (46,000). In most years since 2009, more Asian immigrants have come to the United States than Hispanic immigrants (Budiman, 2020). The influence of an increasingly diverse population on U.S. schools, colleges, and universities is and will continue to be enormous.

Schools in the United States are more diverse today than they have been since the early 1900s, when a multitude of immigrants entered the United States from southern, central, and eastern Europe (C. A. M. Banks, 2005). In 2017, the National Center for Education Statistics estimated that students from ethnic minority groups made up more than 52% of the students in prekindergarten through 12th grade in U.S. public schools, an increase from 39.2% in 2001. Latinxs made up 25% of the children in the United States in 2017; African Americans, 15%; Asian and Pacific Island children, 6%; and American Indians, 1% (Annie E. Casey Foundation, 2019).

Language and religious diversity is also increasing in the U.S. student population. A Center for Migration Studies publication estimated that 21.6% of Americans aged 5 and above (65.5 million) spoke a language other than English at home in 2016 (Camarota & Ziegler, 2017). This percentage has doubled since 1990, and almost tripled since 1980. The significant number of immigrants from nations such as India and China also has greatly increased religious diversity in the United States. Harvard professor Diana L. Eck (2001) calls the United States the "most religiously diverse nation on earth" (p. 4). Islam is now the fastest growing religion in the United States, as well as in several European nations such as France, the United Kingdom, and the Netherlands (J. A. Banks, 2009b; O'Brien, 2016).

The major purpose of the Multicultural Education Series is to provide pre-service educators, practicing educators, graduate students, scholars, and policymakers with an interrelated and comprehensive set of books that summarizes and analyzes important research, theory, and practice related to the education of ethnic, racial, cultural, and linguistic groups in the United States, as well as the education of mainstream students about diversity. The dimensions of multicultural education, developed by J. A. Banks and described in the *Handbook of Research on Multicultural Education* (J. A. Banks & C. A. M. Banks, 2004), the *Routledge International Companion to Multicultural Education* (J. A. Banks, 2009b), and the *Encyclopedia of Diversity in Education* (J. A. Banks, 2012), provide the conceptual framework for the development of the publications in the Series. The dimensions are content integration, the knowledge construction process, prejudice reduction, equity pedagogy, and an empowering institutional culture and social structure. The books in the Multicultural Education Series provide research, theoretical, and practical knowledge about the behaviors and learning characteristics of students of color (Conchas & Vigil, 2012; Lee, 2007), language-minority students (Gándara & Hopkins, 2010; Valdés, 2001; Valdés et al., 2011), low-income students (Cookson, 2013; Gorski, 2018), multiracial youth (Joseph & Briscoe-Smith, 2021; Mahiri, 2017); and other minoritized population groups, such as students who speak different varieties of English (Charity Hudley & Mallinson, 2011), and LGBTQ+ youth (Mayo, 2014).

Rios and Longoria encourage Black, Indigenous, and Teachers of Color to affirm their cultural and social identities, which can help them to recognize and support the cultural identities of their students. The authors write, "A key aspect of the goal of diversifying the teaching workforce, and a focus of this text, is to support you as a BITOC in affirming and sustaining your social and cultural background—that is, your full identity—and helping you find ways to use this to foster the success of all students" (p. 20). The racial, cultural, and ethnic identities of individuals of color, as the authors convey, are *complex, fluid, contextual, and changing*. People of color internalize and exemplify the modal characteristics of their groups to various degrees. Some BITOC teacher education students also internalize the negative racial and ethnic attitudes that are institutionalized within the larger society. In addition, many individuals of color have biracial and multiracial identities, which are also highly fluid and contextual (Joseph & Briscoe-Smith, 2021). Race, social class, gender, and sexual orientation diversity also exist within the BITOC population.

Some teacher education students from racial, ethnic, cultural, and linguistic minoritized groups who historically have experienced institutionalized discrimination, racism, or other forms of marginalization will have a difficult time accepting and valuing their own cultures, languages, and experiences because of the ways in which their languages and cultures are marginalized within the schools and society writ large. To affirm the cultural identities of these students, their teacher education program will need to help them attain a reflective understanding and acceptance of their families and communities, and a comprehension of the institutionalized racist structures that have victimized them (Baldwin, 1985). Banks (2009a) conceptualizes cultural identity in six stages, which include "cultural psychological captivity" (Stage 1)—in which individuals internalize negative attitudes toward their cultural group that are institutionalized within society—and "cultural identity clarification" (Stage 3), in which individuals develop acceptance and positive attitudes toward their own group. An important goal of a teacher education program for Black, Indigenous, and Teachers of Color is to affirm their cultural identities and, if needed, to facilitate their movement to cultural identity clarification and confirmation, as well as to higher stages on this typology, such as "biculturalism" (Stage 4) and "multiculturalism and reflective nationalism" (Stage 5).

This imaginative and interesting book will inspire Black, Indigenous, and Teachers of Color as well as help them to affirm their cultural identities. It provides valuable and empowering information for White teacher education students who are their allies.

—*James A. Banks*

REFERENCES

Anderson, M. (2017, February 14). *African immigrant population in the U.S. steadily climbs.* Pew Research Center. https://www.pewresearch.org/fact-tank/2017/02/14/african-immigrant-population-in-u-s-steadily-climbs/

Annie E. Casey Foundation. (2019). *2019 Kids Count data book: State trends in child well-being.* Author.

Baldwin, J. (1985). A talk to teachers. In *The price of the ticket: Collected nonfiction 1948–1985.* St. Martin's Press.

Banks, C. A. M. (2005). *Improving multicultural education: Lessons from the intergroup education movement.* Teachers College Press.

Banks, J. A. (2004). Multicultural education: Historical development, dimensions, and practice. In J. A. Banks & C. A. M. Banks (Eds.), *Handbook of research on multicultural education* (2nd ed., pp. 3–29). Jossey-Bass.

Banks, J. A. (2009a). *Teaching strategies for ethnic studies* (8th ed.). Pearson.

Banks, J. A. (Ed.). (2009b). *The Routledge international companion to multicultural education.* Routledge.

Banks, J. A. (2012). Multicultural education: Dimensions of. In J. A. Banks (Ed.), *Encyclopedia of diversity in education* (Vol. 3, pp. 1538–1547). Sage.

Budiman, A. (2020). Key findings about U.S. immigrants. *FactTank News in numbers.* Pew Research Center. https://www.pewresearch.org/fact-tank/2020/08/20/key-findings-about-u-s-immigrants/

Camarota, S. A., & Ziegler, K. (2017, October). 65.5 million U.S. residents spoke a foreign language at home in 2016. *The Center for Immigration Studies.* https://cis.org/Report/655-Million-US-Residents-Spoke-Foreign-Language-Home-2016

Charity Hudley, A. H., & Mallinson, C. (2011). *Understanding language variation in U.S. schools.* Teachers College Press.

Conchas, G. Q., & Vigil, J. D. (2012). *Streetsmart schoolsmart: Urban poverty and the education of adolescent boys.* Teachers College Press.

Cookson, P. W., Jr. (2013). *Class rules: Exposing inequality in American high schools.* Teachers College Press.

Eck, D. L. (2001). *A new religious America: How a "Christian country" has become the world's most religiously diverse nation.* HarperSanFrancisco.

Gándara, P., & Hopkins, M. (Eds.). (2010). *Forbidden language: English language learners and restrictive language policies.* Teachers College Press.

Gorski, P. C. (2018). *Reaching and teaching students in poverty: Strategies for erasing the opportunity gap* (2nd ed.). Teachers College Press.

Joseph, R. L., & Briscoe-Smith, A. (2021). *Generation mixed goes to school: Radically listening to multiracial kids.* Teachers College Press.

Lee, C. D. (2007). *Culture, literacy, and learning: Taking bloom in the midst of the whirlwind.* Teachers College Press.

Mahiri, J. (2017). *Deconstructing race: Multicultural education beyond the color-bind.* Teachers College Press.

Mayo, C. (2014). *LGBTQ youth and education: Policies and practices.* Teachers College Press.

National Center for Education Statistics. (2017). *Enrollment and percentage distribution of enrollment in public elementary and secondary schools, by race/ethnicity and region: Selected years, fall 1995 through fall 2025.* https://nces.ed.gov/programs/digest/d15/tables/dt15_203.50.asp

National Center for Education Statistics. (2019). *Status and trends in the education of racial and ethnic groups. Spotlight: Characteristics of public school teachers by race/ethnicity.* https://nces.ed.gov/programs/raceindicators/spotlight_a.asp

O'Brien, P. (2016). *The Muslim question in Europe: Political controversies and public philosophies.* Temple University Press.

Valdés, G. (2001). *Learning and not learning English: Latino students in American schools.* Teachers College Press.

Valdés, G., Capitelli, S., & Alvarez, L. (2011). *Latino children learning English: Steps in the journey.* Teachers College Press.

Zong, J., Batalova, J., & Hallock, J. (2018, February). *Frequently requested statistics on immigrants and immigration in the United States.* Migration Policy Institute. https://www.migrationpolicy.org/article/frequently-requested-statistics-immigrants-and-immigration-united-states-2016

This Political Moment
A House in Disarray?

When we originally proposed the idea for this book, neither of us imagined the political, social, and health upheaval that we began to experience in March 2020. Since the beginning of the COVID-19 pandemic, all of us have had to shift the ways we are living, working, socializing, and learning, among other things. The move to online learning has been a dramatic change for many teachers and, perhaps more significant, for students. The challenge has been exacerbated by significant disarray and delay at the federal level, which has worked its way down to state and local levels.

As important, the pandemic has made compellingly evident, even *more* fully and clearly, the inequalities already existing in our society. That is, we have seen how communities of color have contracted COVID-19 at a more significant level than White communities. This is, in part, because many Black, Indigenous, and People of Color (BIPOCs):

- live in more densely populated areas of the country
- work in service professions (restaurants, hotels, grocery stores, as but a few examples) where telecommuting is not an option
- do not have access to communication about the pandemic that is culturally and linguistically appropriate
- have less access to personal protective equipment when in public spaces

It is also true that as a result of more longstanding underlying health issues and disparities in access to health care for communities of color, higher rates of fatality have occurred from contracting COVID-19. We know that COVID-19 exacerbates the already higher than normal rates of heart disease and diabetes, both of which can lead to increased deaths of BIPOCs as a result of the pandemic.

At the same time as we are experiencing the COVID-19 pandemic, another longstanding pandemic—*racism and White superiority*—associated with (among other things) police brutality and deaths, particularly of those in the Black community, has shone a bright light on existing issues of the racial divide in America. Consider any number of the most recent of these deaths just as we write: Ahmaud Arbery, Breonna Taylor, and Rayshard Brooks. Perhaps nothing stirred the nation quite as much as the videotaped murder of George Floyd in Minneapolis, who pleaded with officers to get their knees off his neck for more than 8 minutes before dying in the street.

For many in the nation, the decades-long critique of the pipeline of mass incarceration experienced by communities of color and their social justice allies was now made visible, undeniable, and concrete. Thousands took to the streets, erected memorials, held town hall meetings, and called for the end of police brutality specifically as well as for the elimination of institutional racism more broadly. For many White people, it has led to greater discussions about white privilege, white fragility, and white superiority than have been witnessed in decades. For Black, Indigenous, and People of Color, it has been yet another moment to draw attention to the ideology of anti-Black racism: These deaths provide contemporary examples of hate crimes (a twist on the public lynching seen during the Jim Crow era) and the state control of Black bodies as an enduring manifestation of slavery. It shows the systemic nature of how racism plays out in the United States. It calls on all people to stand in solidarity toward the greater pursuit of equity and justice alongside the recognition that remaining silent is to be complicit.

Global warming and environmental degradation have sped forward, aided, in part, by those in power who deny climate change and the increasingly toxic air, water, and land that we inhabit. It is well-known that communities of color are disproportionately affected by these toxic environments (consider the Flint water crisis as but one example) and, as a result of having less political power, often are less able to respond to these crises. This toxicity is so great that it is estimated that 18 million people were displaced (forced to migrate) in 2017 alone (Andrews, 2019); consider that the environmental crises were responsible for nearly two thirds of all those displaced. Walia (2018) estimates that there is one new climate refugee every 6 seconds. We know that under the auspices of settler colonialism, a long historical and contemporary "expulsion of minorities from desirable land and communities, the demolition of their neighborhoods, the relocation of minorities to segregated neighborhoods, and the construction of minority neighborhoods in undesirable locations" (Taylor, 2014, p. 3) continues unabated. Add this to the compelling evidence of the disproportionate number of hazardous waste sites and toxic materials within close proximity to minoritized communities (Taylor, 2014).

Immigration restrictions have negatively impacted those climate refugees, as well as all others who have been displaced, and they have become asylum-seekers, due to *neoliberal economic policies* (unfettered, unrestrained, and unrestricted capitalism, or "capitalism with the gloves off," as McLaren and Farahmandpur, 2002, p. 37, describe it), war, and political oppression. At the heart of these immigration restrictions is an increase in political extremist White nationalism—a cornerstone of fascism—with corresponding calls to close the nation's borders. The United States, under the Trump administration, enacted policies aimed at halting immigration, including inhumane family separation policies, deportation without a fair hearing, and expansion of the physical wall between Mexico and the United States.

New immigration is just part of the challenge. The United States currently serves as home to an estimated 10.5 million people living without documentation (Gramlich, 2019). These immigrants and refugees face a pressing identity question focused on what it means to be a citizen and, by extension, on civic identities (J. A. Banks, 2017; Vargas, 2018). These renewed questions ask what citizenship means, to whom it is granted, and under what conditions, given that "citizenship is dynamic, temporal, and spatial but also raced, classed, gendered, and so forth" (Salinas et al., 2016, p. 332). At their heart, these citizenship questions create discussions and debates about what it means to "belong." At the same time, we agree with Grande and Anderson (2017) that these discussions and debates about the very nature of nationhood are layered and contested from a Native American perspective.

In the Trump era, we saw a resurgence of the *culture wars* of the 1990s that included clashes on issues of race, ethnicity, cultural dominance, and political affiliations. The tensions between conservatism and liberalism have become heated in public and popular discourses. As we saw in the 1990s, reforms, reparations, and justice often are interrupted or inhibited by policy and populism. For example, in September 2020, the Trump administration issued an order to begin defunding and blocking any professional development or training on racial justice and Critical Race Theory. The president used his Twitter platform (Trump, 2020) to promote the action, saying that such training was "a sickness that cannot be allowed to continue" and urging people to "report any sightings so [the administration] can quickly extinguish." Actions such as these incite division between racial and ethnic groups, and ultimately perpetuate rather than move to eliminate social inequalities.

Education is a mirror of these broader social inequalities. These include "a retreat on efforts to curb sexual harassment, efforts to assure the human rights and dignity of LGBTQ+ youth in schools, and efforts to disrupt discriminatory discipline policies that negatively affect African American and Latino youth in particular" (Rios, 2018, p. 171). Added to this has been the increasing bias and discrimination, as well as student-to-student hate, that spiked in schools after the election of Trump (detailed in Costello & Dillard, 2019). We explore these developments more fully within the pages of this book.

Following the COVID-19 outbreak of 2020, the schooling landscape saw extended school-site closures and transition to long-term distance and virtual learning. This has had impacts on the nutrition, health and wellness, and academic services that schools provide to children and youth. As the pandemic turned out to be a prolonged event, the debate over whether to open schools saw teachers caught in the middle. The Centers for Disease Control and Prevention (CDC, 2020) issued guidance that recommend schools be reopened despite certainty about the role of children in spreading the virus and the potential

exposure risks to teachers and staff. The CDC rationalized that long-term closing of face-to-face instruction was too detrimental to the development, health,
academic progress, and well-being of children and youth. Teachers also faced
having to adapt to the new technological, relational, and pedagogical challenges
of a sudden change in learning environments and instructional delivery.

While the political moment may have seemed dire, we remained hope-
ful and saw opportunities for real change, led in part by young people in this
nation. Galvanized by the Black Lives Matter movement, more serious conversations began occurring around white supremacy and institutional racism.
Consider that, in Summer 2020, four of the top five books on the *New York
Times* bestseller list for nonfiction dealt directly with racism in America: *White
Fragility* (DiAngelo, 2018); *How to Be an Antiracist* (Kendi, 2019); *Stamped
From the Beginning* (Kendi, 2017); and *So You Want to Talk About Race* (Oluo,
2019).

We were witness to important conversations that questioned the growth
of the police state and called for defunding the police, removing them from
schools, and increasing the number of public health professionals in their place.
Business and industries are feeling pressured to make good on their oft-stated
commitments to value diversity by interrogating their business practices, reviewing their employment decisions, and considering their corporate cultures.
Some states have brought down memorials and statues to those who fought on
the side of the proslavery South in the Civil War, and at least one state (Mis-
sissippi) has removed the confederate flag symbol from its state flag. Many
older activists see important similarities to the civil rights movements of the
1950s–1970s, with a hope that this new movement may advance that agenda
farther and more deeply.

Aside from the specific political challenges you find yourself in while reading this book, we hope you will be reminded that it is important to critically understand the various ways that oppression of a people occurs—in this moment,
white privilege, white supremacy, institutional oppression, silence as complic-
ity, to name just a few—and to commit yourself to anti-oppressive work. We
hope you will be reminded to question taken-for-granted assumptions about
how things work, as well as to forge a vision of the possibilities of social justice.
*We hope you will be reminded that it is important to learn from and appreciate
what has occurred around political activism and education from past movements,
with a creative commitment to making anew social justice movements in your
political moment.* We hope that you will be reminded to listen to the voices of
young people, especially those from the margins, and support their leadership
and leadership development.

Above all, and most germane to this text, we hope you will be reminded
to be fully grounded in those principles most central to who you are; those
values and perspectives that seek to honor your identities and ensure your full
humanness.

As we write this, we recognize that there will be lasting effects to what we have experienced nationally on the health, economy, climate, and political fronts. The impacts on a nation more deeply divided than at any other time in modern history will be felt across generations. We are heartened by the election of the first Black and Indian woman into the Executive Office as vice president, which signals new possibilities and buoys our hope. Along with the turmoil, there is an energetic anticipation and a radical imaginary in our communities, the nation, and the world for whatever results as the new normal. Rather than feeling down and out, we ask for you to courageously push up and into the teaching profession. And, in this regard, we believe the urgency is even greater now than ever to diversify the teaching profession!

Acknowledgments

We appreciate this moment to thank the many people who have supported the development of this book. We offer our appreciation to all those Black, Indigenous, and Teachers of Color who were often the "first and only" from their social identities/backgrounds in their schools and school districts. The pathways created by your commitment to students, families, communities, and schools have been central to the efforts of diversifying the teaching profession.

At the same time, we extend our appreciation to all those current Black, Indigenous, and Teachers of Color (BITOC)—as well as those actively pursuing their teaching credential—for pursuing a profession that very much needs your brilliance, your vision, your passion, and your commitment as part and parcel of the broader social justice project.

We offer our special appreciation to Dr. James A. Banks, who welcomed the idea of the book, offered important insights and suggestions throughout, and provided us with detailed feedback to sharpen our language and our ideas.

We offer our appreciation to the numerous individuals at Teachers College Press who helped us to move this work from manuscript to final text. In particular, we appreciate the guidance and strong support from Brian Ellerbeck at TCP.

This work would not have been possible without the work of activist-scholars who conducted academic research into the lives of Black, Indigenous, and Teachers of Color. It is that scholarship that provides us insight into many of the issues and challenges that we needed to address in this text. Among them, we especially thank Rita Kohli, Conra Gist, as well as several anonymous reviewers of the prospectus of this book for their reviews and recommendations.

Our colleagues and friends at Western Washington University continue to inspire us by their common commitments to the work of equity and social justice broadly and diversifying the teaching workforce specifically. In particular, we appreciate the support and inspiration garnered from Verónica Vélez, Kristen French, Kevin Roxas, and Daisy Padilla. We thank them for their continuing commitments. A special shout-out to three graduate students who supported this work materially as well as socially: Kayla Callanan, Gabriela Serrano, and Hugo Santiago.

I (Longoria) wish to thank Luis Escamilla, whose work pushed my thinking for the better, for his steadfast commitment to BITOCs. Geneva Gay, Dafney

Blanca Dabach, Karen Harris, Karen Mikolasy, Saara Kamal, Raedell Boateng, Winston Benjamin, Renee Shank, Natalie White, Charisse Cowan Pitre, and the growing list of Martinez Fellows have been formative and foundational to my contributions to this book. Giselle Alcantar Soto and Eldred Vidal Vazquez have been inspiring. Mary Ann Chew-Longoria and Richard Longoria have blessed me with unconditional love and support.

While we both have been waiting for a book like this to be written, a spark was set off in a conversation with several Latinx preservice teachers who shared their frustration with their current multicultural education textbook because it centered White students; for these Latinx students, it did not speak to their knowledge, their experiences, and their identities. It is to and for them that this text is dedicated: Natalia Rios, Karanbir Deol, and Karen Monterrosa.

We offer our appreciation to those Black, Indigenous, and Students of Color we have worked with who inspire us about living out an identity-centered pedagogy. Among these, we include Jose C-V., Nathaniel O., McKenzie B., Zachary L., Angelia T., Cindy M-N., Grey W., Chris M., Sukhdip S., Madeline I., Maria R-D., Julia R-H., Caitlyn B., and countless others!

Introduction

Miguel Ignacio Lillo never went to college, but book by book he built a science library that filled his entire house. . . . "My books breathe the air," the sage exclaimed. "I open them and ask them questions. Reading is asking questions." Don Miguel asked questions of his books and he asked many more of the world.

—Eduardo Galeano, *Children of the Days* (2013, p. 293)

Dear Readers:

We are writing this book to you—prospective and practicing Black, Indigenous, and Teachers of Color—because we know and believe you can make an incredible difference in the lives of your students as one part of the greater belief in the importance of diversifying the teaching workforce and the social justice in education project. It recalls for both of us James Baldwin's direct address via his seminal "A Talk to Teachers" (1963) and less well-known but equally important "A Letter to My Nephew" (1962).

We are keenly aware that the ways in which schooling and teacher education programs have been structured have made it difficult to diversify the teaching profession. It begins with much of your own K–12 schooling experience, which, for most Black, Indigenous, and Students of Color (BISOCs), has been fraught with challenges, including efforts to *deculturalize* (Spring, 2016) or subtract your language and cultural background (Valenzuela, 2010). Getting to the university and choosing to become a teacher are, for most, significant achievements in their own right. Flores (2017) uses the analogy that surviving your own school and university experiences and then becoming a teacher are akin to asking you to survive the stormiest of seas and then summoning you to return to those stormy seas to assist those who are still in the midst of the water's turbulence.

We are keenly aware that once you have made the decision to become a teacher, almost every aspect of the recruitment and retention process in teacher education programs, the academic preparation within those programs, and then employment in the teaching profession has been occurring within an "overwhelming presence of whiteness" (Sleeter, 2001). Another way to describe this is that teacher education and the education profession have not been structured around the experiences and needs of BITOCs. It also can be described as structured to keep our presence within the profession at a minimum. This is as true historically as it is contemporarily, as we describe in greater detail in Chapter 1. And those BITOCs who have endured, and currently are enduring, to create a place for themselves within the teaching profession often have had to do so at considerable personal, cultural, and professional cost.

We also are keenly aware, as you will read in this book, that BITOCs are a vital link in the academic success of all students, including and perhaps most especially so for Black, Indigenous, and Students of Color. On one level, your very presence in the profession is a source of inspiration for BISOCs; you often are or will be one of the few Black, Indigenous, and People of Color who are seen in professional and leadership positions in school settings. At another level, we believe that the power of your presence in the profession stems from the social and cultural experiences you bring to classrooms and schools. That is, because of your cultural/linguistic background and identities, because you have survived in a system not meant for you, because you bring commitments to your community, and because you are committed to the personal, social, and academic achievement of BISOCs (among so many other reasons), you are uniquely positioned to help us address pervasive educational disparities—sometimes bemoaned as an "achievement gap," but which we reframe in Chapter 1 as created by an "opportunity gap"—while simultaneously helping to forge a vision of what it means to live in a highly diverse, democratic society.

We also wish to be clear that your presence in the profession, brilliant as it undoubtedly should be, will not by itself create the educational equity our communities demand or close that opportunity gap (Dilworth, 2018). Diversifying the teaching profession is a vital but insufficient response to attaining these important equity and justice goals in schools. Institutional (schoolwide and classroom specific) policies, programs, and procedures, as well as the way we act, think ideologically and conceptually, and talk via narratives and discourses about student success and failure are also central to addressing those opportunity gaps.

A key aspect of the goal of diversifying the teaching workforce, and a focus of this text, is to support you as a BITOC in affirming and sustaining your social and cultural background—that is, your full identity—and helping you find ways to use this to foster the success of all students. Carter and Darling-Hammond (2016) point out that the importance of learning about oneself, most centrally one's identity, runs parallel with learning about one's students. In sharing your identity as part of your teaching practice, you will be inviting students' full identities into the classroom as a humanizing space. This rests on an explicitly stated belief that who you are as a BITOC is as important as what you do as a teacher (Petchauer & Mawhinney, 2017).

Affirming and sharing your social identities are important dispositional foundations of learning in diverse student contexts, as described by Sonia Nieto (2006): a clear mission of what you want to accomplish; a strong understanding of and commitment to your students; the courage to challenge mainstream academic knowledge; a willingness to improvise and creatively respond to professional challenges; and a passion for social justice.

We are committed, through this book, to helping you live out these important aims.

WHO WE ARE AND WHERE WE STAND

We take this moment to introduce ourselves and how we came to this work, so you have a better idea of our own social and cultural locations, our positionalities. This book came about given BISOC critiques that their multicultural education texts were not designed for them. Given that we had recognized the need even earlier, these students' voices activated our efforts to write this book.

Francisco: I grew up in the largely Latinx section of west Denver, at the height of the Chicano movement. It was a tumultuous time, one that was filled with angst but also with hope for change. I went to and graduated from West High School, where 80% of the student population was Chicano/Mexican American. I was fortunate to have participated in the student-led blowouts (walkouts) that were occurring throughout the southwest, including at my high school. We were protesting the lack of Chicano teachers but also the absence of Chicano studies classes where we could learn about our history and see our culture reflected.

As part of the federal War on Poverty programs, low-income youth were offered summer employment. I choose to tutor in a summer alternative school setting for K–6 students called *La Academia del Barrio.* It taught Chicano history, *ballet folklorico,* and math using Mayan math methods, as but a few examples. All the students were Chicano and so were the teachers and staff. It was Chicano-riffic! During the school year, I did after-school tutoring at an alternative middle school for Latinx kids kicked out of the Denver Public Schools.

I also came to nest the work of schooling in the broader cultural community, especially by involvement in several community-based organizations. In Denver, they were mostly youth engagement organizations. But even in college, I connected immediately to the local Latinx community. The organization that was most prominent among these was *La Casa de Esperanza*, where I served on the board of directors, ran a youth-led bilingual community newspaper, directed a summer youth education/recreation program for Latinx youth, as well as served as a tutor and volunteer throughout college and into my first several years as a teacher.

I was inspired to be a teacher by a young teacher who was the first person to talk to me, as an 11th-grader, about going to college. Mr. Vidal, a *Cubano,* was teaching a speech/communications course and singled me out to share his belief that I was "college material." I became a teacher, inspired by Vidal, to see something in others I didn't see in myself, as a way to give back, as a recognition that who I was might be helpful. I earned my high school teaching credential, taught in a technical school for 13 years, and have been working at the university level for nearly 30 years. I tell my students that I still feel like a first-year teacher!

I have been fortunate to have used my service and academic studies to further my understandings around issues of equity, diversity, and inclusion, but most especially around uncovering the assets that BITOCs bring to the profession. This has included researching and reporting about Teachers of Color, running a teacher diversity recruitment program, and ensuring the creation of a Teacher of Color pathway program.

Longoria: The literal borderlands between southern California and Baja California set the background for my schooling and formative childhood experiences. Growing up in El Centro, California, I learned to navigate the complex tensions between race, class, and gender expectations in the community. As a Queer teen I learned to hide my identities around desire and gender in order to match the compulsory *machismo* and White middle-class aspirational conservative values that stifled my self-determination to explore and assert my identities as a biracial genderqueer person with roots to their Chinese and Mexican heritages.

During the school week I was surrounded by other Mexican Americans, White students, a few Asian and Black students, and a strong curricular core of the compulsory patriotism our White teachers promoted. We rarely saw ourselves and our cultural values reflected in the school curriculum. The school was seen as the place for us to learn American (White) culture, and it was expected that we would maintain our Mexican cultural values only at home or in the community. California Propositions 187 (anti-immigrant) and 227 (anti-bilingual education) later would further erode the disconnect between schooling and cultural difference—especially the bitter debates surrounding the values these propositions espoused.

My maternal grandmother, an immigrant from China's Pearl River Delta, filled my childhood weekends with Toisan, our Cantonese dialect, and ensured I was Chinese on the weekends amid the allure of 1980s mainstream American culture. Is it any wonder I have had an affinity in my adult life for championing nuance and intersectionality as they relate to identity? I fundamentally believe that cultural identities matter in education, and further that such identities must be maintained through the schooling enterprise.

In my schooling experiences I had only a handful of BITOCs in spite of my community being majority Mexican American. I would not question this until much later in my higher education journey. I began that journey motivated by it being my ticket out of my rural community but not fully knowing what it entailed. I have had a jagged journey, having dropped out of college twice and accessed community college to help me re-up and eventually finish my undergraduate education.

Teaching high school in Seattle was a subsequent blessing and I regret eventually being pulled away from full-time teaching to pursue an academic future. In my own teacher education experiences and, later, my high school humanities teaching practice, I learned to unabashedly embrace my Chinese Mexican identities to inform my praxis. While there were other BITOCs in my masters in teaching program, it was predominantly White. Even in the 21st century in a large metropolitan school district, I was among only a handful of BITOCs in my school and district. I learned that representation matters to students that hold similar identities and broadly for all BISOCs.

I returned to my higher education journey to pursue being a teacher educator. I came out of that journey with a doctoral degree, research and teaching experiences, and six-figure education debt—all too common for BIPOCs from rural communities who have attempted to access the promise of advanced degrees. Yet I find meaningful joy from my work as a university-based teacher educator and have attempted to find ways to do this work meaningfully and to live out my values and commitments to education and social justice. I miss being a classroom teacher but find incredible rewards in helping to train the next generations of teachers, working with educators to improve equitable praxis and new curricula, and attempting to be worthy of this gift of being a person with the identities I hold in this work. In so many ways, this book is what I wish I had had in those early years of my formation as a teacher—something that was designed and written directly for people like us.

THE FRAMEWORK

We have titled this book *Creating a Home in Schools*. We want to center the use of space/place, more specifically the community and home, as an organizational device. We borrow this notion of a house as a metaphor from Alicia Gaspar de Alba's book *Chicano Art: Inside/Outside the Master's House* (1997). We assert that the house is an apt metaphor to use because it allows us to see how different aspects of what it means to be a BITOC, like different rooms within a house, are connected by a common structure. Importantly, this is an organizational device that we know you probably are already familiar with, given the (perhaps many varied) places where you have lived.

We acknowledge that the kinds of houses we come from are different. Some of you may be more familiar with an apartment, or a hogan, or a yurt, or a teepee, or an iglu, or a tent or camper as your house. An important connection, described by Delgado Bernal (2001), about home and school is that "the communication, practices, and learning that occur in the home and community—pedagogies of the home—often serve as a cultural knowledge base" (p. 623) that will help you succeed in a school system not meant for you.

We also want to acknowledge that we are describing the *house* in the most traditional way. We recognize that too many people are homeless, and the very idea of a house is not part of their present reality. We further acknowledge that we are describing the *home* in the most ideal way. We recognize that the house where people live may not feel like a home at all, given the level of safety and agency that they do not feel there. We are cognizant of and dispirited by the realities of both the house and the home as experienced by some, potentially including you.

What makes a house a home is that it becomes a psychological space you can call your own, especially a place where you have some power and agency to effect change. The shape and texture of what becomes your home are different for each of you; in the same way, your social and cultural identities are different just as teachers are different. What we ask of you is to reconfigure the schoolhouse and classroom as a professional "home" for you and your students, a place where you can feel safe to share identities as you enact change in pursuit of equity and justice. *As we do so, we are aware, as Ladson-Billings (2005) describes, that by getting your teaching credential, gaining a teaching position, and creating a thriving teaching/learning home in your classroom, you are in the house, but you most often are not of the house.*

In using the house as a generic metaphor to organize the text in this book, we acknowledge that we cannot speak to the specific school and classroom where you will find yourself. We cannot speak to the elementary, middle, or high school house where you teach. We will not write about what this means for math, social studies, language arts, music, science, as but a few examples. Given our own positionalities, as shared above, we cannot nor will we try to describe either how the specific experience of being a BITOC differs for people from social-cultural and racial identities different from our own, or the various ways in which these social-cultural and racial identities intersect with other key aspects of teachers' identities. We acknowledge and own the limitations that we have set for ourselves, given that this book project aims at describing a broad vision of schooling and teaching/learning for BITOCs. However, we also hope it serves as an invitation for you to assert your own story of how this plays out and we encourage you to read the work of other Teacher-Scholars of Color who are actively engaged in filling these specific voids.

CHAPTER OVERVIEWS

In Chapter 1, The Community: Mapping the Contours of the Profession, we provide the broadest overview of the context of teaching for BITOCs. This is the setting—the (professional) community context—where the school/house sits and in which BITOCs will find themselves. This chapter includes a brief history of schooling and teaching for communities of color as well as provides a brief demographic profile of schools and the teaching workforce.

In Chapter 2, The House: Finding Your Theoretical/Ideological Foundations, we turn our attention to the structural features of the house, in this instance, the theoretical and ideological foundations of schooling for diversity and equity. In this chapter, we identify the various theoretical orientations that specifically help you to understand race and racism in the context of schooling. These theoretical orientations include both deficiency orientations about our students and communities as well as more liberating approaches, primarily those nested under Critical Race Theory, and asset-based theories of both language and cultural diversity.

In Chapter 3, The Entryway: Representing Through Multicultural and Culturally Centering Education, we focus on those things we hope students and others first see when they enter our house: the public applications of the affirmation of diverse identities as we navigate teaching and learning. In this instance, we are hopeful that upon stepping into the school/house, entrants will see and experience those approaches that honor, engage, and sustain the culturally diverse identities of the teacher, but most especially of the students. After a brief history of multicultural education, we review salient concepts from multicultural education as we segue into a more directed focus on culturally responsive and culturally sustaining approaches to *pedagogies*—a general word used to describe approaches to teaching and learning. We also offer a nuanced discussion of how concepts in multicultural education might be experienced and enacted by BITOCs in ways that their White peers might not consider, let alone navigate.

In Chapter 4, The Living Room: Sustaining Identities Through Teaching and Learning, we move toward the public applications of our identities as we navigate teaching, especially approaches that honor, engage, and sustain the culturally diverse identities that teachers and students bring to their classrooms. We begin with a brief review of diversity in the teaching profession, followed by a description of the assets BITOCs bring to their students, classrooms, and schools. Further, we introduce our concept of identity-sustaining pedagogies. We argue that traditional teacher education programs, and the teaching profession more broadly, exert pressure on BITOCs to subsume their identities into the larger White-dominant identity present in education. To counter this, we offer a framework that can inform BITOCs to enact a creative, intentional adaptation of the methods and practices of the teaching profession in order to honor and sustain their own cultural identities and, in so doing, invite students to do likewise.

In Chapter 5, The Kitchen (and the Closet): Getting Real About Schooling, we further explore the nuances of teacher education programs and the teaching profession as a BITOC. A major theme for this chapter is navigating the tensions between public and private aspects of being a BITOC. We identify several of the most central challenges BITOCs face in the profession. We acknowledge the various "isms" BITOCs encounter in this work, which includes negotiating the tensions around collaborating with other BITOCs, allies, and colleagues. We also encourage an intergenerational approach to this work that honors the experiences and wisdom of those who have come before us and those currently experiencing the profession. We provide strategies for preservice BITOCs to navigate choosing schools in which to work, holding training programs and colleagues accountable for supporting BITOCs, and advocating for communities of color. We end the chapter with loving advice for BITOCs about how to navigate the tensions between the work that must be done within our own communities and the more public work we collectively do in education.

In Chapter 6, The Patio: Re/energizing Yourself in Community, we move toward centering joy and self-care in the work BITOCs do in education. We remind readers that the experiences of BITOCs in schooling are not just a narrative of oppression and marginalization; these experiences are also a success narrative where we celebrate, rejoice with, and care for our communities. Celebration, joy, and care include an acknowledgment that this work is not done by BITOCs alone and highlight the need for seeking and fostering allies. We also stress the importance of self-care and offer practical options for it, building resistance, and finding joy in teaching. Finally, we offer suggestions for movement building, developing pathways to diversify the teaching profession, and activism—especially with allies.

In Chapter 7, The Rooftop: Visioning and Action Planning for Sustainable Futures, we ask you to envision yourself on the rooftop, looking toward the future and thinking of possibilities. This task will include imagining new ways of thinking about yourself and your roles as a teacher in schools. It will include being clear about what those visions of possibilities are, what theories of change might best support them, and how to maintain hope and joy even as you lean into challenges that you may be experiencing. We end by asking you to develop a specific action plan for yourself in relation to your movement into and through the profession.

In the brief Postscript, we come back to our metaphor of the house to share final thoughts and reflections around the importance of making your classroom, school, and profession your home.

In Appendix A, we provide The Toolshed: tools for honing your organizations, conferences, and professional resources, specifically aimed at supporting and sustaining BITOCs. In Appendix B, we provide a Note to White Readers of this text. In Appendix C, we list some Other Goals for Culturally Centering Education beyond those we share in Chapter 3. And in Appendix D, we provide An Action-Planning Worksheet: Crafting Your Story inspired by ideas in this text.

A NOTE ABOUT TERMINOLOGY

We want to be upfront about our use of language. We recognize the power of language, especially those terms and names we use to describe a person's or people's identities; we do not take our use of language lightly. At the same time, we recognize the shifting and dynamic (ever-changing) nature of language, including around social identity descriptors. Consider the terms used just for people within our own Latinx communities: from Mexican or Guatemalan, to Mexican American or Central American, to Hispanic, to Latino, to Latinx, as just a few examples.

We are also mindful that our language often is filled with words that have oppressive origins. Even social justice advocates can be complicit in language that can be denigrating. For example, many individuals have used the term *color-blind* to describe an ideological orientation people have adopted to express a self-perception of racial neutrality and thereby avoid confronting the substantial societal race-based differences and racism. The disability community has pointed out the use of this term, even in the service of social justice, as an example of dismissing members of their community (Erevelles, 2018). To recognize this same ideological posture without denigrating others, we use the terms *color-* (and *power-)evasiveness*.

Each of these terms and words has a different meaning; they are used at a particular political moment for particular purposes. Our decisions to use words in a certain way best reflect where we stand as we write this text. They are not intended to settle these important debates about what the "right" terms are to use to describe a racial, cultural, or ethnic group. We ask for your understanding as we navigate this important element of language use.

To that end, consider the following language used throughout this text:

- In using and capitalizing the term *Teachers of Color*, we are wary that readers may attempt to unnecessarily overgeneralize the experience of this broad distinctive group of people; that is, *essentialize* to the point of glossing over important differences within a category. We ask readers not to assume that the experiences of Black teachers are the same as those of Native American or Latinx teachers. There are experiences that are unique to each group, such as the challenges with language-intensive standardized assessments, which harm Latinx teachers most especially.

  To be sure, there are times when we want to think and talk about this group as a collective, given some common experiences. Using the notion of "strategic essentialism" as described by Philip and Brown (2020), we use both the generic term *Teachers of Color* and, where appropriate and known, the specific racial, cultural, or ethnic identifier. The term *Teachers of Color* then includes Latinx, Southeast Asian, Asian American, and East Asian teachers.

  Relatedly, we recognize that there are other groups that might consider that they, too, fit under the broad umbrella term *Teachers of Color* as a result of historical and contemporary marginalization and oppression of their communities based on race or ethnicity. This might include aspiring teachers who come from low-income communities where their White ethnic identity—such as Portuguese American or Italian American—served as a social identity marker for discrimination. We have no intention of making clear rules around what groups do and do not fit into this category of teachers from "diverse backgrounds" or Teachers of Color.

- We use *Black, Indigenous, and Teachers of Color (BITOCs)* as our standard term throughout the text. We want to be clear that we are making the decision to highlight the Black experience in this acronym because confronting anti-Blackness is so important, as well as confronting the historical and contemporary role of racism (Philip & Brown, 2020). This acronym also highlights the special political relationship Indigenous people have, as a sovereign nation/people, as well as opposes colonization as a political project (Cook-Lynn, 2007; see also Gist & Bristol, in press).

- Much like the use of BITOC, we also will use the terms *Black, Indigenous, and Students of Color (BISOCs)* to describe students, and *Black, Indigenous, and People of Color (BIPOCs)* when referring to people from marginalized backgrounds generally. The reasonings described above also apply when we use these terms.

- We use the specific ethnic/racial identity terms people use in their language to describe the time or identity important to them. However, as a default and when we have a choice, we use *Black* over African American to highlight a shared Black experience across people with African American heritage and people with recent experiences of immigration from the African diaspora around the world. We use *Indigenous* to follow suit with more recent scholarship by Indigenous scholars and use terms such as American Indian and Native American only when context demands. *Latinx* is used over Latino to acknowledge a more gender-neutral form of the term. While Hispanic has been used elsewhere, we have embraced the more inclusive Latinx, while also acknowledging the Whiteness and racialization of the terms. We also recognize that a significant segment of the Latinx community identify as *Afro-Latinx* and/or Indigenous and reject the Whiteness of mainstream Latinx culture. While we use the terms *Asian American* and *Asian Pacific Islander*, we acknowledge that the term *Asian* encompasses a broad continent that includes people with South Asian and Southeast Asian heritages. We also acknowledge that "Asian" is popularly used to refer only to people of East Asian heritage—those people from Japan, Korea, or China.

- While we do not aim to be prescriptive in the terms we use, we acknowledge that identities change over time and some popular terms we use are not reflective of the respective overall communities. We have tried to be consistent and just in the terms we use.

- We will use the word *minoritized* and not minority to capture a key relationship between social identity membership and power. Even though non-Whites are a global majority and were a numerical majority in schools in the United States as of Fall 2014 (U.S. Department of Education, 2016), they still experience policies and practices that, politically and educationally, intentionally result in their being minoritized.

- We will, unless referring to a specific instance, use the general term *oppression* to describe all the specific and various forms of bias, description, and marginalization experienced by members of various social identity categories. These include many of the "isms," such as racism, classism, sexism, heterosexism, linguicism, and ableism, among so many more; for a broader list, see *Rethinking Ethnic Studies* (Cuauhtin et al., 2019, pp. 46–47). They also include xenophobia, misogyny, homophobia, and transphobia, among other terms. Importantly, we do not see these various forms of oppression in competition with one another. Rather, we recognize the ways these forms of oppression overlap and intersect with one another.
- We will use gender-neutral terms (mostly the plural pronoun "they") unless the specificity of gender is central to understanding meaning or acknowledges someone's specific identity. While the *Publication Manual of the American Psychological Association* guides our writing style and endorses using the singular "they," we do so in solidarity with the LGBTQ+ community.

We will use other words and terms throughout the text and will define them as we progress. We hope the clarifications of our working use of these terms will help focus on the central ideas we put forward.

GETTING THE MOST FROM THIS TEXT

We offer the following suggestions as a way to get the most out of this text. To begin, we see this as an open letter to you, aspiring or current BITOC. We share with you our experiences, our knowledge, our questions, and the wisdom we have acquired. We share the words and ideas of this text with you with an open heart and ask that you read them with "a hungry heart," a description we value from our colleague Dr. Kristen French.

We hope you use this text as an opportunity to think about your own identity: how you describe your social identity, how you understand it, how it was developed, and how you can sustain/nourish it. We are focusing on identity because we believe it is your social, cultural, and linguistic experiences—incredible assets that they are—that will serve you and your students well in connecting and teaching across differences. But we also recognize that we are always in the process of "becoming." We see identity as an active, dynamic process. Even when you come from a specific community, such as the Latinx community, returning to that community is a new experience given your new identity as "teacher." Imagine how different and new that experience will be if you find employment in a different Latinx community, in a different region of the United States. Or imagine finding yourself in a highly diverse community, in yet a different region of the United States. Recognize the different identity journey you will be on if you end up teaching in a majority-White and/or suburban school, where you also will seek to use your incredible social, cultural, and identity assets (Petchauer & Mawhinney, 2017). Embrace this identity journey.

We walk a line between radical truth-telling, including the real challenges and pitfalls that you are likely to encounter in schools, on the one hand, and maintaining our hopes and desires for your success as a teacher—hopes and desires we believe you share—on the other hand. As you will read, schools were not set up for people like us to be successful; we were not meant to be here writing this text and you were not meant to be reading it as a prospective or current teacher. Yet somewhere along the way, most of you had a teacher, often a BITOC, who made a profound difference in your life. You may have found purpose and beauty in connecting with students, families, and communities, coming to recognize teaching as one way to give back. Perhaps you recognized the power of learning and the sacred space of classrooms for building living/ learning communities. You may have seen the power of working with colleagues and administrators, as well as with parents and community activists, in making the kinds of institutional change that will foster success for a greater number of students. Keep these latter images of yourself in mind whenever you feel those moments of despair.

We also want to acknowledge the reliance on our own Latinx experiences throughout this book. We do so for multiple reasons. We do not feel it is appropriate for us to represent the experiences of other cultural/racial/ethnic groups to which we do not belong; our efforts would be superficial and inauthentic. We do feel that in sharing with you our specific experiences as Latinx people—experiences we know are genuine—we also are modelling what an identity-sustaining approach to teaching would look like. In addition, we use the language of our ancestors (Spanish),[1] not always translated, when we feel it best conveys our goals for this text and as an act of sustaining our own identities. It is our hope that BITOCs reading this book will find their own cultural connections, identify ways in which ours are both different from and similar to their own, and use that as a guide to make sense of their own experiences.

A note to White students: We recognize that you may be reading this book for any number of reasons: it is a requirement for professional development, you are curious, you want to know how to be a better ally and accomplice to BITOCs, among other reasons. Please recognize and appreciate that the purpose of this text is to center the experiences of BITOCs who are, in almost every other instance, on the margins when it comes to textbooks about teaching and the teaching profession. Whatever your reason for reading this, we hope that you approach this text with a hungry heart, a posture of listening and learning, and a genuine desire to work in solidarity with BITOCs in teacher education programs as well as in classrooms and schools. We will have more to say to you about working in solidarity with BITOCs in Appendix B.

We want to also acknowledge a decision that we have made to focus on BITOCs within the context of education in the United States. We do this even while we recognize that non-Whites are a global majority (Portelli & Campbell-Stephens, 2009) and that the desire to diversify the teaching workforce is being researched and discussed in other countries of the world, especially those with significant numbers of non-White students. We also recognize that international students may find this book helpful; at the same time, we hope you recognize that we did not write this book with international students in mind. We invite you to consider important scholarly work being done on teachers from international backgrounds to understand these important dimensions.

This book has a couple of features that we hope you will find helpful in extending your learning. We begin each chapter with a quote—consider this as advice from scholars. Within the text of each chapter, we will call out important vocabulary and key ideas. We also offer a series of questions in a WONDER ALONE/WONDER TOGETHER text box, the first of which appears here. We hope you will use these questions as an opportunity to both think through your own understandings—that is, "wonder alone"—and then discuss these with others whose opinions you value—that is, "wonder together."

💬 WONDER ALONE / WONDER TOGETHER

What intrigues you about reading this book, thus far? What questions do you hope it answers? What goals do you want to set for yourself as a reader? As a reader of this text?

At the end of each chapter, we include a section called "Make It Happen," where we hope you take up practical applications from what you have learned. We include activities to collect into a personal and professional portfolio of practices and reflections to help you engage more deeply in identity-sustaining pedagogies. We hope this becomes a reflective resource you make for yourself to help sustain you in the profession. At a minimum, we encourage you to keep these reflective activities in a specific place, such as in a portfolio, scrapbook, or computer desktop folder. This resource might be pulled from the shelf to remind yourself, during tough times, why you got into the profession or as a professional portfolio that you might share during job interviews. Additional suggested activities to "Keep It Going!" include reading poetry or watching videos to help extend your learning, enrich your reflection, and inspire your vision. Consider these videos and poems as a kind of culturally centered wisdom and beauty from which to gain inspiration. In doing so, imagine them as a kind of *flor y canto*—flowers and songs—that speak on behalf of our broader communities.

Periodically, we infuse the text with our own testimonies as a way to humanize the key concepts that we are exploring. These testimonies—*testimonios* as we describe them throughout, but which may be told by whatever cultural group is marginalized in the mainstream—are counter narratives and are central to the framework of liberation advanced by proponents of Critical Race Theory. In the Latinx community, they are consistent with the longstanding Latin American genre of sharing spiritual narratives aimed at raising critical consciousness (Chamberlin & Thompson, 1998), both to expose actions designed to oppress as well as to highlight the ways in which individuals and groups enact resistance to that oppression (Pérez Huber, 2009). They allow you to travel along with us on our respective journeys (Cruz, 2012). The intent is for these to be read and understood.

We share these as a gift of ourselves to you as fellow BITOCs. In doing so, we invite you to think about your own experiences, your own stories, and your own *testimonios*. We also wish to be clear that care must be taken when employing *testimonios*. As Pérez Huber (2009) writes:

> However, we must remember the original purpose of *testimonio*—to center the knowledge and experiences of the oppressed. Thus, when adapted in educational research and pedagogical practice, it is important to recognize *testimonio* as a tool for the oppressed, and not the oppressor. *Testimonio* should not function as a tool for elite academics to "diversify" their research agendas or document their personal stories. (pp. 649–650)

Finally, we want to return to an idea we have already shared in this Introduction. We absolutely are pleased that you are pursuing teaching. We need you! And we need you to be successful in every possible way. Diversifying the teaching profession is essential for the work of promoting equity and justice in schools. At the same time, we are clear that no one can or should put all this responsibility on you as new, aspiring BITOCs. We recognize that there are forces—institutional, social, political, and ideological—that also must work in concert to address pressing educational challenges. You are important in this work and your success as a teacher will require professional collaborations with colleagues who share a common goal. But diversifying the profession, a long-term project, alone is not sufficient.

—With solidarity and love, Francisco and Longoria

➤ **Make It Happen:** *Testimonios*

As we mentioned in this Introduction, it is a gift to bear witness to a *testimonio.* This is an active process, and we encourage you to approach *testimonios* in this text with an open heart and orientation toward change. Cruz (2012) implores us to travel, or experience empathy and actively consider how we might rethink our own justice work and experiences. Now is a good time to begin thinking of your own *testimonios* as part of the development of a personal and professional portfolio. As you go throughout this text, you might write them down, record them as voice memos or videos, or artistically represent them. As you encounter others' *testimonios*, collect them in your portfolio, too.

When encountering *testimonios* in this book or elsewhere, we suggest the following practice:

1. Read the *testimonio* in its entirety, at least twice.
2. Consider: How did the *testimonio* make you feel? What points of similarity or empathy did you experience? Did you feel resistance or solidarity?
3. What are the key issues identified in the *testimonio*?
4. How do these *testimonios* exemplify key concepts in the chapter? In the book?
5. Recount any experiences that were similar to what was shared in the *testimonio* or that fostered an experience of your own.
6. What would you have said or done differently? What other interpretations might you have developed?
7. What key learnings can you take away from this *testimonio* into your own work as a BITOC?

CHAPTER 1

The Community
Mapping the Contours of the Profession

> Without question, when the majority of students in public schools are
> students of color and only 18 percent of our teachers are teachers of color,
> we have an urgent need to act. We've got to understand that all students
> benefit from teacher diversity. We have strong evidence that students of
> color benefit from having teachers and leaders who look like them as role
> models and also benefit from the classroom dynamics that diversity cre-
> ates. But it is also important for our white students to see teachers of color
> in leadership roles in their classrooms and communities. The question for
> the nation is how do we address this quickly and thoughtfully?
>
> —Education Secretary John B. King, Jr.
> (U.S. Department of Education, 2016)

When thinking about creating your home anew, before arriving there, you
cannot help but notice the broader community. As you search for that place
where you will teach and live, you will notice housing arrangements, where
businesses are located, spaces and places where the community gathers, among
other things. The locations of these are not haphazard; they are located there
as a result of both historical and contemporary political patterns and decisions
made about that particular place and space. You may notice some disparities in
the types of houses, in the quality of public works such as roads and sidewalks,
in the location of businesses such as grocery stores—convenient for some, but
not for others—among other things. You may notice that there are some spaces
designed for the health and well-being of children such as community centers
and parks, and other spaces that are not healthy such as hazardous waste facilities and abandoned houses. You may notice that certain people live in certain
neighborhoods, and notice who is not present in other neighborhoods. You
probably are thinking about how this new space is both different from and similar to previous places where you have lived and learned.

In this chapter, we begin to provide the broadest overview of the context of
teaching for Black, Indigenous, and Teachers of Color (BITOC). We begin with
a description of the professional community where the school/house you might
envision stands. You are coming into the work of educating children and young

people, work that has a long history—as long as the history of humankind. You also are coming into the professional role of teaching—that is, thinking about schooling—which has an equally long history. And teaching is just one part of the history of what we understand constitutes formal schooling. While the full scope of these histories is way beyond this book, we do provide a brief overview so that you understand the place and space—the professional community— where you find yourself. We also will review some of the central findings from the academic literature that shine a light on the current state of student and teacher diversity.

Before going further, we distinguish between *education*—the passing on of information, skills, and dispositions essential for people to know in order to live in a specific setting or context where they find themselves—and *schooling*—the systematic, intentional, and often decontextualized places (for example, think about what happens in those buildings we call schools) where most formal learning takes place today.

✍ *Testimonio*: She Never Came to School—Francisco

My mom rarely came to school events: not parent–teacher conferences, or assemblies, or plays we were in. At the same time, she always asked about how we were performing in school, looking at our grades and proud when we were doing well. I heard in her voice "estudia mi'jo" in her actions and in her eyes.

After she did not attend a play my sister and I were in during our high school years, we asked why she did not come to see us. She pointed out that school was associated with punishment for her. When she spoke Spanish, even on the playground, she was "fined" a nickel. Coming from a low-income family, she left school rather than continue onward.

It was from this that I first felt that difference between education and school.

We make this distinction with an enduring belief that for all people *education* is valued and valuable. However, as a result of the uneven (at best) and/or negative experiences people have had in the brick and mortar buildings called schools in our respective communities, *schooling* may not be as valued. This distinction is important as we acknowledge that before the conquerors of the Americas arrived, Indigenous people engaged in *education* consistent with the wide variety of worldviews they held and responsive to the specific settings they inhabited (W. Au et al., 2016). In saying this, we recognize the wide range of knowledge that was developed within each nation and the various ways in which that knowledge was taught from one generation to another (Hopkins, 2020; Lomawaima, 2004). Unfortunately, these knowledge systems and ways of knowing were disregarded when it came to *schooling*.

What we present in this brief history is a counter story to what traditional introduction to education textbooks might describe. In some instances, those traditional texts omit this history altogether. In others, it gets a brief mention. What we share here centers the historical experiences of Black, Indigenous, and Students of Color (BISOC) in schools in the United States.

 WONDER ALONE/WONDER TOGETHER

Why is it important to make this distinction between schooling and education? How might it explain minoritized student achievement differently?

AN ALL-TOO-BRIEF HISTORY OF EDUCATION
FOR STUDENTS OF COLOR

We are hopeful that you have had (or soon will have) a chance to explore fully the history of schooling for Black, Indigenous, and Students of Color in U.S. schools. It is a history marked by outright denial, segregation (most often into inferior facilities), marginalization in desegregated schools, assimilation, and cultural subtraction, with wide gaps in achievement outcomes and opportunities to learn. It is also a history marked by resistance from Black, Indigenous, and People of Color to that marginalization via legal means, via community activism and protests, and by resistance within school settings themselves.

The history of educational inequity for communities of color is wide and deep. Any effort we would make to capture this history, in this short section, would be insufficient. Therefore, we are choosing to focus exclusively on school segregation, school desegregation, and school integration. It is important to distinguish these three terms (see, for example, Frankenberg & Orfield, 2007). *School segregation* includes those laws, policies, and practices that exclude groups of students from attending school together. *School desegregation* includes those laws, policies, and practices that bring students together into a common school site despite racial differences. However, just bringing students into the same school building did not always lead to feelings of belonging, educational equity, or cross-racial relationships and understandings. *School integration*, then, encompasses deliberate efforts to foster academic, social, and psychological success of all students within the school walls.

We acknowledge (and apologize) that there are issues around assimilative curriculum and instruction approaches, discriminatory discipline policies, and inequity in school funding, among other issues, that this brief history will not be able to address.[1]

SEGREGATION, DESEGREGATION, AND INTEGRATION:
AN EXTENDED EXAMPLE

What we provide here is an overview of the history of schooling and the roles of teachers focused on one question: Who has access to what kinds of schools? For us, this means looking specifically at the history of schooling with respect to segregation, desegregation, and efforts at integration. We agree with An (2017) that focusing on segregation is instructive as a lens for exploring racism in education both historically and contemporarily. Even today, the many minoritized students attending resegregated schools are more likely to have lower achievement rates, which have great effect on future opportunities, including college attendance and overall income-earning potential (Frankenberg et al., 2019). We hope that focusing on this question of access will illuminate just *some* of the laws and policies that have negatively impacted the historical and contemporary experiences of communities of color in schooling.

Education Since the Early Years

Given the education–schooling distinction we shared at the beginning of this chapter, we want to make three important points that are essential for BITOCs to understand about the early history of *formal*[2] schooling in the United States. As Baldwin (1965) describes, that history is still most often true about education today. He said:

> For history, as nearly no one seems to know, is not merely something to be read. And it does not refer merely, or even principally, to the past. On the contrary, the great force of history comes from the fact that we carry it within us, are unconsciously controlled by it in many ways, and history is literally present in all that we do. It could scarcely be otherwise, since it is to history that we owe our frames of reference, our identities, and our aspirations. (p. 47)

First, formal schooling has been marked by exclusion and privilege (Neem, 2020; Spring, 2016). In the earliest years, wealthy and privileged communities pooled their funds together to pay for a teacher to teach their young, with a strong focus on religion-based learnings. Much like what was occurring in western Europe, boys were exposed to studying the "classics," while girls, when they were provided an education, were offered classes in sewing and other crafts.

Second, early on, at the founding of the United States as a nation, there was a strong understanding that education, knowledge, and learning are political (Spring, 2016). At the end of the War of Independence, the political elite of the new nation asked that British textbooks be abolished. At the same time, those in power sought to create history textbooks that shared a distinctly "North

American" slant, including propagating the narratives, heroes, and myths consistent with the vision of the national identity that was being forged. Even one of the first school-based texts, *The Blue Book Speller*, was created distinctly to emphasis North American—that is, non-British—pronunciation and spelling.

   Third, a general ideal exists that full participation in the nation and the very vibrancy of the democracy require an educated citizenry (Neem, 2020). Early reformers such as Thomas Jefferson advocated for an education—free and public—for all individuals (excluding Black slaves) as central to advancing a strong democracy. While it would take nearly another 100 years after the founding of the United States for public education to come to fruition, the ideal that education equals freedom and democracy endures as a truism for many. Ironically, this ideal was considered true especially by those who most often were denied access to schools. The very small percentage of Black children who became literate believed that literacy and freedom were inextricably linked. As Dumas (2014) details:

> During the years of state sanctioned slavery, white slaveowners would often beat their Black property for attempting to learn to read; for Black people in bondage, learning to read was understood not only as a pathway to economic mobility, but, perhaps more importantly, as assertion of their own humanity, a resistance to being propertied (Anderson, 1988; Dumas, 2014). (p. 16)

💬 WONDER ALONE/WONDER TOGETHER

In what ways do you believe education and democracy are linked? How does linking education and democracy support—or detract from—your work as a BITOC?

Education as the Great Equalizer

Horace Mann in the 1840s recognized that there was great inequality in schooling in terms of both resources and of who was and who was not attending. Mann (1848) asserted the need for a "common school" with a vision of free, public education for all in the public interest:

> It is a free school system. It knows no distinction of rich and poor . . . it throws open its doors and spreads the table of its bounty for all the children of the state . . . . Education then, beyond all other devices of human origin, is the equalizer of the conditions of men, the great balance wheel of the social machinery. (para. 9)

Of course, the question remains whether just having access to an education would, in fact, change the broader social, structural, or political inequalities that have an equally strong effect on an individual's or group's social advancement.

The Early Years of Segregation

Despite this ideal of education as the great equalizer, Blacks were prohibited, by law, from receiving an education. Prior to the Civil War, there was only a 5% literacy rate among Blacks (Spring, 2016). The 5% were educated—most often secretly—by freed Blacks, some slaveholders, and White abolitionists. This era also included some of the first Black schools in the nation. These schools were segregated and created in the best interests of Negro children (Mabee, 1979).

It is important to note that the segregation of Black students in schools was challenged as early as the 1840s, beginning when Benjamin Roberts (*Roberts v. City of Boston*, 1840) sued to allow his daughter to have access to White schools[3] (National Museum of American History, n.d.). Despite his losing the case, the Black community kept up their protests and, in 1855, Massachusetts passed the first state law to abolish segregated schools, almost 100 years before the famous *Brown v. Board of Education* court case did so nationally. With the abolishment of slavery and the help of organizations such as the Freedmen's Bureau, Blacks pursued education, and the literacy rate rose to 70% soon after the Civil War. Those who were taught to read and write soon realized that education, by itself, did not equate to better social opportunities.

The Latinx community's experience with education, in many ways, mirrors that of the Black community. Prior to the Mexican-American War, Mexicans who lived in what soon would become the southwestern United States attended public or religious, primarily Catholic, schools (San Miguel & Valencia, 1998). Although not widespread, these schools served their local communities, promoting literacy, language, and culture. At the end of the Mexican-American War (1848), northern Mexico became part of the United States. The first public schools for students in those areas were engaged in *cultural subtraction* largely via segregation; the justification was the need for these new Mexican American students to attend schools that addressed their English-language needs. In these segregated schools, Mexican American students were exposed to a Eurocentric curriculum, Spanish was prohibited, and corporal punishment was common (San Miguel & Valencia, 1998).

Native American youth have been educated by elders and leaders since time immemorial (W. Au et al., 2016). They learned in the context of living within the specific spaces and places where they found themselves. But they were not allowed to attend public schools because, as one central rationale to their prohibition, they were not *citizens*; most Native Americans were not formally recognized as U.S. citizens until 1924 with the passage of the Citizenship Act (Haynes Writer, 2010). That is, despite being the original inhabitants of the land on which the United States was built, Native Americans were treated as foreigners in their own land. However, as early as the 1860s, public funds, granted to missionaries, were provided to teach Native children, and thus began the first efforts to create segregated boarding schools (Haynes Writer, 2010).

Boarding schools were off-reservation residential schools such as the Carlisle Indian Industrial School in Pennsylvania. The intent of these boarding schools was to separate children from their community (generally) and their cultural and linguistic origins in order to "kill the Indian, save the man" (Pratt, 1892, p. 46). That is, the intent was to "civilize" Native Americans and, in so doing, engage in cultural and linguistic genocide. Those who survived these boarding schools reported the following: exposure to disease, efforts to change their identities (burning their clothes, cutting their hair, and giving them a European name were often part of their initial induction), use of corporal punishment especially if residents used their native languages, psychological humiliation, physical and sexual abuse, and forced labor, among other forms of oppression (Lomawaima & McCarty, 2002).

 WONDER ALONE/WONDER TOGETHER

What have been some common experiences of education for people from these three social identity groups? What has been different and what were the reasons?

Immigration and the Solidification of Segregation

In the early 1900s, the schooling experiences of Black, Latinx, and Indigenous youth were repurposed as immigration tides changed with the arrivals of people from eastern and southern European nations, most notably Poland, Germany, and Italy. At the same time, increasing numbers of individuals were arriving from East Asia, most notably China and Japan. Political leaders believed that public schools would be the best place to begin to "acculturate" these immigrants. Americanization, or the replacing of home culture with a standard curriculum frame associated with being in the United States; citizenship, education, and English became the norm, and deculturalization (Spring, 2016) a principal strategy.[4] In effect, what non-European racial and ethnic minorities had been experiencing in schools was now the norm throughout the nation. *The significant difference was the promise to these new immigrant communities that cultural assimilation would lead to greater social, economic, and political integration given their White racial profile.*

As for non-European racial and ethnic minorities, segregation in all aspects of public life continued as normal and became legitimatized. The Supreme Court ruled in *Plessy v. Ferguson* (1898) that public facilities, including schools, could continue to remain segregated as long as they were equal. Separate but equal become the dominant legal (de jure) doctrine for segregation in schooling as well as in other public facilities for the next nearly 60 years.

Underlying this assimilation and segregation was a belief in the racial/ethnic inferiority of BISOCs and their communities, coupled with a desire to not "contaminate" White students and their culture (San Miguel & Valencia, 1998). This view was supported by the growing eugenics movement—led by White, European American social scientists—which intended to identify Whites as superior and then promote those social groups who exhibited characteristics of White, European American cultural orientations (Stoskopf, 1999). At the same time, efforts were made to have differences from these cultural orientations considered abnormal. While this was not an entirely new idea—Plato described much the same idea in *The Republic*—it really took hold in the early 20th century in an effort to justify privilege to the White, European American, elite social class while simultaneously justifying segregating non-European minoritized and low-income children. Two particularly oppressive school practices, standardized testing and tracking—the deliberate placement of students into a fixed schooling path based on perceived academic ability—were heavily influenced by the learnings from the science of eugenics.

 WONDER ALONE/WONDER TOGETHER

What is tracking and where, if at all, have you seen it in practice? What elements of standardized testing have been used to marginalize students of color?

Beginning of the End of De Jure Segregation?

At the end of World War II, the United States faced a dilemma at home. On the one hand, the narrative used to lure people to support U.S. involvement in the war was the fight against Germany and Japan to ensure democracy and liberty for these and other foreign lands. On the other hand, many Black, Latinx, and Native American soldiers fought bravely in Europe and in the South Pacific. However, upon returning home, they were met with the continuation of segregation and a racist ideology; that is, they did not experience at home the democracy and liberty they had been fighting for abroad.

Recurring court cases advanced by communities of color had been focused on dismantling school segregation. Consider the *Alvarez v. Lemon Grove School District* (1931) case (Donato & Hanson, 2019). The Lemon Grove School District sought to build a new school specifically for Mexican American schoolchildren to ensure cultural subtraction, to foster English fluency, and, in the words of the plaintiff, R. Alvarez, to avoid "the deterioration of American students as a result of contact with the Mexicans." In this case the local court in San Diego ruled in favor of the Alvarez family on the grounds that Mexican

American children were racially White and therefore covered by state protections for Whites (we recognize the problematic nature of using this argument to justify integration). This court case, while notable, had only local significance.

In 1947, the Mendez family sued the Westminster (CA) School District, whose determinations about the school that students should attend were based primarily on the color of their skin; that is, racism was at the core of these determinations (Santiago, 2019). The school district, however, argued that these segregated schools would best address the lack of English proficiency of Latinx students. Interestingly, some of the students who were being sent to the segregated Mexican schools spoke English fluently. Further, the Mendez family argued that integration, not segregation, was better at promoting English-language proficiency and cultural assimilation (we recognize the problematic nature of using this argument to justify integration) (Santiago, 2019). The state supreme court ruled in favor of Mendez and soon after the state of California passed a law ending segregation in schooling.

The Mendez case was one of several that were cited in the *Brown v. Board of Education* court case (Santiago, 2019). The Brown family, along with 11 other families sued the Topeka School District in Kansas on the grounds that their children had to walk past the White segregated school to attend the all-Black segregated school. Interestingly, when the case was at the U.S. District Court level in Kansas, the judges upheld the cause of segregation in schools even while they acknowledged, as argued by the lawyers for the families, that there was indeed a detrimental effect of segregation on the psychological well-being of Black children.

The coalition of Brown supporters appealed the case to the Supreme Court. The lawyers for the plaintiffs argued that segregated schools undermined the equal protection clause of the Fourteenth Amendment. On May 17, 1954, the Supreme Court justices ruled unanimously that the "separate but equal" doctrine, used in *Plessy v. Ferguson*, was unconstitutional; in fact, they asserted that "separate is inherently unequal." Of note, in the following year, the Supreme Court decision in *Brown II v. Board of Education* ruled that desegregation of schools should happen "with all deliberate speed."

De Facto Segregation

As you might imagine, schools did not willingly open their doors to students who had been attending ethnic- and racial-specific segregated schools, despite the Supreme Court decisions. While schools were desegregated by law (de jure), the new fight was to end segregation in practice (de facto). What occurred was yet another decade of outright opposition to allowing Black and Latinx students to attend White schools. One of the most dramatic instances occurred in Little Rock, Arkansas, where nine Black students attempted to integrate the all-White Central High School. As the students attempted to enter the school, television viewers saw the anger, hate, and racism directed by White students, families,

WONDER ALONE/WONDER TOGETHER

What do you imagine it meant for the Little Rock Nine to force integration in this school setting? How do you imagine it would feel to learn in a school where you were not wanted?

and community agitators at these nine Black students. The Governor of Arkansas, Orval Faubus, then ordered the National Guard to prohibit the Little Rock Nine, as they became known, from entering the school. President Eisenhower sent federal marshals to escort the Black youth into the school. It should be noted that even as these students were escorted into the school, they reported being harassed and beaten.

We wish to make three important points here about desegregation in schooling. First, note that the movement of students was from ethnic-minoritized schools to White schools. This meant the closure of these minoritized-serving segregated schools, which, despite their struggle with inadequate resources, often served as the hubs of their local communities. Along with the closure of these schools was position eliminations for tens of thousands of BITOCs who brought with them, in the main, a belief in the potential of the children in their community, an ethic of community uplift, and connections to the culture of the community (Ladson-Billings, 2004a). Second, it meant that these students would be attending these heretofore all-White schools; but the schools did very little to prepare their mostly White school faculty, students, and staff for the integration of these new students. Third, it should be easy to imagine the courage of those first few students, in many schools around the nation, who entered formerly segregated schools knowing that they were not really welcomed.

Civil Rights and the Pursuit of Educational Equity

Given the desegregation court rulings, the political turmoil of the Vietnam War, and community activism via the civil rights movement as well as other social movements of that time, the federal government was compelled to increase its role in moving toward an equity agenda in the 1960s. It began with the Civil Rights Acts, focused largely on eliminating discrimination and segregation (1964) as well as expanding and protecting voting rights (1965). At the same time, communities of color were actively demanding their equal rights in education. Importantly, these included demands to abolish biased standardized testing, enact an inclusive curriculum, increase the number of BITOCs, and expand access to extracurricular participation, as just a few examples. These were central for keeping the role of schools front and center in advancing this equity agenda. While there were some notable efforts to desegregate and integrate schools, there was also continuing resistance. Sometimes this segregation occurred within the schools themselves—within-school segregation—often via tracking.

One other segregation–desegregation court case was notable during this era that makes clear the process of *racialization* (San Miguel & Valencia, 1998), the act or process "of giving a racial character to something; or making it serve racist ends" (Reeves, 1983, p. 173).   Given that in earlier court cases Latinxs were classified as Whites for integration purposes (*Lemon Grove*, for example), several school districts were placing Latinx students with Black students to be able to report the success of their integration efforts. This resulted in litigation in Texas, where one court ruled that Mexican Americans could not be considered White for integration purposes (*Cisneros v. Corpus Christi Independent School*, 1970) and a case in Houston where the court ruled that they could (*Ross v. Eckels*, 1970). The latter case meant that Black and Latinx students could be placed together in schools to serve a school district's desegregation efforts. The question was settled 3 years later in a Denver case, *Keyes v. School District No. 1* (1973). The Supreme Court ruled that Mexican Americans were an identifiable minoritized group and thus could not be included with Black students when reporting integration efforts.

The Backlash

By the end of the 1970s, opportunities were expanding for all students, nearly 85% of whom were graduating from high school, with a majority going on to postsecondary education. Despite these important gains, and also because of these gains, a conservative backlash ensued, and many of these initiatives were revised, recalled, or rolled back.

Schools began to slow down efforts related to desegregation. Even on the legal front, important court decisions ruled against efforts to promote greater school desegregation even when it was voluntary. One court case in this regard was *Parents Involved in Community Schools v. Seattle School District No. 1*; this decision also included a voluntary desegregation plan for the Jefferson County Public Schools in Kentucky. These decisions were following earlier court case rulings that said race, in and of itself, could not be used for school acceptance and placement decisions—even when the goal of racial desegregation and integration was acknowledged as educationally advantageous.

We wish to note that there was one key victory for school access on the legal front. *The Supreme Court ruled that all children, regardless of their documentation status, were entitled to a free public education.* In this case, *Plyler v. Doe* (1982), the state of Texas passed legislation to withhold state funding for those students who were undocumented within school districts (San Miguel & Valencia, 1998). At the same time, Tyler Independent School District, where James Plyler served as superintendent, sought to charge undocumented children $1,000 to attend their local school district, as a result of the loss of state funding. Several families, using the anonym "Doe," sued on the grounds that this violated the Equal Protection Clause of the Fourteenth Amendment, which states, in part, that "nor shall any State deprive any person of life, liberty, or

property, without due process of law; nor deny to any person within its juris-
diction the equal protection of the laws." This was a most significant victory for
the access rights to a free, public K–12 education for all children within the U.S.
borders, whatever their immigration status.

The Resegregation in Schooling

The challenge to school desegregation and integration is far from over. Since
the 1980s, the nation has retreated from the ideal of school desegregation and
school integration, even after over 65 years of *Brown v. Board of Education* court
cases. Schools are becoming nearly as segregated, by some estimates, as they
were prior to *Brown v. Board of Education*. The federal government has made
virtually no federal efforts to promote school desegregation or integration. According to UCLA's Civil Rights Project's report *Harming Our Common Future*
(Frankenberg et al., 2019), the net result is the following:

- The number of Black students attending integrated schools has been
  decreasing since 1988.
- The percentage of minoritized students attending *intensely segregated
  minoritized* schools (where 90% of students are non-White) has
  tripled in the last nearly 30 years from 5.7% to 18.2%.
- Over 41% of Latinx students attend intensely segregated minoritized
  schools.
- White students attend schools that are largely White, while Latinx
  students attend schools that are largely Latinx.

Collectively, this increasing segregation in schooling speaks to the ideas
we presented earlier in this chapter. Unfortunately, we seem to be returning to
the foundational roots of education regarding exclusion and access. We have
recognized how deeply political schooling is, even when it comes to issues of
which school students attend. And we worry that the resulting educational inequalities for our highly diverse student population pose a serious threat to the
nation's democracy. We believe nothing less is at stake.

 WONDER ALONE/WONDER TOGETHER

What are the key factors you see driving the return to hyper-segregated
schools? What are the long-term implications for how we think about
schooling for equity and justice?

The Education Debt

As you read this all-too-brief history of the experiences with segregation–desegregation and lack of integration efforts for BISOCs in schools, we trust you will note that schools have struggled historically and contemporarily with providing the support necessary for student success for all. This history has been marked by exclusion—that is, who has access to public education—as well as the low quality of the education that they receive. It has been marked by efforts to strip students of their cultural and linguistic assets, seeing them instead as deficiencies to be overcome, via efforts at cultural and linguistic assimilation. It has been marked by court cases and public policy decisions that, more often than not, have worked against ensuring educational equity. And, as important, it also has been marked by substantial resistance and efforts on behalf of communities of color that have been on the frontline of seeking quality education for their children.

Given this history, we highlight a question that initially was asked by Gloria

💬 WONDER ALONE/WONDER TOGETHER

Why is it important to think about the broader political context when we think about the role of BITOCs and schooling? What other aspects of this political context would you add to this mix?

Ladson-Billings (2006), in her presidential remarks to the prestigious American Educational Research Association: In working to erase education disparities, what is the *education debt* owed to Black, Indigenous communities and Students of Color as a result of these long histories of oppression?

SCHOOLING AND DIVERSITY IN THE CONTEMPORARY ERA

As suggested, we come into this particular social and political moment with a troubling history that has shaped how we think of schooling in the contemporary era. As with the history of education for diverse communities, we provide a brief snapshot of some of the most compelling contemporary issues we face when thinking about education for our increasingly diverse student population. But we want to be equally clear that these are not the *only* contemporary issues our communities face.

The Demographic Imperative

One thing that is an absolute certainty is that the overall demographic profile of the nation continues its trajectory toward increasing diversity (see Figure 1.1). What mostly stands out is not only the decrease in the White, non-Hispanic/

Figure 1.1. Percentage of U.S. population by race, 2000 to 2017

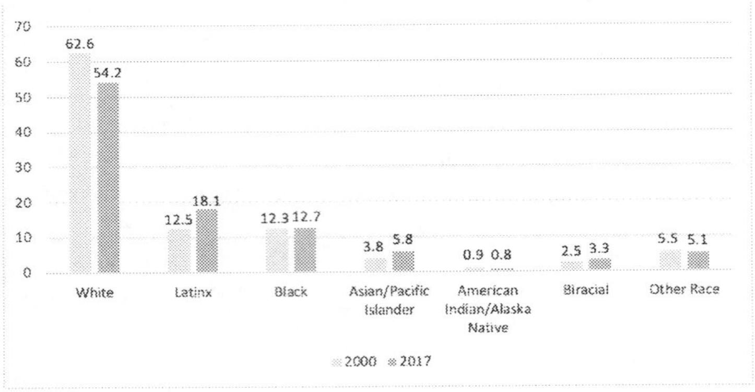

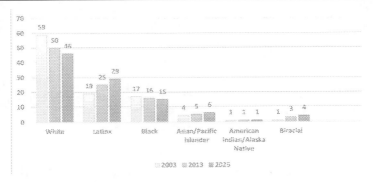

Source: U.S. Department of Commerce, Census Bureau (2012, 2018).

Figure 1.2. Percentage distribution of public school students enrolled in prekindergarten through 12th grade, by race/ethnicity: Fall 2003, Fall 2013, and Fall 2025

Source: Musu-Gillette et al. (2017).

Latino[5] population but the substantial increases in the Hispanic/Latino and Asian and Pacific Islander communities. We must consider that this is not a blip but rather the continuing trajectory of the face of the United States.

Looking at the diversity in schools reveals this trajectory even further, given that it demonstrates the future of our nation (see Figure 1.2). As is evident, between 2003 and 2013, the percentage of White students enrolled in public schools decreased from 59% to 50%, while the percentage of Hispanic/Latino students went from 19% to 25%. There was a modest decrease in the percentage of Black students, and a modest increase in the percentage of Asian and Pacific Islanders as well as in individuals identifying as biracial. *We emphasize the key idea that ethnic minoritized students are now the numerical majority in public schools.*

Figure 1.3. Percentage distribution of teachers in public elementary and secondary schools, by race/ethnicity: School years 2003–04 and 2015–16

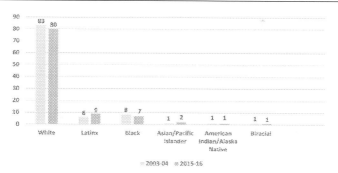

Source: de Brey et al. (2019).

Figure 1.4. Racial and ethnic diversity of students and teachers in U.S. public schools

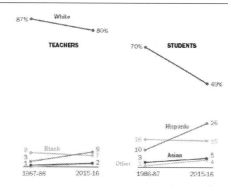

Source: Geiger (2018).

While it is clear that the student population is becoming increasingly diverse, the teaching profession is not particularly diverse. In Figure 1.3, we can see that despite the call for greater teacher diversity, especially over the past 20 years, the percentage of BITOCs has increased only from 17% to 19%. Disturbingly, the percentage of Black teachers actually has decreased (from 8% to 7%). Latinx teachers increased from 6% to 9%, and Asian American teachers increased from 1% to 2%. The percentage of teachers from all the other demographic groups largely stayed the same.

It might be helpful, then, to see how the student demographics and the teacher demographics interact (see Figure 1.4, taken from a study by the Pew Research Center). The mismatch is especially evident when viewing the two side by side. The figure also highlights the oft-cited demographic imperative for diversifying the teaching workforce.

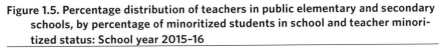

Figure 1.5. Percentage distribution of teachers in public elementary and secondary schools, by percentage of minoritized students in school and teacher minoritized status: School year 2015–16

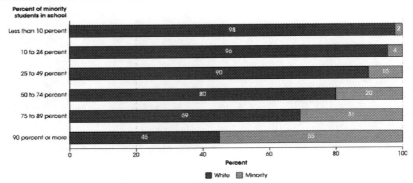

Source: U.S. Department of Education, National Center for Education Statistics (2019).

One of the important characteristics of BITOCs is their desire to work in diverse school settings (see Figure 1.5). From that figure, you can see that as the percentage of minoritized students increases, so does the number of minoritized teachers. BITOCs, for example, make up 55% of the teaching workforce in schools where at least 90% of the students are minoritized. In addition, Geiger (2018) points out that BITOCs are not evenly distributed in schools when considering socioeconomic status. That is, the percentage of BITOCs increases with the number of students who are eligible for free or reduced-price lunch. 74% of BITOCs are in schools where 50% of students receive free or reduced lunch. In essence, BITOCs find themselves in highly diverse and low-income schools (Geiger, 2018). These are described as "hard to staff" schools that BITOCs often seek out for their professional employment (Achinstein et al., 2010).

As is evident, the racial and ethnic demographics of our schools are rapidly changing toward greater diversity. However, a substantial gap persists in the percentage of BITOCs in our nation's schools. The low numbers of BITOCs are not just a historical artifact, as described earlier. Achinstein et al. (2010) engaged a comprehensive study around teacher turnover of BITOCs. After reviewing 70 studies on the issue, they found that BITOCs leave the profession at a substantially higher rate than White teachers. We discuss the reasons why BITOCs leave the profession in Chapter 5.

Educational Disparities

Beyond the growing demographic divide between teachers and their students, there continue to be substantial disparities in education outcomes. Unfortunately, on just about every measure of academic performance, BISOCs are outperformed by their White counterparts. Whites rate higher on measures of

Figure 1.6. Educational attainment by race, gender: 2012

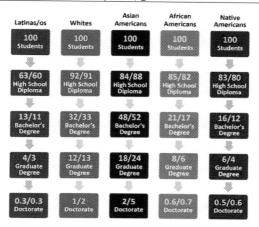

Note. The first number represents females, the second males.

graduation rates, college-going rates, and performance on academic achievement tests. Compared with Whites, BISOCs have higher suspension rates, dropout/pushout rates, and representation in special education programs. We provide a thumbnail sketch of some these performance measures.

To best exemplify the overall educational disparities in our communities, consider Figure 1.6, drawn from data in the 2012 annual American Community Survey, as reported by Pérez Huber and colleagues (2015). Assuming 100 adult-aged people in each of the categories, how many of them would have completed high school, attempted college, completed a bachelor's degree, completed a master's degree, or completed a doctorate or professional degree? These differences in academic attainment levels are another indicator of academic achievement variability among the various social identity groups.

If you were to break this down even further, you also would see disparities, both across and within categories, based on poverty level, sex and gender identity, English-language proficiency, dis/ability, citizenship status, and so on.

As mentioned, it is not only in terms of academic performance that you will see these achievement differences. Consider the school suspension rates for BISOCs, a major driver influencing academic achievement, given that suspension/expulsion begins the road to missing classes and disaffection with schooling. Black, Latinx, and Native American students are more likely to experience longer and harsher punishment than their White peers (U.S. Commission on Civil Rights [USCCR], 2019). These rates are directly correlated to the race-based policies, practices, and procedures that schools employ for student discipline.

This is related to not only what these policies are but how, when, and on whom they are implemented. A major report on the effect of differential school discipline completed by the USCCR (2019) found that while they receive more suspensions, especially involving students who also are identified as having a disability, BISOCs actually do not engage in higher rates of misbehavior. What is significant about the differential application of school discipline policies is that a growing number of scholars show how differential school discipline based on race is related to the "school-to-prison" pipeline (see, for example, Alexander, 2020; C. Clark, 2012).

In addition to these examples, consider the influence of recent political policy shifts with direct impact on BISOCs. Consider the gradual erosion of important human, civil, and educational rights, such as efforts to scale back protections for LGBTQ+ youth and undocumented children, including pending legislation around the Deferred Action for Childhood Arrivals policy decisions.

If that were not compelling enough, after Trump became president of the United States, evidence showed increased levels of bias, oppression, hostility, and stress in schools, including incidents of racism, homophobia, and religious intolerance (Rogers et al., 2017). The Southern Poverty Law Center's *Hate at Schools* (Costello & Dillard, 2019), for example, reported 3,265 incidents of hate/bias in schools in Fall 2018 alone. The report showed that only 5% of these incidents were reported to the media, no one was disciplined in 57% of the cases, and 90% of administrators did not denounce the incidents (or, at a minimum, reaffirm school values). As might be expected, racism, anti-Semitism, anti-Latinx, and anti-LGBTQ+ bias/prejudice were reported as the focus of the

💬 WONDER ALONE/WONDER TOGETHER

What other elements of the politics of education and schooling would you add to this list? Why are they important when you think about schooling for equity and justice?

hate. This is tied, according to the report, to the outright bias and discrimination in the political climate evident at all levels of the political establishment.

The Opportunity Gap

We agree with those scholars who assert that these educational disparities—bemoaned problematically as an *achievement gap*—are less a reflection on students' academic potentialities and more a direct result of an *opportunity gap* (Carter & Welner, 2013; Ladson-Billings, 2006; Schott Foundation, 2016). Shifting attention away from blaming students for causing those educational disparities allows us to focus on policies, practices, and procedures at the *school level*, such as failure to build on the cultural and linguistic assets of students from diverse backgrounds; *community level*, such as unfair and segregated housing policies; and *governmental level*, such as inequitable and inadequate school funding that creates, maintains, and exacerbates these educational disparities (see also National Education Policy Center, n.d.). What is clear is the understanding that these broader structural inequities in education and public policy, not a community's or student's language and culture, best explain ethnic minoritized student underachievement.

✍ *Testimonio*: Across the Tracks—Longoria

Living in northeast El Centro, California, felt normal to me. My grandmother lived blocks away. There were carnicerías and paleta vendors we would frequent in my neighborhood. We lived right next to the train tracks in town and I will always feel at home around the nocturnal rattle of railroad cars trudging by. Like in so many communities, these train tracks represent a dividing line across economic and racial lines.

But I never attended my neighborhood schools. My mom had the shrewd judgment to find ways to send me to the public schools her coworkers talked about, schools in other neighborhoods that were predominantly White, higher socioeconomic status, and with more resources. She found ways to get me to attend those public schools that had gifted and talented education and robust music programs, which I participated in. To be clear, there were problems at these schools, too. I was initially denied admission to gifted programs in spite of high standardized test scores. A White principal once voiced to me, then 10 years old, during a discipline meeting that I did not belong at the school because of where I lived, and threatened action because of it. Nevertheless, the academic and extracurricular opportunities found at these schools boosted my chances at college preparation.

As a teen, I had discovered classical music and sang with a community choir. A member of the choir, a local White teacher, offered to drop me off at home after we had attended a concert together. I will never forget her increasing discomfort as we drove further into my neighborhood. As we arrived across the tracks, she was visibly shocked. Upon arriving at my parents' humble duplex home, she appeared on the verge of tears. In our subsequent interactions she had changed. From then on she frequently shared unsolicited scholarship information, college advice, and would only share musical opportunities that were no-cost. Well-meaning as she was, I had gone from being a singing colleague to an opportunity for charity.

I do not mean to demean my neighborhood; yet it is tough to admit that my educational opportunity was likely boosted by not attending my neighborhood schools. The educational opportunity gap is not some abstract concept to me, but rather a very real lived experience from my own life and the lives of people that continue to live in my neighborhood. In my teaching career, the specter of educational opportunity gaps still haunts the communities where I help train teachers.

I have had to leave my neighborhood to access higher education and economic opportunities. I try to return home every year—or more when I can. Returning to the same home I grew up in—that my parents still live in and finally paid off the mortgage on—is a necessary reminder of where I'm from. I will always be from across the tracks and that has made me who I have been in this education journey.

Of interest is how the opportunity to learn is related to ways in which the curriculum and instruction reflect and sustain students' cultural identities, characteristics, and needs. Toward that end, Carter and Welner (2013) point to the following as a direct way to eliminate educational disparities:

- High-quality pre-K
- Wraparound services for students and families
- After-school enrichment and support
- Adequate, equitable, and stable funding
- Small class size
- Early and intensive reading and math interventions
- Elimination of tracking
- Personalized instruction based on relationships with caring adults
- Culturally responsive instruction
- Strong supports for experienced, expert teachers

It is these last two characteristics of the opportunity gap to which this book is dedicated.

 WONDER ALONE/WONDER TOGETHER

In what ways is it more (or less) productive to think about educational disparities as an opportunity gap? What other opportunity gaps also should be considered?

CONCLUDING REFLECTIONS

We wish to acknowledge that this broad overview is just the tip of the iceberg. The long history of educational inequality and injustice, the demographic divide, and the pressing opportunity gap frame the most central issues facing schools today. Having said this, we believe this overview should provide you with a foundational understanding of the context in which we are asking you to consider making the school where you will teach, your schoolhouse.

We share several key ideas we hope you take from this chapter. First, educational inequality has been and, in too many ways, continues to be the "standard operating procedure" in schools. For BISOCs, this is experienced in racial abuse (Kendi, 2019) as well as oppressive policies, procedures, and practices in schools. Underlying these are white superiority and privilege as well as racism, sexism, homophobia, and other forms of oppression. These are anchored by the tangled web of ideologies (Weiner, 2000) around meritocracy, color- and power-evasiveness, deficiency orientations, and neutrality/objectivity (which we describe in Chapter 2). In this way, we hope you understand the powerful role that race and culture play in influencing schooling outcomes.

A second key idea is that everything you bring, as a BIPOC, matters to teaching and can serve as your greatest resource. A central belief of this text is that who you are as a BIPOC matters as much as anything else in terms of your role as a teacher (Petchauer & Mawhinney, 2017). You often cannot fully understand, or know, the influence you are going to have on the students, teachers, parents, and broader community.

Finally, strengthen your understanding of the school-related issues facing diverse communities of learners to identify those areas in need of growth and improvement. An important ethic will be to recognize that there will always be more to learn. We are all, as Freire (1970/1996; see also Philip & Zavala, 2016) reminds us, unfinished as humans working in institutions that are unfinished, in a nation whose vision of what it means to live humanely and justly is unfinished. Embrace this "unfinishedness."

⇾ Make It Happen: Portfolio Activity—Community Walk

This community walk activity is inspired by an assignment Verónica Vélez and Longoria have used in their Family and Community Engaged Teaching courses. Getting to know the community you serve is imperative. The goal for you as an educator is to become like an ethnographer in order to understand the specific factors, and their intersections, operating at the specific school site and in the specific community where you find yourself. The intent is to uncover those factors that are supporting educational equity and excellence as well as to undermine those negative factors that work against the development of a healthy school environment, especially for BISOCs.

Step 1: You might initiate this process through a walk around the neighborhood of a school of interest. Alternatively, you might drive or use public transportation. Pay attention to what land features (walkways, parks, private areas) are present. Are there areas designed for children and families? Are the conditions safe to walk in at most hours of the day? Is the area accessible to different ability needs? What do the housing patterns suggest about who lives in the neighborhood? What cultural communities are present? What cultural dominance is evident (signs all in English, for example)? What kinds of businesses are most visible? What food accessibility is present?

Step 2: Learn about the history and experiences of diverse groups. Explore the history of a local ethnic minoritized community. What has been the experience of diversity in the local community? What has been the history of oppression and resistance? What has been the history within the school where you are placed/assigned? What has been the history of the school in terms of the diverse groups of students who have attended? What are the current challenges the school is facing with respect to equity and diversity?

Use this reflection to make an initial map of the community and then use the map to make comparisons with official maps such as Google Maps. Compare your mapping with U.S. Census data, official school data, and existing resources about the history of the community. How do any of these reinforce or provide a counter narrative to what you encountered during your community walk? How might this better inform your service to the school community?

⇒ Keep It Going!

- Listen to Malcolm Gladwell's podcast on the history of *Brown v. Board of Education*, on pathologizing BISOCs, and on the power of teachers, especially Teachers of Color: https://dcs.megaphone.fm/PPY7758175647.mp3?key=9fef47de9a8bb8293b802fea42d69 ba4
- Read the poem "Freedom's Plow" by Langston Hughes.
- Read the poem "Maps" by Yesenia Montilla.

CHAPTER 2

The House

Finding Your Theoretical/Ideological Foundations

If we have been gagged and disempowered by theories,
we can also be loosened and empowered by theories.

—Gloria Anzaldúa (1990, p. xxvi)

When considering where you plan to live and work, one of the central features you want to consider is the foundation of the home. When seeing the house for the first time, you will notice whether it sags, whether and where there are cracks in the foundation, whether the paint is peeling, among other things. You will notice whether the house is tall and wide or short and small; whether it is square, rectangular, hexagonal, or circular (consider a hogan on a Hopi reservation). You will notice whether the earth on which it sits is dusty and brown or wet and green.

You also might look at possibilities/needs for improving on the space: an addition given the demands of the composition of your *familia*, a fresh paint job to renew what has become old, strengthening/shoring up window treatments to address areas no longer keeping occupants warm, and even parts of the house that will require a complete remodel because it is no longer habitable. In addition, you would ask the person who is showing you the house questions about the house itself (e.g., how old it is, how energy efficient it is) and about the neighbors and the neighborhood. In essence, you are working to learn the story of this specific house, this specific space, this specific place.

None of the information you are able to gather, in and of itself, is right or wrong, good or bad. Rather what it does is frame the kind of opportunities that you believe are open to you as well as the kinds of challenges you might confront. In essence, it profoundly influences, although it does not determine, the kind of home you will be able to make. At the same time, it offers this caution: If the foundation is weak, the structure may come tumbling down. All of this speaks to the importance of the foundations of your home and the surrounding place—the importance of the physical space.

Education is no different. In education, though, we are concerned with the theoretical and philosophical foundations—the theorizing space (Anzaldúa, 1990)—on which each of us, as educators, stands. We also recognize that each school and each school district also occupies a theorizing space. Just as with the physical space, we may need to touch up, add on, shore up, or transform our theoretical spaces to better ensure that we are thoughtful in meeting the needs of students and communities of color. Likewise, if our theoretical foundation is weak, our conceptual orientations and their related practices will crumble.

Consider whether the school and most of the teachers who work there believe that "children are children" and "everyone should be treated equally," that is, treated exactly the same, no matter what. All students will be exposed to the same curriculum, instruction will be the same for all, classroom organization might include specific rules and routines with no exceptions, and school discipline might be applied in a uniform way across all classrooms, again with no exceptions. These are, among so many other elements of schooling, shaped by the belief that everyone deserves the same treatment; students are to be treated with *equality*.

On the other hand, if the school and the teachers therein seek to welcome the many ways of being in their student population and meet each student's individual needs when learning, they may advance an *equity* agenda. In this regard, they will engage those same key school elements differently, including encouraging and allowing for the exploration of nontraditional voices in the curriculum, teaching small groups differently based on student need, creating a classroom community where differences are affirmed, and adopting restorative justice practices (see, for example, Sullivan & Tifft, 2008) where discussion and problem solving are used in the face of classroom conflict.

In this chapter, we turn our attention to the structural features of the house and its place: in this instance, the theoretical and ideological foundations of schooling for diversity and equity. We identify the theoretical orientations that specifically help you to understand the various ways education for equity and diversity has been and can be thought about in school settings. In doing so, we will share how various forms of oppression can be understood in the context of schooling.

To begin, we will explore dominant theoretical orientations, such as deficiency theories, difference theories, and bias theories, which are the most common approaches to explaining BISOC achievement. We then will describe theoretical orientations particularly those aimed at decolonization, addressing anti-Blackness and advancing a Critical Race Theory. We especially highlight asset-based theories of both language and culture, as well as describe community cultural wealth. In doing so, we are asking you to recognize that while some theories of schooling have been used to justify educational underachievement of BISOCs, there are also theories of schooling that can be illuminating and liberating.

In essence, in this chapter, we invite you to ask the question: What are the theoretical and conceptual foundations upon which you stand as a Black, Indigenous, and Teacher of Color (BITOC)?

What is your understanding of the distinction between equality and equity? How might knowing this difference influence the way you think about the goals you have for your own teaching?

UNDERSTANDING THEORIES OF MINORITIZED STUDENT PERFORMANCE IN SCHOOLS

Before we share the various theories of minoritized students' performance in school, we begin with several key observations about the nature of understanding the academic challenges of our work with students, families, and communities. *First, we know that schools, in the main, are "working" well for many students from certain social identity groups but not for others* (Berliner & Biddle, 1995). Recall that this has been true historically, since schools were constructed for middle- and upper-class White men.

Second, we know that historically and contemporarily, the educational system is marked by racial and class inequities, rooted in poverty and racism. Jonathan Kozol (2012) aptly has called these "savage inequalities." That is, many of the most critical factors facing schools are related to racism and the disregard for people in poverty that lie at the heart of almost all educational marginalization.

Third, given the increasing demographic diversity in schools, these disparities threaten the very fabric of our nation. We consider this a human rights issue, given what we know about the implications of our failure to address these disparities (Osler & Starkey, 2017; Rios & Marcus, 2011). For example, the mass incarceration of People of Color has its origins in schools; Alexander (2020) has called this the new Jim Crow for Black, Indigenous, and People of Color. Indeed, Harvard Professor David Williams and his colleagues (2019) identified oppression as a life or death matter given the adverse effects of racial stress on people's health.

Finally, given that we are aware of these longstanding disparities and their effect on communities of color, we seem to not have the will to do anything about it. We are haunted by the question Nate Bowling (2016), Washington Teacher of the Year in 2017, asked: Does America really care?

As we move into describing specific theoretical foundations, we are reminded that teaching is a deeply intellectual work. As you read this, we call on you to be prepared to engage deeply and critically about the ways in which various theoretical frameworks either demonize our communities or affirm them. It is also important to recognize that our theories often are guided by a set of ideologies: those longstanding, unstated, implied, and rigid sets of ideas. As you progress through this chapter, keep in mind that your everyday teaching for learning practices are guided by your theoretical frameworks, which are influenced by your personal and often unexamined ideologies of what it means to be human, what is good/bad or right/wrong, and what it means to be educated.

WONDER ALONE/WONDER TOGETHER

What are your initial understandings about why BISOCs often are outper-formed by White students on academic achievement measures (as de-scribed in Chapter 1)? How do these explanations reflect your understand-ing of how and why people learn and fail to learn?

We also note that what we present here is just an introduction to these various theoretical and ideological frameworks. Our grandest hope is that you find the theoretical and ideological clarity and intentionality that informs your work as a BITOC.

Deficiency Theories

We begin with a dominant (disturbingly so) group of theories of academic achievement that problematize students, their families, and their communities. Collectively they are called deficiency, or deficit, theories. One such theory posits that it is *biological deficiency*—that is, genetic inferiority—that explains lowered academic achievement. Notably, standardized assessments generally and IQ tests specifically have been the primary tools used to prove this deficiency. While the proposition of biological deficiency has a long history, evident in the eugenics movement where scientists worked to explain intelligence as linked with racial genetics, its modern version can be found in Herrnstein and Murray's *The Bell Curve* (1996).

Another of the deficit theories is called *social deficiency*. This theory focuses on the ways different social groups are structured. As one example, social deficit–oriented theorists blame the family structure, such as single-parent households, which, it is argued, leads to identity and other attitudinal or emotional problems, which in turn lead to delinquent behaviors in and out of school. One important factor often left out when pathologizing Black family structures, for example, is the inhumane, racist practice of breaking slave families apart when they were to be sold (Alexander, 2020; Scott, 1997; see also Coates, 2015, for a discussion of the disruptive role of mass incarceration on Black families).

A third deficiency theory focuses on the values and attitudes of cultural groups; this is known as *cultural deficiency*. For example, one prominent and contemporary focus, embraced by many schools, is related to "the culture of poverty" (Payne, 2005). In this framework, Ruby Payne argues that people in poverty adopt a "present-minded" orientation as well as fatalistic attitude; both lead to a lack of work ethic, thereby explaining the educational inadequacies of students of families in poverty. Notably, several scholars (Gorski, 2008; Hammond, 2015) push against this idea of the culture of poverty. Hammond points out, for example, that *strategies* to cope with poverty are not norms and beliefs, that no one purposely seeks to live and stay in poverty, and that poverty is not a culture.

✍ *Testimonio*: They Have No Language—Francisco

I was invited to come and meet Latinx parents at an elementary school that had seen a dramatic increase in the number of Latinx students in a city that had not seen new immigrants for decades. I was told by the person who invited me that there would be a teacher there who was considered a strong advocate and ally for the parents.

A colleague and I arrived, and I met this teacher-advocate, who mentioned some of the big academic challenges these students were experiencing.

We greeted the parents as they arrived. Soon after, the teacher began by mentioning some of these academic challenges she'd mentioned to me earlier—though this time, in front of the parents.

In describing challenges, she mentioned that the Latinx students come to school and "have no language." Surprised, I said, "No language?" No, she clarified, these newcomer students did not speak English. It was clear that in the mind of this "advocate," English was "valued" and other languages were "worthless."

As I spoke with the parents, I made an extra effort to encourage the parents to continue speaking Spanish to their children, saying that English would come with time, that knowing Spanish would help them with their English, and that their children would, in the end, be *"dotado en dos idiomas"* (gifted in two languages).

As I drove home, my colleague and I lamented that this deficit ideology—besides being demeaning to the parents—may have manifested itself in lowered expectations, such as discouraging a student whose English is still developing from considering higher education because they are just not "college material." It could lead to a justification for denying special services or academically enriching programs (such as gifted/talented or highly capable) because the student just will not benefit (after all, they have no language). It might lead to dismissing the potential power of bilingual education programs because, after all, only one language was valued. Or perhaps this supported the teacher's sense of self: She was teaching in low-income schools so that those students could be "saved" from themselves, their families, their language, and their communities.

If nothing else, it was shocking, inappropriate, and unproductive.

There are multiple problems with deficiency theories. In addition to the fact that the essence of these theories is contested by other researchers and scholars, they *blame the victim*; that is, they blame the students and their families/communities for the students' lack of academic performance. The proposition in these theories is that it is the students' motivation, talent, and experiences outside of school that determine their success inside school.

At the same time, deficiency theories deflect attention away from the role of schools (curriculum, instruction, assessment systems, teaching practices, school policies, for example) in explaining minoritized student achievement, as well as obscuring larger societal causes such as poverty, housing restrictions, and unemployment, among other things. Deficiency theories are ahistorical in that they do not account for the role of schools relative to these parents in this community, let alone broader educational policies that marginalized BIPOCs in the past. Teachers' unexplored theories are left intact; for example, the belief, which is too rarely problematized, that one actually can measure intelligence and that IQ tests are effective at doing so. Deficiency theories do not allow for a focus on how the social dynamics, such as group conflict, or the school culture may be detracting from student learning. Deflecting attention away from teacher and school factors is problematic also because it is these factors that we as educators and activists can most control.

 WONDER ALONE/WONDER TOGETHER

Think about how you learn at home. How is it different from how you were expected to learn at school? Think about how you communicate at home (and in your community). How is it different from the ways you are supposed to communicate at school?

Difference Theories

Difference theories operate in much the same way as deficiency theories but soften the critique of individuals, families, and communities by framing these as "differences." As a result of the cultural values and behaviors taught by caregivers and elders, young children develop culturally specific values, communication styles, and ways of learning. *The central hypothesis of difference theories is that the greater the difference between a student and both their teachers and the dominant cultural values of the school (in terms of home language, values/worldview, community upbringing, ways of learning, among other things), the more challenging it will be for the student to perform well academically.* Conversely, the more *similar* the student is to their teachers and the dominant worldview, the stronger the likelihood that education will be easier. What often is implied and expected is that if students want to achieve academically in school, it will be up to them to change their ways of learning to become more like the dominant culture and teaching styles of the teachers and school.

Researchers have documented many differences between students and their teachers as well as their schools. For example, scholars have focused on several differences that are true for all learners, such as the proposition around "multiple intelligences" proposed by Howard Gardner (2011). In addition, a variety of

Figure 2.1. The Dunn and Dunn learning styles model

Stimuli	Elements

Stimuli:
Environmental
Emotional
Sociological
Physical
Psychological

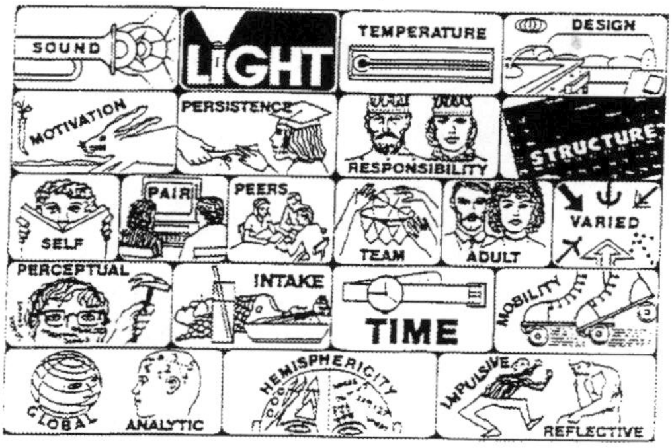

Simultaneous or Succesive Processing

Source: Dunn et al. (1995), Taylor & Francis Ltd, http://www.tandfonline.com

other stylistic differences have been identified by Dunn and colleagues (1995; see Figure 2.1 for several of the most central stylistic differences). As you consider these, you probably can begin to identify some of your own learning style preferences.

For us, the largest two clusters of these differences, with special interactions with culture, fall into learning style differences and communication style differences. We want to preface this discussion of these differences with the acknowledgment that while there are culturally influenced styles of communication and learning, we (and others; see, for example, Paris & Alim, 2017) respond cautiously to a difference orientation because it *essentializes* culture; that is, it assumes one can capture the "essence" of any cultural orientation with a list of traits. It also assumes culture is static (nonchanging) and it implies that culture is monolithic—a grand generalization that becomes a dangerous form of stereotyping. We assert that it is better to assume that there is not one way to learn or communicate as a cultural being.

Learning Styles. The first differences we explore more deeply are in learning style. Scholars have pinned specific learning styles to particular cultural groups. For example, Black children and Latinx children often are described as being more communal than individualistic in their sociological learning orientation (Hammond, 2015). In this instance, teachers would want to create a stronger form of community in the classroom with a strong focus on collaboration as opposed to competition in school-based assignments. As another example, some cultures emphasize learning via the spoken language, while others emphasize learning via the written word. In the former, seeing and hearing are primary modes of learning over reading or being read to by others.

Communication Styles. A second category focuses on communication style differences. This includes culturally based differences in communication, such as use of nonverbals, language/dialect varieties, and sociolingual competence (knowing the culturally appropriate what, when, and how of talk), among other things.[1] It leads to the argument that how you teach, in terms of communication and interaction style, is as important as what you teach.

Three brief examples might serve to make this point. In their review of research, Deyhle and Swisher (1997) point to differences in when Native American students participate. The childrearing customs in some Native communities encourage children to perform tasks only after they have become competent; this is challenging when those same children, now as students, are asked to answer questions whose answers they are not certain about. As a second example, Smitherman and Smitherman-Donaldson (1986) point to the use of Ebonics, also known as African American Vernacular English, by Black students—developed as a synthesis of American English and African language traditions—which resulted in differences such as multiple negation. In this instance, a student might say something like, "Don't nobody don't know that history," perhaps much to the consternation of the student's teacher. A final example comes from Hawaii, where research shows that children, outside of schools, tend to engage in collaborative conversation at the same time, called "talk story" (K. H. P. Au & Kawakami, 1985). In this instance, a teacher may ask a question of a specific child; however, multiple children may contribute to the response in overlapping speech, violating the teacher's expectations.

A key is to keep in mind that "the linguistic form a student brings to school is intimately connected with loved ones, community, and personal identity" (Delpit, 2014a, p. 169).

It is worth reiterating the central proposition: *The closer the learner is to the dominant culturally influenced learning and communication styles of the teachers and school, the greater the likelihood that the student will experience higher academic achievement.* Schools have developed compensatory programs (for example, ESL) to help minoritized students to "catch up"—that is, become more like the teacher and the "ideal" student—or even to teach parents how to support their child's literacy by "reading to them at home," all from a White, middle-class value orientation. This positions minoritized youth as different, and the White, middle-class orientation as the norm. Other researchers in this field of inquiry have called on schools to adjust by seeking to produce cultural continuity or cultural compatibility (see, for example, Cardenas & Cardenas, 1972).

To be sure, we encourage you to recognize and honor how often these stylistic differences reflect the rich cultures that our students bring to classrooms and schools. Indeed, we want to point out that scholars of color, notably Gloria Ladson-Billings (1995) and Geneva Gay (2000), have written extensively about culturally responsive teaching, as described more fully in Chapter 3. For now, consider Gay's (2000) definition of culturally responsive teaching: "using the cultural knowledge, prior experiences, and performance styles of diverse students to make learning more appropriate and effective for them; it teaches to and through the strengths of these students" (p. 29). Culturally responsive teaching includes using culturally specific communication and learning styles, while valuing and integrating the community knowledge of the students in your classroom.

To be clear, we do ask that you think about these stylistic differences in a more complicated, nuanced way that does not essentialize, as we described earlier. A more productive way to engage these is to think less about them as styles that are fixed and to consider them as possible practices used by and within specific communities. This is consistent with the call by Gutiérrez and Rogoff (2003), who urge us to seek to identify the locally specific "repertoires of practice" enacted by and within a specific cultural community. For them, it is these local repertoires of practice that make up "culture" for any specified social identity group in a particular setting.

We end this discussion by acknowledging the resiliency of minoritized students, who often have had to develop multiple approaches to learning to be successful as a learner at home and a learner in school. At the same time, it also means they likely have had to develop two identities, one for home and one for school. While many minoritized students receive a message that they should cast off their learning styles and thereby the cultural identity of their home in favor of the White, middle-class cultural orientation of the dominant culture— which we assert is morally wrong to ask of anyone—we are aware that many minoritized youth successfully have developed a dual frame of learning and being: one for school and one for home (Súarez-Orozco & Súarez-Orozco, 2009). Sometimes this means that BISOCs are able to develop a hybrid identity that brings the home and school together, for the specific purpose of achieving academically in school while also moving comfortably within and through their home community. This is a theme we will come back to more fully in Chapter 4, where we ask that you employ your cultural and linguistic assets in the service of academic achievement in increasingly diverse schools and classrooms.

In the end, these latter approaches highlight how students are developing cross-cultural competencies. We wonder and ask: Do teachers and schools welcome and value the power that comes from this hybridity in terms of being able to operate in multiple cultural contexts as well as to be academically successful?

Bias and Oppression Theories

Another set of explanations for minoritized student failure in schools rests on theories of bias and oppression. On one level, it seems obvious—and something we imagine you have already experienced—that a teacher who holds a strong negative bias against you because of your social identity group membership negatively influences your desire to learn, at a minimum, let alone any actual learning. On another level, you probably have also been in a situation where you felt as if the school rules were unfair to your social identity group. Consider, as

WONDER ALONE/WONDER TOGETHER

How would teaching and learning look different in schools and classrooms where students' cultures and languages were welcomed and affirmed? Can you provide an example from your own schooling experience of how your culture and/or language helped you to be successful on an assignment or in an activity?

one example, policies on paying to participate in after-school activities, which severely limit opportunities for students from low-income families. It is these theories of bias and oppression to which we now turn.

To begin, it is important to identify some specific terms. See Table 2.1.

We hope that you will note that the first three terms—stereotype, prejudice, and (although to a lesser degree) discrimination—are centered on the interpersonal level. These terms help us to understand and describe what one person does to another. This individualistic orientation dominates in the *whitestream*—the bias toward centering Whiteness and White perspectives—where people believe that racism is the result of the views/behaviors of a few "bad" apples (but certainly not them). This logic asserts that if a person constrains their own racist tendencies and those of others, then we can contain racism. To be sure, *individual-level* bias, prejudice, and discrimination are all highly problematic.

At another level, we imagine you already think about how these forms of oppression operate at the *group level*. It is the use of this social-group level of analysis that allows us to look at how oppression is embedded in institutions and in ideologies. This level acknowledges that groups—and not just individuals—vie for power. The group that dominates solidifies its power and then seeks to create and operate institutions so that they work most favorably for those from the dominant social identity group. The group in power also begins to shape the messages (that is, discourses) and beliefs (that is, ideologies) that are employed to justify its domination. The group in power seeks to make this domination invisible and, at other times, asserts that the domination is natural or morally/ethically right. *In essence, Prejudice + Discrimination + Power = Oppression.*

Using a group level of analysis allows us to explore how oppression plays out at the institutional level; that is, to consider the policies, procedures, and practices of the school. For example, there is nothing inherently better about using English as the *only* language for teaching and learning. Every language is capable of conveying every idea, no matter how complex the idea. The decision to make English the only language of instruction advantages English speakers and disadvantages speakers from homes where other languages are spoken. This is an example of institutional linguicism.

Institutions make policies, practices, and procedures about who has access to what classes, what curriculum will be taught and from whose perspective, how learning will be assessed, what teaching strategies can and cannot be used,

Table 2.1. Definition of Terms

Word	Definition
Stereotype	An overgeneralized belief about a group of people that is harmful to that group (J. A. Banks, 2008)
Prejudice	Rooted in stereotypes, a positive or negative attitude or value orientation not supported by facts; these often are guided by oppressive beliefs (J. A. Banks, 2008)
Discrimination	The actions associated, intentionally or not, with prejudicial beliefs. This can occur both interpersonally and institutionally.
Power	The ability to "make the rules" for how institutions operate, the "messaging" or narratives disseminated, and the underlying ideologies guiding their development and implementation
Oppression*	The use of prejudice, discrimination, and power to dominate an individual or a group of people: a. Internalized—What individuals come to believe about the rightness of their own oppression b. Individual—What one individual, because they have power, does to another c. Institutional—The policies, practices, and procedures used by institutions (e.g., judicial system, schools, banks) that advantage some and disadvantage others d. Ideological—The values/beliefs of the powerful, messaged through schools and the media, justifying these forms of oppression or describing them as natural/logical
Hegemony	The imposition of the dominant group's ideology, via institutional systems and majoritarian narratives, on others

* See also John Bell's 4 I's of Oppression as described by Cuauhtin (2019b).
Source: Adapted from Sensoy & DiAngelo (2017) unless otherwise noted.

who can be hired to teach, which schools and extracurricular programs will receive funding and which will not, how relations with parents will be fostered or not, where students will have decisionmaking authority, and so on. Each of these—and the countless other policies, procedures, and practices institutions adopt—have the potential to empower some and oppress others. Again, these decisions often are made to ensure and maintain the success and domination of those in power.

Underlying these institutional decisions are ideologies used to justify how institutions are organized. Several ideologies dominate in the collective consciousness in the United States. One is the belief that we live in a *meritocracy*: the idea that a person's effort and talents determine how much they will achieve. That is, a meritocracy assumes anyone and everyone can earn a living wage, find meaningful work, live in a safe community, attain adequate housing, access

💬 WONDER ALONE/WONDER TOGETHER

What are some of the ways your schools were structured to support groups of students differently? How were students "tracked" into AP or shop classes? When and how were standardized tests used? How were students empowered (or not)? How were families and communities brought into the work of schooling (or not)? Whose stories were central in the curriculum that was taught? How did teaching styles support some—but not others?

health care when needed, and so on. (See Berliner, 2006, for a comprehensive discussion of how all of these are negatively constrained by poverty.)

Several other dominant ideologies work against clarity of understanding around social inequities and injustices. One of these is *individualism*, an exclusive focus on the ability of the individual to determine their life course, bypassing any degree of group-level analysis or collective action. Another of these is *universalism*, a claim that we are all the same, thereby diminishing or dismissing altogether the importance of cultural/racial differences in our everyday experiences. Yet another of these is the belief in one's *objectivity/neutrality* when it comes to understanding social and societal events and trends. This belies the fact that, as a result of our upbringing, education, and experiences, we are all positioned to view things from a certain slant or personal and social-cultural vantage point.

Educators are especially keen on uncovering and examining our ideological orientations related to teaching and learning; that is, our *epistemologies*. Our epistemologies are those values/beliefs centered around knowledge and knowing: what is worth knowing, whose knowledge counts, how do we know what we know, how do we show what we know, among other things related to knowing. For example, you may have heard about the "canon" of an academic discipline, the knowledge generated largely by White scholars for White students that is privileged in schools and thought of as essential and foundational. The canon represents a particular epistemological orientation about whose knowledge counts. As another example of an epistemological assertion—and a dangerous one at that—consider the belief that we actually can measure, especially with timed tests (the implied belief being that speed is an indicator of intelligence), what a person knows.

What we recognize is that there is a vast world of different epistemologies or knowledge systems that people have developed, based on their social and cultural location, to understand their world and to share that knowledge with one another, especially the young people in their communities. Despite this broad range, the whitestream has adopted and enacted a Eurocentric ideological orientation. In doing so, this ideological orientation has devalued so many other ways of knowing. The devaluing of an entire racial group's ways of knowing is called epistemological racism. Importantly, oppression requires the subjugation of these alternative epistemologies. Anti-oppressive work, in contrast, requires us to question this epistemological dominance (de Oliveira Andreotti et al., 2015).

We share a few other key ideas about oppression. First, these various levels of oppression are self-supporting. The ideological and institutional levels of oppression enable (at a minimum) and encourage individual (person-to-person) bias and discrimination; for example, a school's focus on "English only" signals a teacher's right to reprimand a student for speaking their mother tongue inside or outside the classroom.

It is equally important to acknowledge that the individual also can push against the institutional and ideological. That is, teachers and their allies can encourage languages other than English in their classrooms, advocate for support of students' home (primary) languages, and even urge the administration to pursue bilingual education for all students. In addition, teachers and their allies can question those who make sweeping statements about English as a superior language and, instead, can challenge English-only instruction as part of a larger colonizing project (Macedo, 2000). In short, advocates of social justice must question institutional structures, people's social experiences, and the underlying ideologies that support them. Until there is a broader shift in ideologies and institutional practices, it will be nearly impossible to have a broader shift in these coercive relations of power (Cummins, 2009; Dumas, 2016).

Second, *hegemony* is the imposition of one group's ideology on everyone in society (Sensoy & DiAngelo, 2017). Supporting this imposition is the framing of these ideologies as neutral, logical, and natural. These ideologies become so pervasive, so embedded in our systems, that everyone comes to believe them, even those who are the targets of this ideological oppression. The net result is that hegemony allows the group in power to govern without needing the consent of those who are oppressed. *Schools and the media are the primary instruments used to impose one group's ideology on others.* Dumas (2016), describing a specific form of hegemony (anti-Black racism), argues that it "infects educators' work in schools, and serves as a form of (everyday) violence against Black children and their families" (p. 17). For Dumas, individual, institutional, and ideological racism can be described as the "technologies of violence" (p. 14).

A third key idea is that institutional and ideological oppression is an ongoing project. That is, our society continues to engage in oppression projects based on social identities. This is happening, in part, because the dominant group benefits from these oppression projects. The work around "white privilege" has been instrumental in pointing out that members of the dominant group are benefiting from oppressive institutions, social experiences, and worldviews (see, for example, C. Collins, 2018; McIntosh, 2007). Therefore, there is no neutrality to this work: Either you're combating oppression or you're allowing oppression to flourish.

Fourth, we are all being influenced by these forces of oppression. BIPOC—the targets of oppression—are not immune; like everyone else, we are influenced by individual, institutional, and ideological oppression. Sometimes people from these oppressed groups ("us") come to accept and believe what is expressed about our own social identity groups (Kendi, 2019). This is called *internalized oppression*. Of course, we also know that, as a result of the oppressive social and cultural experiences many of us have had, the vast majority of BIPOCs work (and continue working) to develop a sense of critical consciousness and adopt an active anti-oppressive stance more fully. Oppression has been real and personal as well as tied to how others unfairly understand our communities.

CRITICAL THEORIES OF SCHOOLING FOR DIVERSE CHILDREN AND YOUTH

As Anzaldúa's (1990) quote that opened this chapter asserts, theories can oppress us, but they also can liberate us and our communities. This key assertion requires that we seek out those theoretical orientations that frame our communities not as deficient but as culturally and socially rich, full of human and social potential. These theories are not new to us, although they are, without doubt, less well-known. For example, there is W. E. B. Du Bois's (1903) work, which named the forces of racism that negatively affect Blacks, deny them their humanity, and diminish their potential.

Consider more contemporary examples of the many critical theories that could be explored more fully. Several female scholars have advanced ideas around "women's ways of knowing" (epistemologies) (e.g., Belenky et al., 1986; Harding, 2007) as valued and valuable not only for women but for the greater improvement of society more broadly. Patricia Hill Collins's seminal work *Black Feminist Thought* (2002) raised the importance of understanding the intersections of race and gender in theorizing about difference for Black women. Latina/Chicana feminists have been advancing a variety of theoretical frameworks, such as acknowledging the *trenzas* (braids) of Latina feminists' personal, professional, and communal identities (e.g., Delgado Bernal, 2001; Quiñones, 2016). Loutzenheiser (2010) discusses the principles around teaching and learning queerly, while Cruz (2015) explores how Latinx transgender youth enact resistance to what they see as marginalizing conditions given their multiple identities. Erevelles (2018) challenges the "ableism" that is an undercurrent of the U.S. society in favor of one that sees people who are disabled as fully human.

***

Readers, we pause for a moment here to lament the challenge of making decisions about which of the many liberatory theories we highlight in greater detail. As can be seen, there are engaging, insightful, provocative, and productive theoretical orientations emerging, mostly from Black, Indigenous, and Scholars of Color and other minoritized identities, that are worthy of your attention. We recognize this as a challenge to us as writers. At the same time, we challenge you to pursue these when the opportunities to do so present themselves, either in your teacher preparation program or as part of your professional development as a teacher.

We briefly highlight two particularly timely and provocative theories that provide ways of thinking about issue of racial inequality. We hear the call to attend to issues of anti-Black racism and settler colonialism—both of which problematize and push against white superiority—as central to understanding issues of race in the United States as well as around the world. As Tuck and Yang (2018) describe it:

> There is no legitimacy in the field of education if it cannot meaningfully attend to social contexts, historical and contemporary structures of settler colonialism, white supremacy, and antiblackness. (p. 5)

We also focus on asset-based approaches to diversity, such as funds of knowledge and community cultural wealth, within a broader Critical Race Theory, given that they tie more directly into our vision of an identity-sustaining pedagogy for BITOCs.

Anti-Black Racism

Anti-Black racism, as a theoretical framework, seeks to explain the intensely difficult personal, social, and political experience of racism for Black people in the United States. It centers the Black experience with racism and spotlights it as a specific experience in an effort to provide greater attention and clarity to Black bodies and Black thought (Walcott, 2018). It pushes against broader antiracist movements, especially when they minimize the importance of Black suffering. This includes everything from the incarceration of Black people and the devastating effect this is having on their schools and communities (Coates, 2015; see also Laura, 2018, on the need to think of schoolwork as "anti-prison work" [p. 26]), to the staggering number of Black people who have been killed by police officers and self-styled vigilante groups (at the time of this writing, the latest was the stalking and killing of Jacob Blake in Kenosha, Wisconsin). It includes the continuing segregation in housing, state policies aimed at disenfranchising Black voters, increased inattention to the health crises in Black communities, among many other things. According to Dumas (2016):

> The aim of theorizing antiblackness is not to offer solutions to racial inequality, but to come to a deeper understanding of the Black condition within a context of utter contempt for, and acceptance of violence against the Black. (p. 13)

Anti-Black racism theorizes that society (historically and contemporarily) has positioned *Blacks as property* to be owned and controlled. In doing so, scholars argue that Blacks are treated as nonhuman; not just as an "Other" (someone who is different from the whitestream) but as a people who are *other than Human*" (Dumas, 2016, p. 13). As described by Dumas, society "positions Black people as the embodiment of *problem*, a *thing*, rather than a people suffering with problems created by antiblackness" (p. 15, emphasis in the original). What is needed is an abolitionist movement aimed at Black freedom and requiring "the death of whiteness, the end of the Master" (Dumas, 2018, p. 43). The key point for us, as educators, is the need to interrogate the ways in which education has played a significant role in anti-Black racism as it is experienced by Black children in our nation's schools. As Dumas (2016) describes it, "Radical improvements are impossible without a broader, racial shift in the racial order" (p. 17).

Settler Colonialism

Just as Black people have deep scars from the memories and continuing legacies of slavery that continue to influence their identities, as described by anti-Black racist theories, so too have Native Americans experienced intergenerational trauma as a result of settler colonialism. Settler colonialism is deeply embedded in how we think about democracy itself (Grande & Anderson, 2017).

De Oliveira Andreotti and colleagues (2015) assert that settler colonialism is guided by progress, industrialism, humanism, secularism, linear-time flows, and scientific reasoning. It is patriarchal, capitalist, Western-centered, and Christian-centric. Colonization also relies on the subjugation of people whom the colonizers encounter, theft of the land, subtraction of cultural identities and linguistic capabilities, imposition of race-based and racist ideologies, and the elimination of alternative epistemologies (de Oliveira Andreotti et al., 2015). As you consider these processes, note that education plays a central role, historically and contemporarily, in the "deculturalization" of Native identities and languages (Spring, 2016), in the teaching of a racist ideology to justify the colonization that occurred and is occurring, and in the refusal to consider Indigenous ways of knowing in schools.

Decolonization requires us to be more deliberate and intentional about ending the logics of settler colonialism in education—that is, both the ideology and the methods of colonization as described in the previous paragraph—in order to pursue social justice and honor Indigenous sovereignty (de Oliveira Andreotti et al., 2015; Grande, 2004). This requires the restructuring of relations of power from coercive to collaborative (Cummins, 2009). It means questioning epistemological dominance and affirming Indigenous ways of knowing, especially about place and space. And it means advocating for school policies, procedures, and practices that challenge colonization and respond to the needs of Indigenous children, families, and communities.

More specifically, Grande (2014) asserts the need for teachers to imagine themselves as warriors who reject "settler logics" of individualism, competition, accumulation, and immediate return and instead embrace pedagogies of connectedness, cooperation, generosity, and thinking long-term . . . resist knowledge as "production" and see knowledge as a "relationship" to place, to history, to self, to other, to community, and to higher senses of being. (p. 19)

 WONDER ALONE/WONDER TOGETHER

How do you see schools positioning themselves in these anti-Black and colonization projects? How do we make sense of our roles in schools as hegemonic sites of anti-Blackness and colonization? How can schools engage in anti-oppressive projects that seek to abolish anti-Blackness and decolonize? What does your most radical imagination of schools, and teaching/learning, look like given this, as Tuck and Yang (2018) ask?

Funds of Knowledge and Community Cultural Wealth

Pierre Bourdieu, the French educator/theorist, argued that schools are structured around middle-class value orientations and that, as a result, the students from the middle class enter schools with a cache of cultural and social capital (Bourdieu & Passeron, 1977). That is, middle-class values, tastes, culture, demeanor, speech, writing, among many other things, dominate in schools in comparison to working-class values. Similarly, as Affolter (2019) describes it, "schools cater to white middle and upper-class students' speech, habits, and basic dispositions" (p. 102) in the United States, and this is a basis for educational oppression. The net result is that this advantages middle-class youth via a robust, personal, and human set of relationships and other institutional support systems within schools. Bourdieu and Passeron (1977), in this instance, were challenging the ways schools were *not* working for those from low-income and working-class communities.

This set the stage not only for critiquing schools for what cultural and social capital was valued but also for asking the opposite: What are the forms of social and cultural capital that students from marginalized communities bring to schools? This served as the basis for asset-oriented theories, including the pioneering work by Luis Moll and his colleagues (1992), who argued that we need to understand the "funds of knowledge" that students from diverse social and cultural backgrounds bring, and build on these funds of knowledge in schools and classrooms. We hope you, as do we, see this as a deliberate "talk-back" against deficiency theories that identified what people were missing in terms of values and knowledge; rather, it seeks to identify the assets (i.e., cultural capital) of a particular social group that illuminate what people do know and can do—even when these knowledges and experiences are not recognized, let alone valued, in schools.

WONDER ALONE/WONDER TOGETHER

Think about all of the things you learned at home, prior to going to school, but which may not represent directly learning to read or write. What did you learn that was helpful for you as a student later in life (working in community with others, taking care of siblings, helping to translate for a parent, among many other things)? Think about all the things a person whose parents are farmworkers know. What knowledge and skills might these parents have and share with their children?

To illustrate, consider this extended description by Lisa Delpit (2014b):

If we're going to ensure that all children learn to read, I believe we have to turn our notion of "basic skills" on its head. What we call basic literacy skills are typically the linguistic conventions of middle-class society. . . . What we call basic skills are only "basic" because they are one aspect of the cultural capital of the middle class. What we call advanced or higher-order skills—analyzing new information, evaluating the relative merits of concepts and other problem-solving skills—are those that middle-class children learn later in life. But many children from low-income families learn them much earlier because their parents place a high value on independence and real-life problem-solving skills.

So children come to us having learned different things in their four-to-five years at home, prior to formal schooling. For those who come to us knowing how to count to 100 and to read, we need to teach them problem solving and how to tie their shoes. And for those who already know how to clean up spilled paint, tie their shoes, prepare meals and comfort a crying sibling, we need to make sure that we teach them the school knowledge they that haven't learned at home. (pp. 18–19)

In short, Delpit asks us to understand that the dominant institutional culture of most schools values White, middle-class orientations of what it means to be school-ready or literate. She asks us to identify the knowledges and skills students bring from home as powerful assets in the growth and development of young people in schools and society (see also Delgado Bernal, 2001, on pedagogies of the home).

Building on the idea of funds of knowledge, scholars have been working to identify the collective wealth of specific minoritized communities. Many of these forms of community cultural wealth (CCW) are specific to various ethnic minoritized communities, such as the *community uplift* capital or ethic in Black communities. Or it may be the cultural capital associated with respect, responsibility, reciprocity, and caring relationships (Lee & McCarty, 2017) important to Native American communities.

Consider the work of Tara Yosso (2005, 2013). Yosso wanted to talk back to the oft-cited critique that Latinx parents "just don't care" about education (see also Valencia, 2002). Educators make this assertion because Latinx parents may not participate in schools as expected, given middle-class orientations. The parents (often because they cannot do so) may not go to parent–teacher meetings or organizations, may not help students with homework, and may not create a quiet place for children to learn at home, among other normative ways of participating in schools. Yosso (2005), working in a specific Latinx community, asked parents to share how *they* believed they *were* supporting the education of their children. From that, Yosso identified six forms of CCW, and others have identified other forms of CCW beyond the initial six identified by Yosso (see Table 2.2).

We want to be sure you recognize that these forms of CCW were identified in specific communities. We know that the forms of CCW that are operating in your own local community—your home community or the community where your school is located—may be different; in fact, you should *expect that there will be* other forms of community cultural wealth at play. They may be specific to a particular region. You might, for example, find that the cultural capital developed by a Latinx community in an urban, historically Latinx community (think East Los Angeles) was different from the cultural capital required of those in a Latinx community in a rural area of the country that only recently saw new Latinx immigrants (see Hamann et al., 2015, for descriptions of the diaspora in the Latinx community).

The central implication is that rather than assuming the kinds of community cultural wealth exhibited in the community where you are located based on the descriptions of other scholars doing work in other communities, it is better to consider yourself a learner of your students by asking: In what ways do the families and communities who send their children to these schools support the dreams for their children's education?

Critical Race Theory

We end our description of liberatory theories by describing Critical Race Theory (CRT). CRT emerged from legal studies that showed that the judicial system is not, in fact, neutral and fair but is a racist and unjust institution. This principle soon was applied to education (Ladson-Billings, 1998; Ladson-Billings & Tate, 1995). CRT in education "asks such questions as: what roles do schools themselves, school processes, and school structures play in helping to maintain racial, ethnic and gender subordination?" (Solórzano & Yosso, 2000, p. 40), as well as whether schools can help end racial, gender, and ethnic subordination (Zamudio et al., 2011).

Critical Race Theory is guided by several theory-to-practice principles that can be applied to schooling (Solórzano & Yosso, 2000) as follows:

- Foregrounds race and racism as central in U.S. society and sees these as deeply engaged in society and in schooling
- Attends to intersectionality by showing how racism intersects with other forms of subordination

Table 2.2. Descriptions of community cultural wealth

Capital/Asset	Description
Aspirational	The ability to maintain hopes and dreams for the future even in the face of barriers
Linguistic	The intellectual and social skills learned through communication experiences in more than one language and/or style
Navigational	The skills of maneuvering through social institutions
Social	The network of people and community resources one relies upon, including adults and teachers as important others
Familial	The cultural knowledges nurtured among *familia* (kin) that carry a sense of community history, memory, and cultural intuition
Resistant	The knowledge and skills cultivated through behavior that challenges inequality
Political	The political consciousness around understanding how oppression works and ways in which one is actively engaged in politically (Cuauhtin, 2019c)
Ancestral	The knowledge, talents, and ways of being that come from ancestors (Cuauhtin, 2019c)
Ecological	The ways in which people connect to the land and the environment, and see themselves as an interdependent species (Cuauhtin, 2019c)
Spiritual	A strong belief, rooted in a connection to a reality greater than oneself, as a form of resistance and resilience (Galván, 2006)
Cultural*	**The ability to share and apply one's cultural knowledge and the specific skills of well-being in ways that foster action (knowledge + reflection + action = praxis)** (Cuauhtin, 2019c)

*We bold this form of capital because we believe this is a central asset for BITOCs; we focus on this in Chapter 4.
Source: Yosso (2005) unless otherwise noted.

 WONDER ALONE/WONDER TOGETHER

As you look at this list of community cultural wealth, which forms (if any) were developed in your home and community? Provide an example. What might be some other forms of CCW that were developed in your home/community but are not listed here? How might you, as a teacher/social justice advocate, affirm, enhance, and/or sustain these with the young people you encounter? Finally, how might we leverage these forms of capital to resist oppression and injustice in schools and communities?

- Challenges the ideology of neutrality/objectivity, color-evasiveness, and meritocracy as well as deficiency orientations
- Reframes the master narrative via counter narratives by focusing on people's real experiences—via *testimonios*, storytelling, narratives, chronicles, family histories, scenarios, biographies, and parables—that draw on the lived experiences that BISOCs bring to the classroom and views these experiences as sources of strength
- Utilizes a transdisciplinary approach (history, law, women's/ethnic studies, for example) to understand race in schooling
- Commits to social justice by helping students develop a critical consciousness and then acting to eliminate racism, sexism, and poverty from people's lives

Critical Race Theory also uncovers specific and unique issues affecting how different groups experience racism. For example, *LatCrit* focuses on issues of immigration, language, ethnicity and culture, identity, skin color/phenotype, and sexuality for Latinx communities (Solórzano & Delgado Bernal, 2001). *TribalCrit* focuses on colonization, land dispossession, identity, sovereignty/autonomy/self-determination, and government-to-government relations for Indigenous communities (Brayboy, 2005). *AsianCrit* focuses on "model minority" myth busting, immigration, language, and disenfranchisement issues as experienced by Asian communities (Chang, 1993).

In schools and classrooms, educators who are guided by CRT push against institutional racism by fostering *school organization* with a focus on expanding opportunities to learn, including what classes are offered, who teaches (including teacher diversity) which classes, which students are placed in which classes (college prep or special education), what school programs to enact, the role of student voice and governance, and support for parent and community engagement, among other ways of participating in schools (Yosso, 2002). Parent outreach would be responsive to when and how parents can participate (given language, childcare, and transportation needs as well as work constraints), sensitive to how parents are positioned ("they don't care about education"), and supportive of efforts by school staff to go into the community to learn about the "pedagogies of the home" (Delgado Bernal, 2001).

Relatedly, *classroom organization* would attend to how chairs/tables are laid out, what posters are hung on the walls, what classroom rituals are enacted, how classroom management is implemented, when differential discipline is employed, and how languages other than English are used and affirmed, among other things. Instruction would include active learning and critical thinking versus passive and rote learning. Teacher expectations would view all learners as a promise, a potential. The curriculum would work to actively confront epistemological racism by pushing against the dominance of the Western canon in the curriculum (textbooks, standards, assessments, for example) and, instead, connect to the everyday lives of students of color (see Zamudio et al., 2011, for an extended discussion of school-based practices consistent with CRT).

Resistance Theories

Students, families, and communities do not passively accept the conditions they encounter in school settings. Freire (1970/1996) reminds us that while we are social products (conditioned by our respective societies), we are also social agents who seek to navigate, in creative and important ways, the toxicity of the conditions we encounter. Our communities have long histories of opposing their oppression via legal and political actions as well as via public demonstrations and protests of oppressive conditions in schools. Sometimes these are large, public, and national demonstrations such as those many witnessed on May Day 2006 (see Zamudio et al., 2009, for a description of how this occurred in one city). More often, smaller, local, and collective acts of resistance tend to occur, including daily individual acts such as going to school but refusing to engage; Herbert Kohl (1994) calls this "willful not learning."

We call on you to consider how you will resist those forms of oppression you likely will encounter in school settings where you will teach (Chapter 5 will extend this discussion). Yosso (2005) would urge you to develop your "resistance capital," which will enable you to challenge inequality through oppositional behaviors. Cuauhtin (2019c) adds the need to develop "transformative resistance capital," which requires you to understand the oppressive school structures in order to transform them. We believe you will be assisted in doing the above by developing theoretical and ideological clarity, challenging deficit ideologies, and pursuing asset-based pedagogies.

 WONDER ALONE/WONDER TOGETHER

Think of a person (historical or contemporary) who has engaged or is engaging in either resistance capital or transformative resistance capital: What is their motivation and what actions (or inactions) do they take? Think of a time when *you* resisted something at school because it violated your identity or integrity: What was *your* motivation and what did you do? What cultural resources do students draw upon to navigate oppressive constraints?

CONCLUDING REFLECTIONS

We offer some concluding remarks for your consideration. We acknowledge that you may decide that there is no one overarching, all-encompassing, decontextualized (accurate for any setting) theory of teaching and learning in diverse contexts. Rather, a contextual interaction lens would tell us that school failure is a result of a variety of complex factors unique to each setting. Sometimes these factors are different depending upon the unique and specific student, school, and community. Sometimes it is a combination of factors, interacting with one another (e.g., poverty in the community and lower funding to the local school, which minimizes support programs), that are at play. Sometimes the factors are a product of histories of schools and people's experiences in them. Sometimes there are national factors, as described by Rogers et al. in *Teaching and Learning in the Age of Trump* (2017). As we write, a global challenge is the COVID-19 pandemic and how it is profoundly influencing teaching and learning on a massive scale.

We end by asking: What are the theoretical foundations upon which you hope to make a home within the schoolhouse that you envision?

➻ Make It Happen: Portfolio Activity—Theory Mapping

Reading and engaging in theory sometimes can lead us to forget that real people's lives inform our own theory making. This activity has two steps:

Step 1: Visit students' families and communities through home visits, attending community events, or spending intentional time in valued spaces. This allows you to relate to your students as more than just "bodies" in the classroom, but also as social and cultural beings connected to a complex social and cultural network. Moreover, by becoming familiar with students' home lives, you gain insight into the influences on the students' attitudes and behaviors.

Step 2: Use these visits to begin making connections to theories you have learned about and to inform your teaching practice. We provide a theory table for you to add to your portfolio. In addition to making connections to other theories, we ask that you reflect on practical and local applications of the theories you encountered in this chapter. Be sure to make connections to your community walk and mapping.

Portfolio Theory Table

Theory	Related authors	Connections to other theories	I see this in my community/ schools . . .	I see this in my life . . .	I am still wondering about . . .
Theory 1					
Theory 2					
Theory 3					

➨ Keep It Going!

- Read the poem "Tony Went to the Bodega but He Didn't Buy Anything" by Martin Espada.
- Watch the documentaries *Precious Knowledge* and/or *Fear and Learning at Hoover Elementary*.

CHAPTER 3

The Entryway

Representing Through Multicultural and Culturally Centering Education

> Multicultural education, like other kinds of teaching, is a moral enterprise that requires deep personal engagement, commitment, advocacy, and agency from those who participate fully and genuinely in the enterprise.
>
> —Geneva Gay (2003, p. 6)

It is common in many houses, when going in the front door, to find an entryway. The entryway is unique and different for each kind of house. Often, we deliberately consider what it is we want others to know about us when they first enter our house. To that end, we may display family photos, artwork, plants, and cultural artifacts that are important to us and reveal a little about who we are. Because we recognize it is the first thing people see about us, we might "fuss" about this room as much as any other. In a way, the entry room is text, telling those who enter something about who we are, what we value, and what we want others to know about us from the onset. Because it creates first impressions, front and center, we are intentional about what we place there.

At the same time, as you return home through the front door, the entryway becomes that moment when you can begin to decompress from the day. You may hang up a coat, take off your shoes, and drop keys in a basket. It is also a mental signal that you are entering into your home space, where you find personal energy as well as are revitalized, and where you are affirmed and valued.

In much the same way, we are hoping that you will consider diversity in teaching—multicultural and culturally centering education—as one of those places where you will "fuss" about yourself in the profession. We sincerely hope it is what people see when they first enter your classroom. It is visible in everything from the student artwork and poetry on the walls to how they see you teaching and fostering student engagement, especially your commitment to equity in teaching, which most Black, Indigenous, and Teachers of Color exemplify (Philip & Brown, 2020). In essence, we hope that when people come into your classroom, they see, perhaps above all else, that you truly affirm diversity in education. At the same time, much like in our description of your own arrival through the entryway, we believe that you will find your efforts to engage in diversity a place from which to draw energy, to be reenergized, and to be affirmed.

Affirming diversity in education is the manifestation and public application of our identities and worldviews as we navigate teaching. In this chapter, we review salient concepts from multicultural education; we then focus on culturally centering education. We use *culturally centering education* as an umbrella term under which several approaches might fit—which we discuss more specifically—including culturally responsive, culturally relevant, and culturally sustaining pedagogies. We also offer a nuanced discussion of how concepts in multicultural and culturally centering education might be experienced and enacted by BITOCs in ways that their White peers might not navigate.

It is these approaches to multicultural and culturally centering education that serve as the foundation for identity-sustaining pedagogies. These are central because we believe that traditional teacher education programs and the teaching profession exert pressure on BITOCs to subsume both their commitment to diversity in teaching/learning and their identities into the larger whitestream present in much of education. To counter this, we describe how BITOCs might adapt the methods and practices of multicultural and culturally centering education into their work as teachers.

Identity-sustaining pedagogies (the focus of Chapter 4 and a central focus of this text) can play out via several curricular frameworks. However, we assert that multicultural education generally, as well as culturally responsive, culturally relevant, and culturally sustaining pedagogies specifically, are particularly well suited to help you navigate teaching in ways that honor, engage, and sustain the culturally diverse identities that you bring as teachers and your students bring to their classrooms. Therefore, we detail those frameworks that we believe are best suited for an appreciation of identities and for forging identity-sustaining pedagogies.

🗨 WONDER ALONE/WONDER TOGETHER

We imagine that you may have heard the term *multicultural education*. What is your current understanding of what it is and how to enact it? What about culturally responsive teaching? Culturally sustaining pedagogy? What questions do you have about these? To what degree and how have you experienced these either in your K–12 schooling experiences or your experiences in higher education? What are possible reasons you have or have not experienced these?

Figure 3.1. Word cloud of words students associate with multicultural education

MULTICULTURAL EDUCATION: OUR HISTORICAL ROOTS

We begin with multicultural education because this academic discipline preceded culturally centering education: culturally responsive, culturally relevant, and culturally sustaining pedagogies. Multicultural education opens a wider lens on the many aspects of education (writ large) that need to be considered from an equity and diversity perspective. You might be like our students who shared the words they associate with multicultural education (see Figure 3.1). The span of possible understandings and meanings is both important and informative.

The earliest foundations of multicultural education come from scholars who challenged the racist attitudes the whitestream had about People of Color. [1] We think of the scholarly work of W. E. B. Du Bois, John Hope Franklin, Manuel Gamio, Bruno Lasker, Carlos Bulosan, Carter G. Woodson, and others whose writings advocated for valuing and affirming the racial and/or cultural identity, as well as the incredible assets, of their communities. [2] They were writing in the 1900s and forged the foundational scholarship around understanding how race and racism played out in the United States as well as advocated for ethnic pride, empowerment, and social action.

The mid-1900s, especially around the World War II era in the United States, saw the emergence of the intergroup relations movement (C. A. M. Banks, 2005). The focus of this movement was on the origins, values, and outcomes of (individual) bias, prejudice, discrimination, and oppression. The intent was to foster positive interactions among people who shared a common (democratic) cultural aim. This movement included people like Gordon Allport, Lloyd Cook, Septima Clark, Hilda Taba, Kenneth Clark, and Mamie Clark, among others. The Black psychologists Kenneth and Mamie Clark played an instrumental role in the *Brown v. Board of Education* case (described in Chapter 1) by demonstrating how racist ideologies, including the segregation of schools, led Black students to favor Whiteness over their own skin color, in this instance, shown by the preference for white dolls over black dolls (K. B. Clark, 1963). In other words, they were able to tangibly demonstrate the psychological influence—internalized oppression—of oppressive ideologies and institutional practices such as segregation on the identities of Black, Indigenous, and People of Color.

This foundational research and scholarship were instrumental in the development of the ethnic studies movement that would emerge from the civil rights movement of the 1960s–1970s (J. A. Banks, 2004). Many in the civil rights movement had become impatient with the intergroup relations approach and its underlying ideology, given that it focused on oppression at the level of the *individual*. Activists during the civil rights movement asserted more directly that deliberate and specific *institutional* policies, procedures, and practices were largely responsible for the academic, political, and social challenges their children faced.

While many communities of color were protesting race-based admissions policies that were keeping their young people out of college, they also were protesting the lack of knowledge about their communities, given the absence of those communities in the curriculum once Black, Indigenous, and Students of Color did enter universities. Ethnic studies began with a focus on specific social-cultural identity groups, as evident in academic programs such as Black/African American studies, Chicano/Latinx studies, American Indian/Indigenous/Native American studies, Asian American studies, and also Women/Gender/Sexuality studies. They sometimes were brought together under a broader "ethnic studies" umbrella. Ethnic studies scholars brought many of those earlier scholarly works to the surface but also engaged in the creation of new knowledge, especially aimed at documenting and affirming the cultural heritages of their respective communities (Sleeter & Zavala, 2020). These early ethnic studies scholars included Harry Kitano, Rudy Acuña, Betty Lee Sung, Vine Deloria, Jr., and Alex Wong, among so many more.

Arising from the civil rights and ethnic studies disciplines were demands for greater acknowledgment, inclusion, and affirmation of the various social-cultural groups that constitute the United States, as well as demands to push against institutional practices that limited access to opportunities. That is, ethnic studies is rooted in a culturally affirming and valuing orientation as well as a politically conscious, socially active, and antihegemonic project.

The foundations of multicultural education rest with those ethnic studies scholars and activists whose work advanced a positive and constructive vision of education for marginalized communities. Its contemporary emergence was spurred by James Banks, Jack Forbes, Geneva Gay, Carl Grant, Gloria Ladson-Billings, Sonia Nieto, and Christine Sleeter, to name but a few. It began with questions around how to move from ethnic studies, with its focus on a single ethnic identity, to multiethnic education as a way to address the needs of schools across the United States that were typified by classrooms where students from a variety of ethnic, cultural, and racial heritages sat next to one another (see, for example, J. A. Banks, 1981).

Shortly thereafter, multicultural education took hold as an acknowledgment of the many diverse identities—beyond race and ethnicity and their intersections—that students brought to schools. It also provided a jumping-off space to move from a focused recognition of the importance of the curriculum to attending to the many other dimensions of schooling (pedagogy, class/school climate, policies/procedures, community/family engagement, as examples) that also required scrutiny, given the ways these practices denied students opportunities to be academically and socially successful. In addition, many multicultural education scholars embraced the need to understand how schools were nested in wider social structures, advocating for an even broader focus on societal reforms. For critical multicultural educators, these include things like the increasing economic divide driving more into poverty, homelessness and the housing crisis (as well as housing segregation), the health crisis, mass incarceration, and immigration policies, among other things (Sleeter & Delgado Bernal, 2004).

 WONDER ALONE/WONDER TOGETHER

What are the key ideas you can glean from this brief history of multicultural education? What concepts were embedded from the earliest days that are still relevant today? Why is knowing this history important to you as a BITOC?

DEFINING MULTICULTURAL EDUCATION

While there are many perspectives and theoretical orientations of multicultural education (Grant & Portero, 2011)—indeed, given the variety of both labels and frameworks, we might think about the field as multicultural educations—we find the definition by Nieto and Bode (2007) especially productive. They defined multicultural education as:

> *a process* of comprehensive school reform and *basic education for all*. It *challenges and rejects racism* and other forms of discrimination in schools and society and accepts and affirms the pluralism (racial, ethnic, religious, linguistic, economic, and gender, among others) that students, communities, and teachers reflect. Multicultural education *permeates the school's* curriculum and instructional strategies as well as interactions among teachers, students, and families, and the very way that schools conceptualize the nature of teaching and learning. Because it uses *critical pedagogy* as its underlying philosophy and focuses on knowledge, reflection, and action (praxis) as the basis for social change, multicultural education *promotes democratic principles of social justice*. (p. 44, emphasis added)

We have italicized the key terms in this definition that speak to the characteristics of and aims for multicultural education.[3]

An additional tool for understanding multicultural education is to consider the five interrelated dimensions of multicultural education developed by J.

WONDER ALONE/WONDER TOGETHER

As you read the Nieto and Bode definition as well as the dimensions of multicultural education outlined by Banks, what stands out for you as central elements of multicultural education? What parts of this definition/these dimensions do you feel you need to know more about?

A. Banks (2004) based on his extensive review of educational research literature and work in the evolving field of multicultural education at the time. The dimensions are *content integration, knowledge construction, prejudice reduction, equity pedagogy*, and *empowering school culture*. Each dimension offers a broad concept for understanding or applying the corresponding aspect of multicultural education—including how it might intertwine with other dimensions in the framework.

Content integration is most concerned with curricular interventions, including adding diverse voices or perspectives not typically seen within a discipline's canon. *Knowledge construction* aims to acknowledge the ways a discipline's canon is constructed from dominant cultural values and seeks to empower students to interrogate the various ways that knowledge is actively valued, devalued, and transmitted, while also helping students see themselves as knowledge producers. *Prejudice reduction* seeks to confront bias and oppression. *Equity pedagogy* is concerned with supporting academic achievement by making meaningful changes to teaching in order to attend to the cultural needs present in the classroom. In many ways, these dimensions typically—although not exclusively—address multicultural education as practiced within the classroom. Extending beyond the classroom's walls, an *empowering school culture* is concerned with building an environment throughout the school that attends to the diverse needs of all members within its scope and influence.

In her review of the field, Ladson-Billings (2004b) asserts that multicultural education is to be lauded for taking a strong ethical stance about the need for educational equity. Multicultural education is critical of cultural assimilation ideologies and favors cultural pluralism. It has been productive in responding to new knowledge and new ways of talking about equity and diversity. Its conceptual and theoretical aims are clear about the importance of having a strong social justice focus that includes broader social issues and challenges. Perhaps most important, when teachers do this work well, significant gains in academic achievement (even on standardized measures), but also student interest, motivation, engagement, and confidence, have been reported (Aronson & Laughter, 2016).

There have been critiques of multicultural education as well. One critique suggests that the general concepts have been largely misunderstood (Shannon-Baker, 2018) and, correspondingly, poorly implemented (Ladson-Billings, 2004b; Ladson-Billings & Tate, 2016). While most schools say they value multicultural education, the net result has been minor tinkering versus substantially changing the cultural and structural aspects of how schooling is implemented. That is, multicultural education gets watered down as it mixes with the hegemonic logics of institutions (V. Vélez, personal communication, October 2018). Another critique is that multicultural education has not had a significant impact on real-life material circumstances for BIPOC (Jay, 2003).

Ladson-Billings and Tate (2016) offer two additional critiques. First, multicultural education has been overwhelmingly concentrated on serving the needs of White students and White teachers, not BISOCs or BITOCs. Second, it has been practiced mostly in superficial celebrations of diversity within current social and political structures of inequality, thereby preventing opportunities for genuine educational transformation. This latter critique suggests that multicultural education is epistemologically grounded in principles of *liberal pluralism*: celebrating difference while ignoring the inequalities resulting from social, political, and economic structures and uneven power dynamics, inequalities that, if addressed, could lead to real transformation (Daniels, 2008; see also Farahmandpur & McLaren, 1999).

A final critique is that, as a result of moving away from the various approaches to ethnic studies, issues of race and racism have become watered down. Over 30 years ago, McCarthy (1988) lamented that "multicultural education, specifically, must be understood as part of a curricular truce, the fallout of a political project to deluge and neutralize Black rejection of the conformist and assimilationist curriculum models solidly in place in the 1960s" (p. 267). Indeed, when the Tucson Unified School District's Mexican American studies program was disbanded by the State Superintendent of Arizona in 2010, the program was rebranded a multicultural education program. In many ways it could be asked whether this was a contemporary example of the curricular truce that McCarthy spoke of earlier.

We argue that acknowledging both the strengths and limitations of multicultural education is important and healthy, providing opportunities to reflect and reconsider. Indeed, the growth of the field relies on being pushed to think about and respond to the complexity of issues and challenges confronting schools and societies in a wide variety of political, social, and cultural settings. Given its important historical roots and strong theoretical orientations, rather than rejecting multicultural education, we invite you to consider how to respond to these critiques in ways that advance the field and foster success in the schools and classrooms where you find yourself.

💬 WONDER ALONE/WONDER TOGETHER

As you read these affirmations and critiques of multicultural education, what stands out for you? How might you strengthen those things that multicultural education is doing well? What might you do to address its critiques?

CULTURALLY CENTERING EDUCATION
AS MULTICULTURAL EDUCATION

Partly in response to the critiques of multicultural education—especially the lack of guidance about how it is to be implemented but also the superficial ways in which culture and identity are understood—a variety of models of culturally centering education have been developed.

As with multicultural education, there were important antecedents to the contemporary culturally centering education approaches. From the 1800s through the first half of the 1900s, a dominant justification for having Black teachers working with Black children was the belief in their ability to motivate the Black children in their classrooms (Mabee, 1979). Another catalyst was sociocultural studies of specific cultural communities. Consider, for example, Jack Forbes's (1969) description of education for the "culturally different" in thinking about Native American students. Cardenas and Cardenas (1972) called for schooling for Latinx children and communities that was "culturally compatible." K. H. P. Au and Jordan (1981) advanced a description of "culturally appropriate" instruction for Hawaiian children and communities. Mohatt and Erickson (1981) asserted the need for "culturally congruent" approaches to working with Native American communities. The term *culturally relevant* was used as early as 1981 to describe the education needs of English language learners (Cazden & Leggett, 1981).

We wish to make a few key observations here. First, the theory-to-practice of culturally centering education was occurring at much the same time multicultural education was starting out and, in many ways, their paths were both similar and overlapping. Second, both multicultural education and culturally centering education approaches have broad aims around social justice and the ways in which social justice can be enacted in schools and classrooms as central to their visions (Aronson & Laughter, 2016). Third, much of their difference is less in the kind of characteristics they are advancing and more in the degree to which they emphasize one characteristic over another. Importantly, as you will read next, culturally centering education approaches keep, front and center, the notion of "culture" as a central element of teaching/pedagogy for diverse learners.

Under the culturally centering education auspices, we will describe culturally relevant pedagogy, culturally responsive teaching, culturally sustaining pedagogy, critical culturally sustaining/revitalizing pedagogy and Indigenous education sovereignty, community responsive pedagogy, and ethnic studies pedagogy as culturally responsive pedagogy.

Culturally Relevant Pedagogy

The most current iteration of academic and educational interest in culturally centering education began with the use of the term *culturally relevant pedagogy*

WONDER ALONE/WONDER TOGETHER

Where do you see the overlaps between multicultural education and culturally centering education? Where do they diverge?

(CRP) by Gloria Ladson-Billings in the 1990s, with a focus on teachers who were identified by the Black community as being particularly successful for Black students. Stemming from this research, captured most fully in her book *The Dreamkeepers* (1994), she wrote the seminal work on this in 1995: "Toward a Theory of Culturally Relevant Pedagogy."

CRP has three primary goals, as summarized by Muñiz (2019). First, CRP must result in academic achievement for BISOCs. Second, CRP must support the development of students' positive cultural identities resting, in part, on academic achievement. And third, CRP must help students to see, understand, critique, and challenge social inequalities. Underlying this work is Ladson-Billings's (2014) desire to push against deficit ideologies, to advance the positive possibilities of cultural identity and learning, and to uncover those teaching practices that lead to cultural and academic identity development.

Culturally Responsive Teaching

Geneva Gay, writing as early as 1975, had a specific focus on how to develop a curriculum for diverse youth that spoke to the many dimensions of their personhood (beyond academic identities). Gay asserted the need for a focus on teaching practices and approaches that were rooted in the cultural orientations that learners bring to schools and classrooms. For Gay (2010), the central goals of culturally responsive teaching are to use the "cultural knowledge, prior experiences, frames of reference, and performance styles of ethnically diverse students" (p. 31) to ensure that learning is both relevant and effective. While the focus is on teaching, it is important to note that Gay also discussed relationships in the classroom, classroom climate, and self-reflection as central to culturally responsive teaching.

Gay (2018) asserts that culturally responsive teaching rests on eight qualitative attributes:

- Validating—it "teaches *to and through* the strengths of these students" (p. 36, emphasis in original)
- Comprehensive and inclusive—it addresses the needs of the whole child (social, psychological, academic, cultural, and so on)
- Multidimensional—it includes changes to the curriculum but also includes all aspects of schooling
- Empowering—it helps students to be better people and to succeed in ways they would not otherwise

- Transformative—it pushes us to think about other ways to do schooling, including focusing on asset-based pedagogies, sharing power/decisionmaking, and engaging with knowledge production
- Emancipatory—it unleashes human potential, especially when collaborative and cooperative, while it questions those taken-for-granted truths that have been used to oppress
- Humanistic—it is concerned with human rights, the dignity and welfare of people, and helping students to value those different from themselves
- Normative and ethical—it is the right, honorable, and necessary way to teach in highly diverse classroom contexts

Both Gay's and Ladson-Billings's approaches share significant commonalities. Both are committed to promoting positive student cultural and academic identities as essential for strong academic performance. Both recognize that cultural diversity is a prominent feature in classrooms and can be instrumental in students' academic achievement. Both root their work in seeing the classroom as a place where social justice can be enacted. Both push against deficit thinking. Both see their approaches to teaching diverse learners in opposition to typical (whitestream) approaches to teaching/learning and even acknowledge resistance to these new approaches. One way we see in which they differ is that Ladson-Billings is describing a teacher's (dis)positions in this work, while Gay is more interested in teachers' practices (Aronson & Laughter, 2016).

We wish to be clear that culturally centering education approaches to diversity, like the varying approaches to multicultural education (Sleeter & Grant, 2007), are dynamic. Just as with all scholarly work, they change as new insights and new understandings emerge. Indeed, even Ladson-Billings and Gay have "updated" their approaches over the years. In many ways, this is especially true as we have begun to understand the dynamic nature of culture, given that cultures themselves and our understanding of them are constantly changing. As Ladson-Billings (2014) describes, "Such revisions do not imply that the original was deficient; rather, they speak to the changing and evolving needs of dynamic systems" (p. 76). This is also true for the varied approaches around culturally centering education. On the other hand, much like multicultural education, what gets described and implemented as culturally centering education is often a mere shadow of its original conceptual vision, even though poor efforts at these approaches may be labeled as culturally centering education by misinformed scholars and practitioners (Ladson-Billings, 2014).

Culturally Sustaining Pedagogies

A more recent iteration of culturally centering education comes from the work of Django Paris (2012) and their colleague Sammy Alim (Paris & Alim, 2017) around culturally sustaining pedagogies (CSP). Paris and Alim make three

WONDER ALONE/WONDER TOGETHER

As you read these two approaches, what stands out for you as key to any approach to culturally centering education? What adaptations would you make given your own schooling experiences as a BISOC?

significant contributions to our understanding of culturally centering education.

The first contribution is a deeper understanding of what "culture" means and, as important, how it influences our identities. Culture is not a thing but a way of living in a particular social location. It has both a *heritage dimension* (long-lasting ways of understanding/employing race, ethnicity, language, and ways of being) that changes slowly, as well as an *evolving dimension* that adapts to changes in arts, music, film, sports, and politics, among other things (Muñiz, 2019; Paris & Alim, 2017). Relatedly, it centers the understanding that individuals develop (hybrid) unique identities based on the various (multiple) social-cultural communities to which they most connect. As such, it acknowledges that our students' identities, like cultures themselves, are complex as well as deeply rich and creative in terms of practices, language use, and various literacies (Paris & Alim, 2017). Paris and Alim describe it this way:

> As we seek to perpetuate and foster a pluralist present and future through our pedagogies, it is critical that we understand that the ways in which young people are enacting race, ethnicity, language, literacy, and their engagement with culture is always shifting and dynamic. (p. 7)

For Paris and Alim, culturally sustaining pedagogy fosters these evolving identities and advocates for "cultural dexterity as a necessary good" (p. 1).

A second feature of CSP is the emphasis on *sustaining*—not just *responsive* to or *relevant* for—"the lifeways of communities" (Paris & Alim, 2017, p. 1). This posture begins with a refusal to see students' cultural and linguistic identities, along with the lifeways of communities, as problematic, as deficit, or as pathologies. Rather, it sees these as assets, as strengths, as additive and whole. From this posture, CSP asks educators and teachers to imagine not only how to affirm these social-cultural identities—complex as they are—but also to develop pedagogies aimed at "sustaining them in ways that attend to the emerging, intersectional, and dynamic ways in which they are lived and used by young people" (Paris & Alim, 2017, p. 9). Indeed, as Ladson-Billings (2014) describes, this is a new acknowledgment about the role of identities and how they get represented in the classroom.

Given these first two features, CSP offers an invitation to educators to create pedagogies that speak to the students and communities where the educators are located. Recognizing and acknowledging this deeper, complex, and dynamic

💬 **WONDER ALONE/WONDER TOGETHER**

As you read about culturally sustaining pedagogies, what speaks most to you about the ways in which they extend the earlier works by Ladson-Billings and/or Gay? In what way do you think they speak more fully to needs of BISOCs?

understanding of culture and identities—and the need to sustain them—will require a plurality of various context-specific pedagogies. Consider, for example, the dynamic cultural identities being developed when students live and learn in multiracial, multiethnic communities and schools. These identities easily might be influenced by multiple languages, multiple dialects, multiple literacies, multiple elements of popular culture, and multiple cultural practices, among other things. It is not too difficult to recognize, given this setting, that students will develop a hybrid of cultural identities. As Paris and Alim (2017) relate:

> As youth continue to develop new, complex, and intersecting forms of racial/ethnic identification in a world where cultural and linguistic recombinations flow with purpose, we need pedagogies that speak to our shifting cultural realities or, as Pennycook (2006) put it, pedagogies that "go with the flow." (p. 9)

One final brief note about the perspectives Paris and Alim share with respect to CSP. They recognize that the development of hybrid identities is not unproblematic, especially given those elements that students might adopt that represent forms of oppression. In essence, CSP asks educators to work with students to develop a critical self-reflexivity that resists misogyny or homophobia, as but two examples. As Paris and Alim relate:

> Our goal is to find ways to support and sustain what we know are remarkable ways with language, literacy, and cultural practice, while at the same time opening up spaces for students themselves to critique the ways that they might be—intentionally or not—reproducing discourses that marginalize members of our communities. (p. 11)

Variations on the Culturally Sustaining Pedagogy Theme. We want to acknowledge that there have been other variations on culturally centering education (see Cuauhtin, 2019a, for a listing of several of these). We share three noteworthy additions here.

Native American communities have been deeply invested in language revitalization as a goal central to their nation's uplift. In this vein, Lee and McCarty (2017) have called for a *critical culturally sustaining/revitalizing pedagogy and Indigenous education sovereignty.* The central elements of this approach are resistance to longstanding efforts at colonization and, instead, the pursuit of self-determination. This requires reclaiming and revitalizing those aspects of Indigenous ways of living that were displaced, disrupted, or destroyed as part of the colonization project, most notably (in this instance) language loss and control over education policies (Hopkins, 2020). The central feature of this pedagogy is the incorporation of community values reflected, most generally, in the 4 Rs: respect, reciprocity, responsibility, and caring relationships (Brayboy & McCarty, 2010). The urgency of this approach was highlighted by Ladson-Billings (2014), given that this approach links "their work to the very survival of people who have faced systematic extinction. For these authors, teaching Indigenous students is not merely about propelling them forward academically; it also is about reclaiming and restoring their cultures" (p. 87).

Tintiangco-Cubales and colleagues (2015), working within ethnic studies and looking at teaching practices in that field, proposed the development of a *community responsive pedagogy.* It acknowledges the longstanding commitment of most ethnic studies programs to the communities from which they emerged. Community responsive pedagogy has three overlapping elements. The first is the development of a critical consciousness, mostly around learning to think analytically and critically about the challenges being experienced in local communities or within the schools themselves. The second element is the development of agency through direct community engagement around both understanding the challenges in the community and also identifying actions that can be taken to address those challenges. The third element is the growth of transformative leaders; that is, a focus on leadership skills necessary for community growth and development.

Cuauhtin (2019a) proposes a model of culturally responsive pedagogy interlaced with ethnic studies pedagogy. The model is described as ethnic studies pedagogy as culturally responsive pedagogy-X, or *ethnic studies pedagogy as CxRxPx.* What is intriguing about this model is that it harkens back to the foundations of multicultural education and culturally centering education, while also recognizing that the return toward ethnic studies can deepen and enrich culturally responsive pedagogies (evidenced by the "x" in the model). Consider the many additional meanings each of the letters in the CxRxPx model can include (Cuauhtin, 2019a). The Cx, besides *cultural,* can include caring, critical, community-based, creative, and collaborative. The Rx, besides *responsive,* can include remembering, racial identity development, reflective, reflexive, and rehumanizing. And the Px, besides pedagogy, can include the plurality of literacies and discourses, power balancing, purposeful, postcolonial, and praxis, among others. We are intrigued—and hope you are too—with the possibilities of regenerating culturally centering education with ethnic studies pedagogies.

WONDER ALONE/WONDER TOGETHER

As you read these other approaches to culturally centering education, what most stands out for you as something you will want to employ as a BITOC? What elements are most intriguing for you? What elements are you most uncertain about or do you wish to learn more about?

TEACHERS OF COLOR:
EXPLORING YOUR OWN PRINCIPLES OF PRACTICE

One of the most important characteristics that has been identified in BITOCs is their greater interest in and willingness to enact a culturally centering education. That includes a keen interest in centering culturally relevant education in the curriculum and instruction in ways that do not trivialize what culture is and what it means in our lives. That is, we believe you understand the value of and have or seek to have the skills to enact a culturally centering education based on your experiences in your own social-cultural communities, as well as on how your own education was or was not relevant, responsive, sustaining, or revitalizing in light of that background.

Additionally, we believe you know how to connect to communities of color, given the broad cultural repertoires of practice you have gained that are essential to culturally centering education. We believe that you already bring an asset orientation around your own cultural community, around the potentials of BISOCs, and around teaching for and through diversity more generally. And we believe that you understand the salient role of students' social-cultural identities and are willing to share with BISOCs how you have navigated these identities in school settings.

Toward that end, we ask that you begin to consider and develop a list of those principles (characteristics, aims, and goals) that you most want to achieve as a teacher committed to culturally centering education. We encourage you to look at the descriptions of the various approaches in this chapter and develop both your own *posture* around diversity as well as your own set of *practices*.

As one example, consider this set of eight competencies associated with culturally responsive teaching, generated from a review of the literature and reported in New America's *Culturally Responsive Teaching* (Muñiz, 2019). The eight competencies are listed here (with a complete description available in the report) and shown in Figure 3.2.

- *Reflect on One's Cultural Lens:* a general understanding and appreciation for diversity evident in the lifeways/paths of other cultures. It includes being critically and keenly aware of areas of possible bias.
- *Recognize and Redress Bias in the System:* an ability to see how systems have been set up to disadvantage some students and privilege

Figure 3.2. Eight competencies for culturally responsive teaching

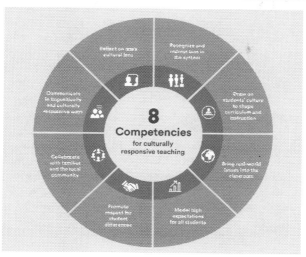

Source: Muñiz, 2019.

others. It includes a willingness to disrupt institutional bias in school- (and district-) level policies, procedures, and practices.

- ***Draw on Students' Culture to Shape Curriculum and Instruction:*** an awareness, appreciation, and respect for students' cultural backgrounds. It includes planning, selecting, and using materials that accurately represent those backgrounds and link those backgrounds to new ideas/knowledges.

- ***Bring Real-World Issues Into the Classroom:*** an ability to ensure relevance in teaching and learning by connecting topics to students' lives. It includes being willing to construct assignments that engage students in complex, authentic, and real-world issues for the purpose of understanding complex causes, unseen consequences, and creative solutions.

- ***Model High Expectations for All Students:*** an unshakable belief in the promise and potential of each student. It includes providing the necessary "scaffolding" so that students can be successful with assignments, and sharing these high expectations in all aspects of one's communication with students.

- ***Promote Respect for Student Differences:*** an understanding that teachers need to cultivate the kind of caring culture and peer-to-peer respect/support for one another's differences. It includes teaching students how to address behaviors by one student toward another that are disrespectful, prejudicial, or bullying, among other things.

- ***Collaborate With Families and the Local Community:*** a recognition that strong home–school relationships are essential and that parents/

caregivers value those relationships. It includes learning about the community, local community-based organizations, and families, as well as becoming part of those communities at the same time that parents/caregivers are welcomed in schools and classrooms.

- *Communicate in Linguistically and Culturally Responsive Ways:* an appreciation for learning, valuing, and responding to culturally inspired ways of communicating. It includes honoring and accommodating home languages, including advocating for school and district translation services.

As we hope is evident, a key strategy is to develop a list of goals that best speak to who you are (including your strengths and weaknesses), who your students are, and the school and community context as a basis for determining what your approach might be to culturally centering education. We provide a description of other goals for culturally centering education for your consideration in Appendix C.

CONCLUDING REFLECTIONS

We began this chapter with a description about people (you and others) coming into the house via the entryway. We end by acknowledging that this is also the place from which they, and you, leave the house. As you prepare to go out, you grab your keys, put on your shoes, and choose outerwear according to your guess about the day's weather. But you also may take one final glance into the mirror by the door and take one final deep breath before heading out. We hope that as you move forward into your school-/workday, you are reminded in these final moments in the entryway about the things that are most important to you and who you are.

➵ Make It Happen: Portfolio Activity—Interview a BITOC

Multicultural education is a complex field, and we invite you to wrestle with its multiple aims. One way we encourage you to do this is by interviewing a BITOC about how they understand and implement multicultural education and/or culturally centering education. Choose a BITOC whose opinion you value to seek loving advice. Hopefully this will include an opportunity to visit the teacher in their classroom as well. If you don't have access to a Teacher of Color, consider talking to a community or family member about your desire to be a teacher.

Focus Area #1: General Introduction. Why did they decide to become a teacher? What were their primary motivations? Talk with the person about how they bring their cultural assets into the classroom and school. Have them share the challenges they've experienced along the way and how they've navigated them. Ask them what are those things that keep them going and sustain them.

Focus Area #2: Teaching. How have they carved out a professional home in the school where they teach? What are their understandings about why schools work for some but not for others? How do others within the school make sense of why the school may be inequitable? What are their grandest visions and ambitions for schooling for their respective communities?

Focus Area #3: Multicultural Education. What role does theory about curriculum play in their teaching practice? Then, turn your attention to multicultural education and/or culturally centering education. What do those terms mean to them? What is easy or challenging about this approach to teaching and learning? What supports or facilitates this important work? What works against it? How do they address those barriers? Finally, what special obligations and opportunities, if any, do BITOCs have with respect to multicultural education and/or culturally centering education?

End the interview by sharing with them what it is you see and admire about them as a teacher.

⇒ Keep It Going!

- Read the poem "Rayford's Song" by Lawson Inada.
- Watch the short videos or read the profiles of educators honored with Learning for Justice's "Award for Excellence in Teaching" (available at https://www.learningforjustice.org/award/award-for-excellence-in-teaching). In particular, consider reading profiles (2011, 2012, 2014, 2016) or choosing videos (2018) by awardees who are BITOCs. What is it about how they position themselves or how they enact culturally sustaining practices that most catches your attention? What are things you can glean for yourself or ways that you can extend what they're doing in your own classroom? If nominated, how would you like your profile to describe your teaching for diversity?

CHAPTER 4

The Living Room

Sustaining Identities Through Teaching and Learning

> I am in the process of my own learning, and it is not my goal to arrive at a final resolution. Rather, I am in continual discovery. Identity and self are multiple and continually remade, reconstructed, reconstituted, and renewed in each new context and situation.
>
> —Sofia Villenas (1996, p. 726)

We turn our attention now to the living room. This is both the most public and the most intimate space in a home. We gather here for celebrations. Often, we convene here around the television for news and important programs. At times, our living room is cluttered; at other times, it is made tidy for company so as not to show too much of our casual sense of self if we are not quite ready. The living room is a versatile space that reflects who we are and what we value via the art or pictures on the walls, the heirlooms sitting on our end tables, and even the furniture that we have inherited, now used for our guests and families. Our living rooms are a multipurpose space that, for some, is large and expansive while for others is humble yet meaningful.

Of course, in some homes, there is no entryway before entering into the living room or main room. The front door opens right onto the action of the living room. At a gathering in a home without an entryway, you get no respite to transition to another space. Our identities function much the same as this metaphor. It illustrates how we all have a variable gradient to the public nature of our identity. In some spaces—depending on how they are constructed and the power and privileges at play—we get a chance to curate our identities (much like in an entryway) and in others, we are on full display without this opportunity.

In our living rooms, we redecorate and remodel through contemporary fashion trends and we include objects that reflect our current values. The living room is both our most interior representative space and yet, because it is so central in our home, its most guarded. Only guests and family members are invited in. These first impressions of identities are not always the most illustrative, accurate, or meaningful, especially if we are not intentional about what we choose to share.

Tatum (1997) offers that our identities hold dominance or subordination. When identities hold dominance, they set the agenda and general character-istics for an identity group. Our stereotypes and shared experiences often are based on this dominance. Within identity groups there are those that are per-ceived as less than and often provide nuance and sometimes stark contrast to the dominant group. These identities are subordinate. The relationship between the groups is unequal. This tension between dominance and subordination in-forms how we curate our identities and implores us to caution against relying solely on dominant notions of identity as we consider how we sustain them as Black, Indigenous, and Teachers of Color (BITOC).

In much the same way, our identities are sometimes really messy. Some-times they are tidy. Particularly when we first meet strangers or outsiders, we put our best foot forward. But we always have aspects of our self that we cannot or do not desire to hide, in much the same way that in our living room there might be some papers in the corner and some used glasses that need to be washed.

In this chapter, we ask: How do we as BITOCs preserve and sustain our own identities while navigating the sometimes-competing professional pres-sures of teaching? Further, how do we navigate these identity questions so that the very aims and practice of social justice education serve us most deeply?

 WONDER ALONE/WONDER TOGETHER

As you read this brief history of the teaching profession, what factors most negatively impacted diversifying the teaching profession? What aspects of this legacy are still evident today?

DIVERSITY IN THE TEACHING PROFESSION

Historical Overview

We take a moment here to briefly share the history of teaching and the teach-ing profession for BITOCs. The primary group employed as teachers in the earliest years of formal schooling in the United States were White men who most often used teaching as a steppingstone in their career path.[1] Horace Mann bemoaned the lack of training of teachers, while advocating for a substantial increase in the number of common schools (the forerunners of today's public schools). At the same time, while colonization (read: land grab) was occurring in the western United States, one factor used to lure White people from the East toward the West Coast was the promise of schools. Given these trends, the need to increase the teaching workforce grew substantially, and normal schools (teacher-training programs in a higher education setting) proliferated to prepare new teachers. Besides filling a workplace need, White women were described as a better fit to teach children, as more compliant to authority, and as less expensive (given lower salaries) than men. When White women did accept positions to work in schools, the employment often came with strict limitations. To be sure, White women often resisted these poor working conditions (Teitelman, 2015).

During this period, each community of color was engaging with the education of their young, often in informal and natural settings. Educational historian Anderson (1988) points out that with the end of the Civil War and the proliferation of public schools, Blacks had a compelling interest in creating "Black common schools" as a means to foster liberation. Black parents and community members would start their own schools, fundraise for them, and pursue policies and practices (as well as legislation) that would best meet the hopes they had for these schools.

With the tide of increasing racial tension and racism of the early 1900s, including the rise of the Ku Klux Klan, the hyper-segregation period of U.S. schooling began. Walker (2000), in her review of the research, points to both the intense challenges these schools faced (especially lack of adequate resources) as well as the tremendous benefits for the African American community, largely as a result of the large number of African American teachers these schools employed.

As suggested, before schools were desegregated, there were substantial numbers of BITOCs working and serving in these segregated settings. Teaching was, in fact, one of the few professions open to Black, Indigenous, and People of Color. Despite the unequal and inadequate physical, financial, and curricular resources evident in most of these schools, many of these BITOCs were engaged in culturally sensitive approaches to teaching and committed to community uplift.

At the end of the segregation era, the number of BITOCs would decline (Dilworth & Brown, 2008). The primary practice was to allow Black, Indigenous, and Students of Color to attend previously segregated White schools; after all, the segregated schools these BISOCs attended were, in fact, largely underresourced. Most of these BITOCs, then, lost their jobs, while a select few were hired in these newly integrated schools. Epps (2002) asserted that 38,000 Black and Latinx teachers in 17 southern states lost their positions from 1954–1965. Thus, when thinking about the lack of BITOCs, we point to historical factors that exacerbated the problem.

Contemporarily, we worry about the influence of federal and state policies, including the federal policy legacies affecting teacher accountability and certification constraints of No Child Left Behind, serving as a barrier to increasing the diversity of the teaching workforce. We are especially worried about the role of standardized tests as a gatekeeper to the teaching profession.

The State of Teacher Diversity

As mentioned in Chapter 1, the demographics of our schools are rapidly changing toward greater racial and ethnic diversity. However, a substantial gap persists in the percentage of BITOCs for our nation's schools. The low numbers of BITOCs are not just a historical artifact but a contemporary reality.

Before going farther, we want to be clear that we believe the teacher is but one of the most important factors influencing student academic achievement. As we have been asserting, the quality of teachers is not the only within-school or outside-of-school factor influencing students' academic, cultural, and social achievement. We also believe that teachers who are equity and justice warriors (Grande, 2014) can be found across all social identity characteristics. We believe that all teachers benefit from quality teacher preparation and professional development that speak to enacting an equity and justice agenda. We believe that students—all students—benefit from having an array of teachers from a variety of social identity locations. And we believe that BITOCs, most often as a result of their unique set of social-cultural experiences, have played and continue to play a significant role in the positive academic achievement of all students, particularly BISOCs. We are reminded of Gay's (2000) important caveat here:

> Knowledge and use of the cultural heritages, experiences, and perspectives of ethnic groups [of students] in teaching are far more important to improving student achievement than shared group membership. Similar ethnicity between students and teachers may be potentially beneficial, but it is not a guarantee of pedagogical effectiveness. (p. 205)

Motivations to Teach

Some of the earliest books around diversity in teaching focused on Black teachers, including S. P. Clark and Brown's *Ready From Within* (1986) and Foster's *Black Teachers on Teaching* (1997). One of the earlier empirical works written about a broad range of teacher diversities was June Gordon's book, *The Color of Teaching* (2000). When interviewing BITOCs, Gordon sought to answer the question, What motivates BITOCs to pursue the teaching profession? She found that BITOCs mentioned teaching as a way to tangibly/concretely "give back" to the community (that is, community uplift), and that they saw education (although not always schooling) as valued within their respective communities. BITOCs also reported a degree of agency, given that schools and teachers make critical decisions about what knowledges, languages, and stories to include; that is, BITOCs recognized that schools and classrooms can be structured differently. They also believed that, as BITOCs, they had to be "change agents" to make schools more responsive. In essence, BITOCs were committed to forging the schools they wanted, and not the schools where they currently were employed.

WONDER ALONE/WONDER TOGETHER

Think about a BITOC that you had. What was different about them as a result of their being a BITOC? If you didn't have a BITOC, what do you think you were missing or what did you want?

Approximately 15 years later, Farinde and colleagues (2015) conducted a research study that identified some of the same themes identified by Gordon. In this study, Black teachers mentioned their love of schools, of teaching, and of opportunities to work with students as primary motivations for teaching. In addition, these teachers pointed out that sometimes they learned what it means to be an effective teacher, and shaped their own teaching approaches, by reviewing their own experiences (positive *and* negative) with teachers and in their student teaching.

The Assets of Black, Indigenous, and Teachers of Color

For over 30 years, scholars (mostly scholars of color) have been working to identify the value BITOCs bring to their profession (for example, see Irvine, 1988; Quiocho & Rios, 2000; Villegas & Irvine, 2010, among so many others). Most generally, what this research asserts is that BITOCs understand their students' cultural experiences and are more likely to enact a culturally responsive curriculum and strengthen the connections between home and school. Achinstein and her colleagues (2010) found that BITOCs often bring with them humanistic commitments (commitments to making a substantial difference in the lives of their students and/or to give back to their cultural communities) and add to the multicultural capital of schools (a willingness to raise issues of oppression and privilege, and to enact culturally responsive and sustaining pedagogies, for example). Cherng and Halpin (2016), in particular, point to the power of high expectations that BITOCs have for their BISOCs. Also of importance is acknowledgment that BITOCs have a positive influence on White students as well as on BISOCs (Cherng & Halpin, 2016; U.S. Department of Education, 2016).

Around the same time that Gordon's book was published, Quiocho and Rios (2000) provided a comprehensive review of research that sought to identify the social-cultural and political assets of BITOCs. The intent was to go beyond the much-identified (and yet still important) need of BITOCs to serve as role models for BISOCs (see Gershenson et al., 2018, for an extended discussion of positive role-model effects). The research showed that BITOCs have learned how to navigate the differences between their home culture and language and that which is valued at schools, at both the K–12 and university levels. This provides a real-life text for others to follow. BITOCs often share these border-crossing experiences with their peers/colleagues and students in ways that affirm their home community and their community's cultural assets, and

BITOCs often are willing to serve as cultural mediators between other teachers and the local ethnic minoritized community. They bring a commitment to advancing connections with the local community as a resource for advancing learning.

 WONDER ALONE/WONDER TOGETHER

As you read about these general assets that BITOCs bring to the teaching profession, to schools, and to students, how does knowing these help you to think about your future career as a teacher? What do you need to know to strengthen some of these more important assets for yourself personally and professionally?

In working with students and affirming their cultural and language assets, BITOCs often bring culturally relevant ways to motivate students (Kohli, 2009; Quiocho & Rios, 2000). They can understand and be empathetic with those students who, due to school–home culture mismatch, are struggling to succeed in school. Importantly, they also help White students re/imagine their perspectives on People of Color. They often are committed to (indeed passionate about) implementing a culturally sustaining, antiracist pedagogy while promoting a classroom-level and school-level climate for diversity.

As demonstrated in Chapter 1, BITOCs often seek to work in highly diverse, low-income schools (which most new teachers seek to avoid) while, at the same time, seeking to be part of a professionally nurturing community. They have become skilled at "coping and resistance" mechanisms while, at the same time, being willing to identify and name racist (hegemonic) practices in both their school and university/teacher education. BITOCs often serve as advocates for BISOCs while, at the same time, holding positive yet realistic expectations for them. They also see their own efforts as central to students' success while, at the same time, holding themselves, their colleagues, and their institutions accountable for student academic achievement.

A variety of scholars have verified and extended the findings of the Quiocho and Rios research review, offering a more nuanced look at the positive influence of BITOCs. Milner (2006), for example, found that when Black teachers were working with Black students, they employed culturally relevant classroom management, pedagogy, and curriculum. A central part of this curriculum was the use of counter narratives on behalf of their Black students. They developed culturally informed relationships with students, including mentoring and role-modeling with students and connections with parents.

Whiteplume and Rios (2010) described the assets that Native American teachers bring to their students. Despite the long, painful, and deculturizing experiences with schooling that constitute much of the Native American academic experience, they report that Native American teachers bring foundational cultural and linguistic knowledge central to their community, especially

WONDER ALONE/WONDER TOGETHER

How do you imagine the experience of being a BITOC differs across racial/ethnic lines? How do these racial/ethnic differences interact with other differences in identity, such as class, gender identity, and sexual orientation?

efforts around language revitalization, as part of their work around promoting positive identities as Native people. They bring tribal values around respect, reciprocity, and responsibility into school settings (see also Brayboy & McCarty, 2010). Native American teachers see themselves as role models for their students in terms of living in and committing to their particular place and their local cultural community. These teachers also find ways to modify the curriculum, with attention to the spiritual in ways that are consistent with local tribal communities' values; this includes what to bring into and what *not* to bring into the classroom.

Ramírez and colleagues (2016) paint a profile of Latinx teachers who enact a culturally specific pedagogy consistent with life on the border. The case study points to how these teachers enacted, although differently given their own sociocultural experiences, principles of *cariño* (culture-specific approaches to caring), *conocimientos* (knowledge of both one's internal and external locations), and *conscientizacíon* (critical consciousness toward action). The key takeaway was an understanding of how these teachers, as "border crossers" and *neplanteros*, were able to use these principles to help students navigate the psychological, cultural, and institutional borders they were experiencing in the school and community.

In addition to research focusing on the culture-specific advantages of BITOCs, especially when in the presence of students from their own cultural community, is research focusing on what BITOCs do to be successful in schools. One such study, by Souto-Manning and Cheruvu (2016), involved early-career teachers in early childhood education programs. Despite significant and sustained challenges they faced, BITOCs negotiated their identities as teachers, as well as their identities as People of Color, with intersections especially around gender and sexual orientation. These teachers engaged in transformational resistance as professionals in ways that "challenged and reappropriated institutional (power) discourses, reauthorizing them agentively" (p. 9); that is, these BITOC worked to create their empowerment in the school setting by challenging language and narratives used about the institution.

While it is important to identify (just a sampling of) these important assets, it is equally important to point to the positive impact that BITOCs bring to the aims and purposes of education. Several studies over the past 20 years have identified increases in standardized testing scores (Dee, 2004; Gershenson et al., 2018), reductions in discriminatory practices in school discipline, increases in multicultural awareness schoolwide (Meier et al., 1989), increases in school attendance and decreases in dropping out, and increases in BISOCs opting to go to college.

✍ *Testimonio*: **Exemplary BITOCs—Francisco**

I had four exemplary BITOCs in my own schooling experiences. Ms. Dukes, an African American educator in my middle school, was what has been described as a warm demander.[2] She had the highest of expectations for us to learn language arts (we *were* going to learn English!) while at the same time showing us that grace, care, and intellectual prowess do go hand in hand. *From Ms. Dukes, I learned that teaching and learning are academic and intellectual activities.*

While in the art classroom of Ms. Saucedo, a Latina teacher, I felt the pride in her Mexican heritage that exuded from her as she taught us about the master artists of Mexico: Rivera, Siqueiros, Orozco, and Kahlo. In fact, I felt like she was an incarnation of Frida Kahlo in how she dressed, talked, and moved about the room. She taught us about the murals being painted in and around our own community that told the story of nuestro pueblo. *From Ms. Saucedo, I learned that teaching and learning are cultural activities.*

I took my first Chicano studies class from Mr. Acosta. I would see Mr. Acosta at almost all of our community's events: baseball games, theatrical presentations, and political rallies. This Chicano teacher wanted us to know about the various Latinx communities' experiences with oppression and marginalization but also about our communities' resistance and resilience. *From Mr. Acosta, I learned that teaching and learning are political activities.*

Besides being the first person to talk to me about going to college (as described in the Introduction), Mr. Vidal developed a relationship not only with me but also with my family as we explored, together, what going to college—and being successful—might entail. Besides coming to know my family, he would meet me at the public library to begin to show me how to do scholarly research. *From Mr. Vidal, I learned that teaching and learning are relational activities.*

Collectively, we assert that the need for BITOCs goes beyond the need for teachers as role models. They bring so much to the teaching profession as a result of their social and cultural assets—the essence of their identities. It is these identities that we turn to next.

💬 WONDER ALONE/WONDER TOGETHER

How might being a BITOC who brings a strong and active commitment to social justice add to the complexity of your role as a teacher? What might this stance entail?

ON IDENTITY

Identity is complex and its implications for teaching are manifold. Cultural identity encompasses race and ethnicity but includes all the identities, beyond these markers, that make up who we are. Our identities are *intersectional*; this means that our race and ethnicity are interconnected with other aspects of our social identities, including our language, gender, faith, sexuality, and geographic contexts, to name a few salient ones (Crenshaw, 1991; P. H. Collins, 2002).

Importantly, not every identity holds the same power and privilege. We constantly are navigating which identities have privileges—given that decisions about who belongs and who has power are both arbitrary and historical depending on the spaces and institutions where we find ourselves. To navigate these, we sometimes identity-switch in much the same way that one code-switches linguistically. That is to say, we might highlight certain identities in some spaces, and hide or downplay some identities in other spaces, particularly if these aspects of our identity are not immediately visible.

Recently, teachers and academics have come to understand the central role that identity has in teaching and learning. Teachers want students to think of themselves as capable learners. Teachers recognize that identity is key to advancing students' potential in the content areas: thinking of themselves as readers and writers, scientists, musicians, artists, and so on. Heritage-language teachers, for example, want students to see themselves as good at learning languages as a key to facilitating their abilities to learn multiple languages well. Cummins and colleagues (2015) argue that

> issues related to identity negotiation, investment, and affirmation are directly related to patterns of achievement and underachievement among social groups. Our starting point is that societal power relations, and their reflection in patterns of identity negotiation in schools, operate as causal factors in explaining underachievement among students from socially marginalized communities who have experienced discrimination and restricted educational and employment opportunities, often over generations. Educational responses to underachievement that fail to address the causal role of identity devaluation, and its roots in historical and current patterns of coercive power relations, are unlikely to be successful. (p. 556)

Consider, for example, students who identify themselves as academically competent (i.e., "smart"). They will put greater energy and effort into their studies than those students who do not see themselves as smart. These identities are stunted (in the case of coercive relations of power) or nurtured (in the case of collaborative relations of power) via interactions between teachers and their students. In short, we now have a deeper understanding of the importance of and connection to identity in teaching and learning. When students develop these academic identities, learning will be deepened.

Our identities encompass our core beliefs, practices, assumptions, and, most important for educators, our beliefs about teaching and learning. Recall that Tatum (1997) implores us to keep in mind the dominance and subordination of identities—even within cultural groups. We also are reminded that we hold both individual and shared identities. All of these are informed by "culture." Culture includes everything from what we eat to how we speak; and some of the most important aspects lie deeper in those things we are less aware of, like our value orientations and our worldviews. Culture is also something that we share with others. In this way, we can regard culture as a kind of "collective unconscious" (Jung, 1981). Thus, our shared or collective identities are culturally influenced.

Mindful that our identities are derived from our personal and communal histories, even when those histories (and resulting identities) are born out of opposition, we appreciate Galeano's (2007) important description of these:

> Our collective identity is born out of the past and is nourished by it—footprints which our own feet follow, steps which foreshadow our paths in the present—but does not crystalize into nostalgia. Certainly, we are not going to find our hidden face in the artificial perpetuation of ethnic dress, customs and objects which tourists demand of conquered nations. *We are what we do, and above all what we do to change what we are: our identity resides in action and struggle.* That is why the revelation of what we are implies denunciation of what prevents us being what we can be. We define ourselves through defiance and through opposing obstacles. (p. 19, emphasis in the original)

A central tenet of this book is that given all of our identity dimensions, we have the right to self-determination, the right to be who we are and to define and make visible any and all of our racial, ethnic, sexual, and gender identities as we choose.

Why is it important to sustain one's cultural identities? As BITOCs our unique identities and perspectives are often much needed and, at times, lead to creative innovations in teaching and learning in the schooling milieu. We do not point this out to be dramatic and self-serving, but rather to highlight the immense importance of your presence in schooling.

Further, in many of our communities, our elders transmit key knowledge—often without having advanced degrees, but rather as a result of their lived experiences. We carry their wisdom in our care of youth, our service to communities, and our everyday practices in the teaching profession. In this way, we need you to see yourself as a cultural guardian for our children, their families, and our communities (Flores, 2017). We ask you to consider how you might honor and sustain such knowledge in your pedagogical endeavors in a way that centers this wisdom rather than treating it as some curiosity erroneously seen as exotic to the dominant cultural values of schooling. *In identity-sustaining pedagogies, BITOCs serve as a conduit between our communities and the public space of the classroom.*

WONDER ALONE/WONDER TOGETHER

What are examples from your own school experiences where you felt your identities were invited into the classroom? How did that experience make you feel? How did the teacher model this?

Given that schooling in the United States comprises classrooms filled with students compulsorily bound to receive their free, public education (a human right), it seems honorable to intentionally center our identities pedagogically. Further, in this humanizing approach to teaching, we provide a powerful model for all BIPOC to not feel compelled in the very public space of schooling to hide or diminish the importance of their cultural identities.

Identity at the Core of Schooling

We believe that identity affects and informs how we both teach and learn. To not recognize identity as at the core of schooling is to deny the centrality of this key aspect of learning. Yet, as we detail later in this chapter, teacher education programs and, by extension, the teaching profession often make our identities invisible. Granted, identity may be discussed, learned about, or referenced in classrooms and schools, but we maintain that these instances are often fleeting and rarely, if at all, do they center identity. We dare to say that schooling is identity neutral or, worse, identity averse.

In teaching, being identity neutral is often the default practice. This might be grounded in an assumption that all teachers hold a similar identity and therefore do not need to navigate cultural differences. It might be grounded in a belief that your identity as "teacher" is the only one that matters given the roles and responsibilities prescribed for you. This is a problematic assumption for serving the needs of BITOCs, for whom their cultural identity is a central part of who they are. We make the distinction here between a professional, practice-centered, culture-neutral teacher identity and a BITOC's identity, which we see as largely informed by cultural values in concert with professional practice.

One way to consider this is to think about teacher identity development as *socialization*; that is, "our systematic training into the norms" of the profession (Sensoy & DiAngelo, 2017, p. 36). It comprises not only learning new knowledge and new pedagogical practices but also the development of one's professional identity (Neto et al., 2017). Much of this process is established early on, from the first time you enter a classroom as a student. Before entering a university, you have 12 years of schooling during which you have begun to develop a mental model of what being a teacher means, even before you take your first teacher education course. Lortie (1975) called these thousands of hours of observing teachers—which he argued are a more powerful factor in learning to teach than even your teacher education program—an apprenticeship of observation.

Teacher identity also might be seen as something put on during teaching—a kind of character or persona one enacts as an actor might on a theatrical stage. We point out, however, that there are likely insidious implications of this kind of false identity in teaching. Perhaps more anecdotally, we can relate a popular, but misguided, piece of advice to novice teachers that a more forceful or, in some cases, meanspirited identity (the adage goes "do not smile until December") is the only way to gain respect or compel students to comply with instruction. This kind of false identity runs counter to the vision of identity-sustaining pedagogy we present here.

Not everyone is on the same journey or on the same leg of their journey. We acknowledge that education, especially today, encompasses a dynamic, changing space for identity-sustaining pedagogies. As a novice educator, you may not have language at this time to articulate all facets of your identities and their implications for teaching and learning. Yet you undoubtedly have lived through experiences that attest to your identities as a student in this particular moment. Some of you have lived through learning multiple languages, crossing cultural and national borders, serving as cultural translators (Irvine, 2003), and navigating racial trauma in schools (Philip & Brown, 2020). Admittedly, not all BITOCs have the same experience, and it is erroneous to presume that membership in a cultural group guarantees universal experiences. *It is important to see identity-sustaining pedagogies as both inner-oriented, reflective work and part of a lifelong trajectory toward sustaining your identity.*

Cultural renewal, too, is work you must do for yourself and for your communities. In order to sustain your identities, you first must know what they are, how they are understood, and how these understandings have shifted over time (historically). It also would be important to know how people like you have migrated across geographic borders or across generations, and how students and teachers with those identities experience the current context in schooling. Being able to situate and articulate your identity in these contexts is imperative. Further, you renew and rejuvenate your cultural identities—and heritages—as you learn more about their historical contexts on both micro (personal) and macro (social) levels in order to articulate your individual way of being. Some scholars refer to this as social location (Kirk & Okazawa-Rey, 2004). Expect in this process to rethink, reexamine, and understand more fully your own identities.

We encourage you to have some real talk with yourself about what you need to begin this lifelong journey of re/discovering, re/articulating, and re/forming your identity. This often starts with an honest reflection about your social and cultural experiences. If you do not have the language to name your experiences, we have included some resources in the toolshed in Appendix A to help you in this process.

WONDER ALONE/WONDER TOGETHER

Looking back at your childhood experiences, what did you learn from your family and caregivers about your cultural identity? What were examples of how these were lived out in your home? How did people in your community demonstrate their cultural orientations? What happened to these as you went to school?

The Expected Role of Identity in Teacher Education

It is impossible for most BITOCs to suppress their identities upon entering the schoolhouse door. Whitestream expectations in the teaching profession abound and are largely unproblematic for White teachers. Yet for many BITOCs there are competing implicit and explicit expectations to hide or downplay their cultural identities. Kohli (2014) found in her qualitative examination of BITOCs' beliefs and practices that racial hierarchies were perpetuated in teacher education programs. In these hierarchies, White students' identities were seen as superior to BIPOCs' identities. BITOCs necessarily look toward their teacher education programs, as their primary introduction to professional practices, for guidance on how to bring their whole self into the classroom. However, they often are met with vague guidance and empty celebration of their identities.

Another example in teacher education can be found in how novice teachers are assessed for licensure. The edTPA (a teacher *performance* assessment) is a high-stakes portfolio exam submitted by teacher education candidates that is required by multiple states in order to receive initial licensure. As part of the assessment, students make and submit instructional plans, record and analyze their teaching and assessment practices based on such plans, and justify their instructional choices through written reflections. Students are scored on rubric criteria according to the subject area for which they are seeking certification. Overall, the assessment requires that teachers demonstrate only minimal knowledge of students' cultural assets. Moreover, it restricts identifying information and does not give clear guidelines on culturally responsive teaching or culturally sustaining pedagogies, let alone anything that might look like explicitly social justice–oriented teaching. Rather, teachers are expected to demonstrate understanding of the students' cultural and academic context, but are not asked to unpack how their own identities influence instruction. Since this is a major assessment tool for the profession, one might deduce that novice teachers must demonstrate a generic objectivity and neutrality regarding their identities as an expected form of professionalism. Similarly, invisibilization of teacher cultural identity can be seen in inservice teacher evaluation systems.

 WONDER ALONE/WONDER TOGETHER

When (if at all) have you observed teachers bring their full cultural identity into the classroom? How did they do so? With what impact?

Figure 4.1. The expected role of identity for BITOCs

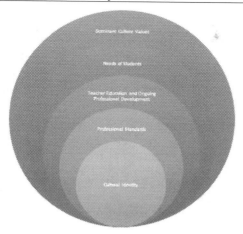

Figure 4.1 illustrates the expectation about the *buried* role we believe a BITOC's cultural identity plays in professional practice. This includes how you are taught as well as how you are expected to teach, to assess, and to evaluate in your teacher preparation program. While your cultural identity is central to you and how you see the world, most teacher education programs ask that you subordinate this to other expectations placed on all teachers.

In the current education landscape, schooling is oriented toward White teachers whose cultural identities are not subordinate to the dominant culture. This can read as necessarily taking on your teacher training as a BITOC as endeavors that actively suppress your cultural identity. According to your training, expectations, and evaluations, attention must be paid to professional standards (including curricular standards in your content area), training and education through your teacher preparation program, and ongoing professional development provided by your school and district. Your identity also is expected to be subsumed to the generic needs of students (and their families and communities) and to attending to and transmitting dominant culture values. All of these are in increasing importance and weight of influence on your teaching, whether explicitly stated or implied.

To counter these expectations, we pose an alternative. In this, you might read Figure 4.1 as a guide to how a BITOC's cultural identity is *foundational* to all other practices. We ask that you consider this reorientation as you learn about identity-sustaining pedagogies in the next section.

Lunenberg and colleagues (2007) posit that teacher educators can be a powerful model for teacher practice but might themselves be understudied and underemphasized given their role in the development of teachers. The authors also argue that teacher education practice is, in general, understudied. Zeichner (2009) argues that teacher education programs have made gains in welcoming more diverse teacher candidates, but they have struggled with structural changes to keep or grow the numbers of Black, Indigenous, and Teachers of Color.

Our experiences as teacher educators can attest to this. It is important to acknowledge that identity-sustaining pedagogies will need to be modeled for teacher candidates in their teacher education programs. It might be that White teacher educators will need to interrogate and model how their own identities inform their teaching practices. These processes will need to include acknowledging their own cultural dominance, questioning beliefs about the role of identity in teaching, and examining their own commitments to identity-sustaining pedagogies. While imperfect, this approach might lay the groundwork for BITOCs to be well-supported in enacting their own identity-sustaining pedagogies.

 WONDER ALONE/WONDER TOGETHER

In what ways have you found yourself hiding parts of your identity in schooling? In what ways do you feel free to include your identities in your teaching?

IDENTITY-SUSTAINING PEDAGOGIES

Earlier, we raised the point that a BITOC's cultural values can and should be central to their teaching practice. While a teacher's general training and professional expectations might downplay this centrality, we pose that cultural identity must remain intentionally foundational to a BITOC's practice. We call this identity-sustaining pedagogy, for it is an act of cultural preservation to sustain one's own cultural perspectives, values, communication methods, and ways of being in the world in enacting curriculum and instruction. We do not suggest here that identity-sustaining pedagogies are some feeble act of celebrating diversity within schooling. Rather, to enact an identity-sustaining pedagogy is to liberate both the teacher and all students from an invisibilization of the centrality of identity in instruction.

Identity-sustaining pedagogy is deeply rooted in the equity pedagogy dimension of multicultural education (J. A. Banks, 2004). We see identity-sustaining pedagogy as complementary to culturally responsive teaching (Gay, 2018) and culturally sustaining pedagogy approaches (Paris, 2012; Paris & Alim, 2017), as described in Chapter 3. Whereas these authors have focused largely on encouraging educators to enact practices that benefit and sustain students' cultural identities, we offer that identity-sustaining pedagogy is the BITOC equivalent to nourishing and advancing their own cultural survival in education. *As BITOCs enact identity-sustaining pedagogies, we believe that they will be more fully present—in an unprecedented way—in the enterprise of education.* This presence means that BITOCs do not deny, hide, or shy away from their cultural, linguistic, political, and intersectional identities in the planning and enacting of curriculum and instruction.

Returning to Figure 4.1, we pose that identity-sustaining pedagogy does not eschew professional standards, teacher education experiences, knowledge of students' needs, or the dominant culture. While a critique of teacher education is implicit in the figure, it illustrates the gargantuan task BITOCs navigate in enacting identity-sustaining pedagogy, given that the dominant culture pervades all aspects of teaching. Nevertheless, BITOCs navigate and incorporate their professional expectations while at the same time enacting an intentional, critical self-preservation in their daily pedagogies. No choice is too big or too small. In introducing yourself at the beginning of a term, you might insist on pronunciation of your name that holds fidelity to the linguistic tones of your family's tongue and not kowtow to an Anglicized version of their name. You frequently might offer a *testimonio* from your childhood experiences. And you might code-switch to the language you would speak in your home community as you illustrate a key idea.

We acknowledge that identity-sustaining pedagogies might seem to some a biased, self-centered approach to teaching. We reject this solipsistic simplification of our argument here. BITOCs are not simply rejecting all notions of pedagogy or other cultural contexts and hierarchies, nor are they creating their own teaching practices in isolation of professional expectations or generally accepted instruction. Harding (1993) argued that stronger objectivity comes from an intentional examination of one's own biases in the pursuit of a more robust and critical objectivity. Given Harding's notion of stronger objectivity, we argue that identity-sustaining pedagogy is a stronger, more substantial, more authentic instructional practice than inauthentic, superficially objective approaches.

BITOCs who center their cultural values are not encouraged to do so in a blind, uncritical praxis. To be clear, identity-sustaining pedagogy does not aim to be a feel-good vision of education that intentionally embraces a misguided focus on the positive or uncontroversial. Anti-oppressive approaches to education embrace uncertainty and surface issues that are often uncomfortable, difficult, and rarely talked about (Kumashiro, 2000, 2002). Identity-sustaining pedagogy seeks to embrace criticality and antibias, antiracist, and anti-oppressive praxis.

BITOCs are presumed to be honest in their instruction when sharing their cultural values (a topic we return to in Chapter 5). We assert that rather than shying away from biases, cultural assumptions, or stereotypes that we may hold, centering cultural values implicitly demands interrogating harmful, violent, denigrating, and problematic cultural values. We all have been socialized into cultural values that are not politically neutral. Although the teaching profession often expects teachers to embrace some form of professional neutrality, we argue this comes at the cost of productive critical analysis and revision of teaching practices. This is difficult work, albeit necessary.

Figure 4.2. Four core actions for identity-sustaining pedagogies

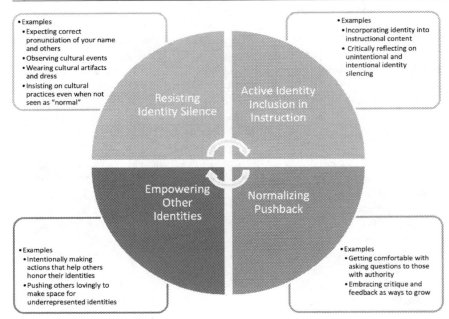

- Examples
  - Expecting correct pronunciation of your name and others
  - Observing cultural events
  - Wearing cultural artifacts and dress
  - Insisting on cultural practices even when not seen as "normal"

- Examples
  - Incorporating identity into instructional content
  - Critically reflecting on unintentional and intentional identity silencing

Resisting Identity Silence

Active Identity Inclusion in Instruction

Empowering Other Identities

Normalizing Pushback

- Examples
  - Intentionally making actions that help others honor their identities
  - Pushing others lovingly to make space for underrepresented identities

- Examples
  - Getting comfortable with asking questions to those with authority
  - Embracing critique and feedback as ways to grow

A Framework for Enacting Identity-Sustaining Pedagogies: Four Core Actions

We offer a framework for enacting identity-sustaining pedagogies that we hope informs your teaching. As shown in Figure 4.2, this framework has four core actions: resisting identity silence, active identity inclusion in instruction, normalizing pushback, and empowering other identities. We hope this framework guides not only your classroom teaching but all of your work outside of it—with colleagues, with families, and in the community.

These four actions are ongoing, iterative, and nonlinear; they can overlap and work in tandem with one another. We hope you see this framework as a kind of menu of options to inspire (or remind) you that your identities are essential to the teaching profession, as well as help you generate ways to make their presence more meaningful in educational spaces. Also keep in mind that these four core actions do not fit cleanly into all of the topics we describe in the rest of this text. Rather, we give you some guidance throughout with examples of how to think about them. We invite you to think about further examples of these four core actions you might take as you read through what follows.

We offer some brief examples here to help you better understand these core actions. In later chapters, we expand these and offer additional examples to support your identity-sustaining pedagogies. We argue that in spite of all expectations and restrictions placed on you in the teaching profession, BITOCs

WONDER ALONE/WONDER TOGETHER

Before reading further, what is your initial reaction to these four core actions for identity-sustaining pedagogies for BITOCs? Which of these core actions most immediately speaks to you?

have the most agency over their classrooms and pedagogies. Therefore, these are the most powerful and effective sites for identity-sustaining pedagogies. We hope you draw inspiration from the following four core actions.

Resisting Identity Silence. While the core actions are nonlinear, we logically might order them in discussing how they might be effected. We start with resisting identity silence as it is often the catalyst for other actions. As discussed earlier in this chapter, teacher education and schooling often work implicitly to suppress our identities. This can be as subtle as Anglicizing the pronunciation of your name—different from what you might hear in your homes and communities—or insisting you wear your hair or dress in a more "professional" manner. This coded language has served to silence our collective identities as BITOCs in order to compel us toward a more so-called neutral identity presentation. In your teacher education programs, this might come in the form of feedback you receive from a university supervisor to be more identity neutral or to downplay your identities in your teaching style. In these instances, insisting on the centrality of your identities is important.

To facilitate this, you might find that you have to first learn to analyze more deeply the ways—both implicit and explicit—that your identities have been silenced or discouraged. You might not at first notice when your identity is being silenced. Awareness is an important initial step toward more effective action. It is important to recognize that this awareness is an important catalyst, but not a complete realization of this core action.

This action also seeks to encourage you to insist on keeping your identity as core to your teaching practice. We realize that for some of you, this is permission to continue to do so. For some, it is an invitation to find ways to do so for the first time. Another way of doing this work is to learn more about your own identities, including the ways in which the local school context has treated people like you. Have people with your identities experienced joy in schooling? Have they found meaningful ways to make contributions to the community? How have you, your family, and your ancestors come to the local community? In addition, this action also invites you to engage in deep reflective work about how your assumptions about teaching, learning, content-area expertise, and youth care are all informed by cultural lenses.

Active Identity Inclusion in Instruction. Instruction is at the core of teaching and insisting on an active inclusion of our identities in the classroom is paramount. This core action draws upon guidance from culturally centering education, as described in Chapter 3. To iniatiate this action, we encourage you to think about the ways culturally centering educational pedagogies might be applied in your practice in order to sustain your own identities.

In this action, teachers actively find ways to include their identities in their instruction. Actions include, of course, a teacher intentionally incorporating their own cultural identity into curriculum. For example, when discussing Halloween, a teacher might take the opportunity to also discuss the Day of the Dead as enacted in many Latinx communities around the world. This action encourages the teacher to include this context both for student learning and to preserve the teacher's own epistemological cultural beliefs.

Recall that these actions can work in tandem with one another. For example, in the previous action, a teacher first might notice that they are silencing their own identity by not including their own traditional Chinese medicine practices in a unit on health. By sharing these, the teacher could model for students a more realistic, complex understanding of health in the real world. Teachers also can intentionally include opportunities for students to reflect on their own identity and cultural contexts, as appropriate to the curriculum. This ultimately helps students consider a more complex understanding of course content and the ways it is applied in the world.

Normalizing Pushback. We hope that you do not romanticize the inclusion of your identities into your teaching practice as a perpetual vignette of feel-good cinematic moments. Insisting on the visibilies of our identities in educational spaces will be an endeavor filled with rewards, setbacks, resistance, and joy. This core action insists on you preparing for and normalizing pushback to those in power and those students and families you serve as a teacher who are resistant to identity-sustaining approaches to instruction. We encourage you to embrace the inevitability of resistance or pushback.

This also may come from unexpected sources, such as other BITOCs, a mentor, or an administrator, including someone who evaluates your teaching. Knowing that pushback from others will happen, you will be better prepared to respond to it with the knowledge that it is a regular part of identity-sustaining pedagogy. Effective actions to support this work include practicing responses to resistance, collecting resources to share with unsupportive colleagues, finding ways to deal with the frustration as (regrettably) part of the process, practicing self-care, and finding a supportive community with whom to vent and share frustrations, for this is difficult work. We return to these themes in later chapters.

Empowering Other Identities. Key to liberatory education is to help liberate others. Just as there is a reflexive and reciprocal benefit in enacting identity-sustaining pedagogies, this core action encourages you to seek ways to help others sustain their own identities. To be clear, this includes White students and those that hold power and privilege. This does not mean sustaining problematic elements of such identities (Paris & Alim, 2017). A better way of envisioning this type of empowerment is to encourage a *critical* sustaining of all identities. This would mean not engaging in a blind maintenance of identities, but rather confronting problematic or dehumanizing cultural beliefs and sustaining this criticality alongside joyous and meaningful cultural values (Paris & Alim, 2017). But we do not encourage you to center dominant identities in this work; rather we ask you to ensure that other nondominant identities find empowerment to nourish and sustain their own cultural values. In this action, we encourage you to embrace advocacy and allyship as core practices in helping all educators critically sustain their identities.

As with the other core actions, there is a reflective, reflexive action that is a necessary precursor to empowering other identities. A White-passing Latinx person might need to do deeper reflective work, such as reflecting on, confronting, and actively dismantling anti-Blackness in their teaching practice as a way to seek to empower others. This core action also encompasses more structural work that seeks to critique, push on, and dismantle policies or practices that ultimately render identities invisible or dehumanize others.

We find much pedagogical and practical value in the work developed by Cummins and his colleagues (2015), who describe the value of creating *identity texts* that bring students' lives together with their language repertoires while supporting literacy development. Identity texts are literacy products described as follows by Cummins and Early (2011):

> Students invest their identities in the creation of these texts—which can be written, spoken, signed, visual, musical, dramatic, or combinations in multimodal form. The identity text then holds a mirror up to students in which their identities are reflected back in a positive light. When students share identity texts with multiple audiences (peers, teachers, parents, grandparents, sister classes, the media, and so on) they are likely to receive positive feedback and affirmation of self in interaction with these audiences. Although not always an essential component, technology acts as an amplifier to enhance the process of identity text production and dissemination. (p. 3)

For us, any class-based activity where you invite students to bring their lives, their cultural viewpoints, and their home languages into the creation of academic products serves to empower students' identities.

Identity-Sustaining Pedagogies in Teacher Education and the Formation of Teachers

Here we offer advice for two groups: students in teacher education programs and faculty for teacher education programs who want to be advocates for preservice BITOCs around identity-sustaining pedagogies. As seen in Figure 4.1, we offer a critique that teacher education programs pay little, if any, attention

WONDER ALONE/WONDER TOGETHER

Now having read about these four core actions for identity-sustaining pedagogies, what is your general reaction? How do you imagine these four core actions would change the way you have been thinking about how to be a BITOC?

to preserving BITOCs' identities. Further, BITOCs are discouraged from using their identities to inform instruction. Standardized assessments, such as edTPA, in teacher education and performance evaluations in the teaching profession do little to assist BITOCs in validating the informed use of their identities in instruction.

Achinstein and Aguirre (2008), in complicating assumptions of "cultural match" between BISOCs and BITOCs, have demonstrated that teacher education programs fail to adequately prepare new BITOCs to negotiate their racial identity within the school context. Such lack of attention leaves them in positions where they must make sense of their racial identity as teachers without the support of their preparation program, often making them particularly vulnerable to attrition (Parker & Hood, 1995; Villegas & Davis, 2008). In sum, teacher education offers a one-size-fits-all program designed primarily for White teacher candidates. We hope an identity-sustaining pedagogy framework offers a useful addition to re/visioning teacher education.

Identity-Sustaining Pedagogies in the Classroom and Community

As a teacher, you have little agency over many things. A child's home life, global pandemics, snow closures, fire drills, pep assemblies, and your own health issues can all arise as unanticipated factors that change your teaching. Yet it is in the classroom, and the practices that you enact, that you enjoy much agency. An identity-sustaining pedagogy centers your cultural values in planning, enacting, assessing, and reflecting on your instruction. We offer more concrete examples in the following chapters on how you might specifically enact identity-sustaining pedagogies. We emphasize that this work is important in your everyday pedagogies.

As a teacher, you also navigate spaces outside your classroom—places where you have less agency. Nevertheless, it is important to be intentional in enacting identity-sustaining pedagogies. In Chapter 5 we share how BITOCs can enact and advocate for identity-sustaining pedagogies in community spaces. We will go into more depth about applying these to your teaching practice in later chapters.

CONCLUDING REFLECTIONS

Returning to our living room metaphor that began this chapter, we contemplate the ways this public space might serve identity-sustaining pedagogies. A good host seeks to have welcomed guests feel at ease, comfortable, and accommodated, even though they may be strangers in the space. To be fully present here—to preserve one's own continuity of identity—a host should invite all to come as they are. To facilitate this, the host may share their own stories and invite guests to do so in an effort to build dialogue and community. And in this way each person in the space preserves their own identities—their narratives and lineages—while resisting a temptation to try to conform inauthentically to some arbitrary notions of neutrality and detached respectability. As we metaphorically let our hair down, and learn more about where people and their ancestors have come from, we start to see where people stand on issues. In doing so, we can enjoy a level of real talk far more profound than any small talk that might have occurred. Even as we disagree, or argue, we have seen enough of one another authentically to be bound by a kinship that leads to a deeper invitation to find ourselves in this home together.

As the 2020 global pandemic and rapid changes to schooling in response to COVID-19 have demonstrated, we have had an unprecedented invitation into our homes for teaching and learning. Many have home offices improvised on dining tables, studio-grade lighting, and emergency camera-ready clothing for last-minute meetings. Identity-sustaining pedagogies might be even more appropriate in these moments. We encourage you to find authentic ways to center your identities in these practices.

⋙ Make It Happen: Portfolio Activity—Identity Text

For your portfolio, we invite you to create a text of your identities. Understandably, this may change over time. But who are you in this moment? Take stock of your identities through some initial reflection. Identify up to five artifacts that represent your identity. For example, these may be books, keepsakes, foods, or photographs. Reflect on how these represent your cultural identities. Which identities are most salient? Which must you still wrestle with or learn more about?

Additionally, consider your personal and family histories. What early experiences and familial events have contributed to your understanding of your identities? Be sure to acknowledge membership in different groups. As you recognize and acknowledge your affiliation with various groups in society, how do you understand what it means to belong to each group? How does belonging to one group influence how you relate to and view other groups?

Using this reflection, recall the four core actions for identity-sustaining pedagogies. How might your chosen artifacts help you intentionally sustain your identities in your teaching? In what ways are you already enacting the four core actions? In what ways might you set goals to sustain your identities?

Be creative about how you capture these for your personal and professional portfolio.

⇒ Keep It Going!

- Read the poem "Poem About My Rights" by June Jordan.
- Explore personal and family histories. There are many tools available today to explore these and we encourage you to critically engage with them. Consider Sleeter's (2020) essay titled "Critical Family History: An Introduction" for inspiration on how to engage your own critical family history.

CHAPTER 5

The Kitchen (and the Closet)
Getting Real About Schooling

So now my young Indian child does not want to go to school anymore
(even though we cut his hair). He feels that he does not belong. He is the
only Indian child in your class, and he is well-aware of this fact. Instead
of being proud of his race, heritage, and culture, he feels ashamed. When
he watches television, he asks why the white people hate us so much and
always kill our people in the movies and why they take everything away
from us. He asks why the other kids in school are not taught about the
power, beauty, and essence of nature or provided with an opportunity to
experience the world around them firsthand.

—Robert Lake (Medicine Grizzlybear), "An Indian Father's Plea" (2000)

As we move ever deeper into the home, we find ourselves in the kitchen, the
place where things are getting cooked up. An important fixture of the kitchen
is the kitchen table. It is here that we sit sipping café con leche or eat arroz con
pollo while, at the same time, sharing with loved ones the happenings of the
day, debating recent political challenges, or engaging in tough conversations
about our interpersonal relationships. At the kitchen table we share our vulnerabilities, even if we share them with a sense of caution.

The kitchen is a space that is private to the outside world, typically private
to guests in our home, yet it is not our most private space. An even more private
space is the closet in the kitchen. In the closet, we keep cleaning supplies, junk
food, or anything we hastily might have stuffed in there to hide from those that
find their way to these less public spaces. These more private spaces reveal our
complications and growth areas that we do not always want others to know,
even those we hold in relationship.

In this chapter we turn toward ways of enacting an identity-sustaining pedagogy in your teaching practice. We provide advice to guide your decisionmaking to more fully engage identity-sustaining pedagogy. Key to this discussion
is exploring the notion of what is public and what is private—especially how
to make that distinction relevant to identity-sustaining pedagogy as central to
your teaching practice.

You likely have begun thinking already about the more public actions you might take in carrying out identity-sustaining pedagogy. These are important. At the same time, we invite you to think deeply about what must remain *private*—whether at the kitchen table or deeper into the most private space in your house. That is, you might need to keep some of your identity-sustaining pedagogy practices private in order to ensure job security, sustain professional relationships, or practice care for students, youth, and communities. And sometimes you keep them private because they are knowledge and practices sacred to your sociocultural community (Whiteplume & Rios, 2010).

In this chapter, as authors, we step into our roles as mentors and provide advice for your journey through your teacher education programs and development as teachers. We hope our suggestions inform your practices, encourage you toward a meaningful practice of identity-sustaining pedagogy, and assist you to survive and thrive in this profession.

FINDING NUANCES BETWEEN PUBLIC AND PRIVATE SPACES

The division between public and private spaces is not clean. We offer a framework here to help you think more deeply about public and private spaces as an important context for your decisionmaking in carrying out identity-sustaining pedagogy. Public spaces—such as the classroom, the school, and your teacher training program—are ubiquitous in your experiences. Private spaces often are found among other people that share your identity and those with whom you hold deep interpersonal relationships. Even more private might be those reflective spaces you hold for yourself and that you share via a journal, or the thoughts you have while walking alone.

Further, there is nuance between these two dimensions of the public and the private. The kitchen represents a type of public-private space, for it is not the most private space you might experience and still sits within a public space. It is in these spaces that we can push, stretch, and question others in loving ways. We also acknowledge a deeper, sometimes more personal space—an inner-private one—which we discuss in the next section of the chapter. Overall, we suggest that there are ways to enact the four actions for identity-sustaining pedagogy in more private spaces and we articulate some examples here.

We also acknowledge that there is sometimes a tension between academic discourse and our own lived experiences and *testimonios*. Recall that in earlier chapters we discussed the different knowledge systems and cultural contexts that are at play in schooling. Often, the dominant culture dictates what counts as official knowledge and it undercuts other forms of knowledge or ways of being. We embrace this tension and believe that offering *testimonios* of our lived experiences as counter narratives is important. We, Francisco and Longoria, enact our own identity-sustaining pedagogy here by insisting on relating our *testimonios* and perspectives in these chapters to both sustain our own identities and help illustrate this praxis.

Paying attention to public-private contexts is key to your work in the teaching profession, especially the work that you will do outside of the classroom. This encompasses how you navigate interpersonal relationships with colleagues and determine who might be an ally and who might not be ready for allyship, and whom you most rely on for personal growth.

Consider this chapter a public-private space that we are opening up to you. In these spaces, we more easily might encounter insider knowledge—including systemic knowledge—that is crucial for success. We hope to relate some general knowledge about being a Black, Indigenous, and Teacher of Color (BITOC) in the hope that it helps you be more successful in enacting identity-sustaining pedagogy and supports your teaching practice.

In this chapter, we also want to share the other side of the story of being a BITOC. In Chapter 4, we highlighted the incredible assets BITOCs bring to their students, their schools, and their communities. We hope that reading that chapter inspired you toward being fueled by the essential nature and importance of your role as a BITOC in schooling. In what follows, we detail some of the most salient challenges you might face in the profession and some ways you might persevere and work through them.

💬 WONDER ALONE/WONDER TOGETHER

How does this distinction between public and private spaces make a difference for you in terms of how you think about your work personally? Professionally?

THE CHALLENGES OF BEING A BITOC

We wish that we could tell you that—having succeeded in schools, a university, a teacher preparation program, and teacher licensure—you will enter a profession that will embrace you fully. Just as schools were not made to affirm the wonderful cultural and linguistic diversity of our young people from marginalized communities, as well as their potential to be active citizens, neither are schools structured to support the diversity and potential of BITOCs. We share these challenges not to scare you away; in fact, you probably can imagine these on your own. Rather, we share these to help you to be prepared, as best you can, to navigate—accept, disrupt, question/challenge, move around—them in ways that assist you in being the best possible teacher for our communities.

While scholars have identified the substantial assets BITOCs bring to the profession, studies also have identified the numerous challenges BITOCs face along and throughout the pathway from deciding to become a teacher, through college and a teacher preparation program, and into the profession. We offer this overview here.

Within teacher education programs, BITOC candidates experience a curriculum that normalizes Whiteness (Ullicci & Battey, 2011), talks about BISOCs

WONDER ALONE/WONDER TOGETHER

As you read these challenges of being a BITOC, what is your general reaction? Which of these are not new to you, given what you have read/heard before about challenges to BITOCs? Which are new?

as objects (Montecinos, 2004), and overlooks the significant assets that BITOC candidates bring to the program and the profession (Kohli, 2009). The result of these experiences, as summarized by Kohli (2016), is that "teacher candidates of Color are often silenced, invisibilized, and alienated" (p. 311).

Within school settings, BITOCs entering and within the profession have identified the following challenges, as summarized descriptively by Dixon et al. (2019):

- Experiencing an antagonistic culture in their schools
- Feeling overworked and undervalued (in terms of both compensation and recognition)
- Lacking a sense of agency and autonomy to teach in culturally sustaining ways in order to be responsive to the school's student population
- Facing intensive psychological and financial strain, the "high cost" of being a Teacher of Color
- Missing the kinds of social, psychological, and professional supports that will enable BITOCs to be successful in the profession for the long haul

Much of the scholarship also explores issues related to developing an identity as a BITOC. These include how you see yourself, how you perceive others, and how you think others perceive you. It is because this is such a crucial factor that we have centered an identity-sustaining framework in this text. We acknowledge that there is often a lack of opportunities to discuss, navigate, and negotiate what it means to serve in the role of a BITOC. Many BITOCs have had too few models to glean a clear image of what it means to be a BITOC. Often in teacher education programs, as in the teaching profession, there are too few other BITOCs as fellow travelers to share your emerging understandings of what it means to be a BITOC, as well as too few opportunities to do so. Add to this the even fewer opportunities to consider your identity as a BITOC as it intersects with other salient aspects of your identity (around gender identity, sexual orientation, dis/ability, immigration status, as just a few examples).

Often because BITOCs are so few within a school setting, they feel as if they have to carry the full load in addressing pressing school issues vis-à-vis ensuring educational equity; in short, they have to don their cape and play the role of "super" teacher. At the same time, because of their experiences being racialized and questions from others about their qualifications to serve in the role of a teacher, BITOCs often begin to doubt their own legitimacy. This manifests itself in feeling like "imposters" who do not belong in the profession and in a particular school.

BITOCs' identities, in interaction with the school culture, also are largely implicated in the challenging experiences they face (Achinstein et al., 2010). Souto-Manning and Cheruvu (2016) found that, at times, BITOCs are *hyper-invisible* when it comes to listening to and acting upon opinions shared within the school, consideration for important professional development and leadership opportunities, and career advancement. At other times, BITOCs are *hyper-visible* when, for example, it comes to leading "cultural diversity" events, addressing parents and community representatives, and dealing with BISOCs who are disaffected with schooling. This can be added, as Souto-Manning and Cheruvu describe, to experiences with subliminal racism (tokenism and essentialism) and deficit ideologies about BITOCs' language and/or culture, as well as seeing "Whiteness" normalized. The collective influence of these implicit messages is a devaluing of one's cultural and linguistic assets.

Kohli and Pizarro (2016) described the specific challenges of BITOCs who bring a social justice orientation aimed at transforming educational opportunities for students. To begin, these teachers want to have deep connections to and with their local communities. This conflicts with the culture of most schools, which, given their hierarchical stance (that is, schools as superior), have framed communities and families as the "problem." This often leads to social and professional alienation and isolation for these BITOCs.

Challenges: How to Work Through Them

Recall that core actions for identity-sustaining pedagogy include resisting identity silence and normalizing pushback. *Indeed, we assert, sometimes your mere presence is an interruption of business as usual.* With respect to normalizing pushback, we encourage you to expect pushback and resistance to your identities and presence in the teaching profession. We do not relate this to discourage you, but rather to be realistic about the marginalization and oppression so many BITOCs experience. We also caution that this need not be the full sum of the characterization of being a BITOC in schooling and, as we discuss later in this book, that there is joy in this work, too.

We feel like we do not need to say (but perhaps do not say often enough) that you inevitably will experience oppression; that is, "the -isms." Whenever this occurs, it may cause you to feel dejected, hurt, or even depressed. A way to move through this oppression is to game plan how you might confront resistance and disrupt bias. Gorski's (2013) equity literacy is a useful framework to support this ability to resist and disrupt bias in a purposeful way, as we describe here. It includes four abilities focused on recognizing, responding to, and redressing bias, and then cultivating and sustaining an equity focus.

The ability to *recognize* even the subtlest biases and inequities begins with attending to those factors we often do not formally think about, but which send messages to students about who is welcomed in the room. These include tools like classroom materials—books, posters, classroom setup, as just a few examples. They include how interactions occur in the classroom (which student voices are affirmed and which are silenced). They certainly include the curriculum itself. Underlying this is the special skill of recognizing how the curriculum, instruction, classroom organization, and assessment might reflect a deficit ideology as opposed to an asset-based framework.

The ability to *respond* skillfully and equitably to biases and inequities in the immediate term requires knowledge around equity issues and the interpersonal skills to intervene when evidence of bias occurs. It also points out the special role you have as an educator to teach this knowledge and skills to your students so that they too can begin to recognize bias in the classroom setting and respond accordingly. Additionally, it includes the knowledge and skills associated with raising these issues with peers and school-based administrators so that all sense their collective and institutional responsibility to respond to bias.

The ability to *redress* (that is, to make right) biases and inequities that have occurred requires understanding of various ways that bias is a result of institutional culture and then rectifying this bias. It asks equity-minded educators to recognize, respond to, and redress biases at their institutional roots—especially regarding school-based policies, procedures, and practices—as well as to learn to advocate for equity-based practices. It requires educators to "remember that celebrating diversity and multiculturalism is not the same as antiracism or dismantling white supremacy" (Kleinrock, 2020).

The final ability is centered on the need to *create and sustain* equity by way of developing an ethic and commitment to equity in every decision made, as well as to continue these commitments even in the face of discomfort or resistance (Gorski, 2013). This means holding high expectations for all students, filling the gaps for those who do not have access to learning resources, thinking responsively about how to increase family engagement, and creating a school-based culture where students feel free to share their thoughts and feelings with honesty and integrity.

Being thoughtful and intentional about how to respond to bias and oppression (the "-isms") that you experience demands that you be prepared to confront these in a strategic and systematic way. You might need to first develop your ability to identify biases and inequities before being fully able to respond to them productively.

We add that paying attention to public versus private contexts is important when thinking about when and how to respond. Keep in mind the metaphor of the house we have used and consider it guidance as you think about ways to engage Tatum's (1997) notion of dominance and subordination. Sometimes you must be more public in how you respond to challenges and sometimes you must work through them in a more private context.

WONDER ALONE/WONDER TOGETHER

As you read about these four approaches to responding to the challenges faced by BITOCs, how do you imagine these guiding your professional actions? What other elements do you imagine would be valuable to you as you address challenges you might be likely to face?

You will find that you must advocate for yourself as a BITOC within the teaching profession. At times this will encompass the identity-sustaining pedagogy action of resisting identity silence. You might find that you must insist on correct pronunciation of your name by colleagues and students alike. It might, at times, consist of needing to educate others on the cultural roots of your hairstyle against perceptions that it is "unprofessional." Coupled with Gorski's (2013) equity literacy framework, it is imperative that you not see such opportunities as trivial or unimportant. It is in these everyday moves—where little things are big—to resist identity silence that we must offer our own pushback to practice identity-sustaining pedagogy.

✍ *Testimonio*: We Don't Have to Do That Anymore—Francisco

I was newly out of graduate school, having completed my doctoral degree at a top-tier public university. I was in my 2nd year as a tenure-track faculty member and was asked to chair a search committee for a new hire in the college. Accepting the assignment, I scheduled our first search committee meeting. At the meeting we discussed the job description, the places it would be posted, and the search process we would use, among other things. Toward the end of the meeting, I asked the members, What do you most hope we find in a new colleague? Some spoke about special experiences, others about areas of scholarly research, others about personal qualities. At the end, I shared many of these and I also included I hoped we would be successful in having a diverse pool of candidates so that we have faculty of color to consider.

Alison, a White, more senior member of the committee, chimed in: "Oh, no, we don't have to do that anymore. The last person we hired was an affirmative action hire and wasn't the most qualified applicant. So we don't have to do that anymore." I was stunned since, as I and all the committee members knew, I was the last person hired.

I checked in with a friend on the committee to confirm what I heard and what I thought it meant. My friend agreed, saying, "That was clearly a cut at you." I was stunned. My years teaching, my advanced degrees, and even my emerging scholarship were not enough to shield me from the insidious nature of racial abuse.

I consulted a senior Black faculty member, who gave me good advice: Confront the person, describe what occurred, listen, and then share how these kinds of statements would not lead to the kind of professional relationships we should all pursue in the college.

I did so and the person just looked at me, without responding. Right after that meeting, I went to the Dean's office and said that if Alison were in any position to evaluate me, I would file a discrimination charge. After all, she had already determined, before looking at what I had accomplished, that I was unqualified for the position. The Dean agreed and placed a letter in my file saying, in effect, that Alison could not serve as an evaluator of my file.

Microaggressions

One of the challenges all BIPOCs experience—and then confront—is racial microaggressions (Solórzano & Pérez Huber, 2020). As much as we would like to believe that our education, our experiences, our talents, and our commitments should stand on their own merits, you still should expect that there will be those who will question your existence and your right to be a teacher. While some of this will manifest itself in outright bias, prejudice, and discrimination, you also will experience it as microaggressions. Derald Wing Sue (2010) used the term *racial microaggressions* to describe those "brief and commonplace daily verbal, behavioral, or environmental indignities, whether intentional or unintentional, that communicate hostile, derogatory, or negative racial slights and insults toward people of color" (p. xvi).

The prominence of theorizing and detailing racial microaggressions was instrumental in demonstrating—tangibly and concretely—acts of marginalization and oppression of BIPOCs (see, for example, microaggressions.com for an extended description of these). This theorizing also was intended to show how power and privilege were often at the core of microaggressive statements. What is central is that a single one of these, by itself, often is thought of as "no big deal" by the person committing them. Indeed, it is in the collective where they become instruments of dehumanization for BIPOCs; collectively, they create a hostile work or home climate. This can result in psychological, emotional, and spiritual trauma (Sue, 2010). It speaks to the saying, as the poet Stainslaw Jerzy Lec (1969) describes, "No snowflake in an avalanche ever feels responsible" (p. 9).

We certainly want you to keep in mind that all oppressive incidents cannot be described as microaggressions. In some instances, a deliberate, oppressive attack is really a macroaggression. For us, institutional policies preventing student success or limiting student opportunities are considered macroaggressions. To strengthen the real impact of all of these, Kendi (2019) asks that we consider all of them as racist abuse.

Combating Racial Microaggressions. Responding to microaggressions can be difficult, especially for a novice teacher. It is important to always keep in

WONDER ALONE/WONDER TOGETHER

In thinking about microaggressions that you have experienced, what are some of the patterns that you can identify? How have you responded? What worked? What did not work?

mind your own personal dignity and that you are entitled to calling attention to and seeking reconciliation for the abuses microaggressions effect. If the microaggression does not need to be immediately addressed, it likely will be best to think strategically about how to proceed. It will be best to think about how you might affect the core action of empowering others.

Some things to consider in this are the relationship you hold with other individuals and the short- and long-term implications of your actions. A peer might be easier to confront more directly, whereas a supervisor's microaggressions will demand that you seek input from their supervisor or one of their peers in order to confront or rectify the microaggression.

A short-term action might be to call out the microaggression, in the hope that it results in the behavior being immediately stopped. But inviting a colleague to understand how their language or actions were experienced as a microaggression might better serve in the long term, helping them to rethink their problematic behavior and transform their teaching. There are no set rules, but we think it is important to help guide you in confronting microaggressions instead of feeling that you perpetually must work to shut them down in every instance.

Beyond the short- and long-term implications, we recognize that you also must be true to who you are, to your heart and soul; it is from there that you feel compelled to speak out. In thinking about speaking out, feminist scholar Audre Lorde (1984) advises us to transform our "silence into language and action" (p. 28). Lorde urges us to recognize that our silence is oppressive to ourselves, while speaking up is a form of personal liberation. As Lorde posits, "I have come to believe over and over again that what is most important to me must be spoken, made verbal and shared, even at the risk of having it bruised or misunderstood. That the speaking profits me, beyond any other effect" (p. 28).

THE CLOSET:
OPENING OURSELVES AND BEING VULNERABLE . . . OUT OF NECESSITY

Few guests to our homes ever see our closets. Often, off the kitchen is a closet where there might be additional foodstuffs, brooms, dust pans, and aprons, among other things. These are things that we often don't want to show to guests. or make public—sometimes even among our own household members. Sometimes in the closet we also find those things we meant to "get at" long ago but we have not yet dealt with, and even cleaning supplies: those tools that can help us clean up our messes.

Of course, there are extravagant walk-in closets and entryway closets for guest outerwear, closets that may be intended for guests to use or even for showing off. We do not invoke these closets; rather we are discussing those closets which hold our deeply hidden feelings or realities we would rather others not see—our proverbial skeletons in the closet. In these closets, we hastily might have placed surprise birthday gifts for a partner or clutter we would rather guests not see before a gathering. We also, as in the borrowed metaphor of the Queer closet, may hide our identities and our truer selves out of fear of rejection.

In this section, we lean ever deeper into this notion of what has been private; in doing so, we confront and hesitantly engage with what is ugly and damaging to our communities and collective survival. The public acknowledgment of intergroup conflict is perhaps dangerous to perceptions about our communities, especially the perceptions of outsiders. Yet to most fully sustain our identities within education and schooling, we must confront these conflicts in an honest and justice-oriented way. This means we must admit to ourselves—and indeed to outsiders—that we have room to grow, that we are imperfect, and that the work of justice and liberation is an ongoing process that even communities that experience marginalization must engage. *None of us is immune to the ideologies of oppression, even with one another.*

For those reading this from outside of our communities, we encourage you to think about ways that this privileged information that we share here demands a nuanced understanding in order to not perpetuate oppressive attitudes toward marginalized communities. We do not approach this section lightly and understand that there might be consequences to revealing the skeletons in our collective closets. Nevertheless, we assert that to sustain our identities, we must engage in all aspects of them, especially those which we sometimes hide from public view.

We recognize that power and privileges exist within and between our own communities and there is, at times, intergroup conflict. We acknowledge that this aspect of being a BITOC is not one that usually is shared in public spaces and, if understood out of context, would be damaging to our collective work. We discuss the interpersonal challenges for BITOCs, especially addressing one's own internalized racism and biases, given that it is a truism that all people, regardless of their social and cultural identities, are influenced by (and often internalize) racism and white superiority (Kendi, 2019). *We assert these are issues and challenges we, within our respective communities, have to address.*

Our Inner-Private Spaces

In our practice of identity-sustaining pedagogy, there are undoubtedly beliefs, attitudes, insecurities, or behaviors that we uncover in our critical self-reflection

WONDER ALONE/WONDER TOGETHER

What are some of the "private" issues your own cultural identity group needs to address as not being helpful to the broader social justice project? How do you imagine it would work best for your cultural identity group to address them?

and critical self-reflexivity, yet we rarely make known to others, even within our own intergroup communities. We must push on ourselves to critically engage with and enact a vulnerability in our inner-private spaces in order to effect a more fully realized identity-sustaining pedagogy. We understand that admitting our problematic attitudes or assumptions might be damaging to us when viewed by outsiders. Admittedly, we must be strategic about with whom we share these inner-private journeys and the confrontations of our problematic or oppressive attitudes and behaviors. Sometimes this is work done in small community with others that share your identities. At other times, this is work you engage with by yourself in honest reflexivity. Nevertheless, we believe that to not do so only serves to inhibit or interrupt identity-sustaining pedagogy. Worse, the hesitancy to engage with this work might be fueled by fear. In many ways this is the most difficult part of enacting identity-sustaining pedagogy.

We borrow from Picca and Thompson-Miller's (2020) backstage–frontstage framework for discussing race to articulate our thinking on the power of engaging in work done in backstage or closet spaces. In their work, they envision that some of the deepest pushing on oppression can be performed backstage—within those private in-group spaces—and would never be addressed or resolved in more public and mixed-group spaces. Similarly, we believe that these inner-private spaces can be the site of the greatest transformative identity-sustaining pedagogy. *A critical engagement with our identity does not mean that we passively work toward sustaining our identity; rather it means that we work to sustain the best of our identities.* This means that we must root out oppressive behaviors that do not serve to empower others.

 WONDER ALONE/WONDER TOGETHER

What are some of the "private" issues you would identify as important for you to address? How do you imagine you can get at these so that they are not debilitating to yourself or to others?

✍ *Testimonio*: **Making Space by Being Visible—Longoria**

You might have noticed that my name is atypical. I do not use my birthname in my professional or personal life. The "A" I use professionally is merely a placeholder as I prefer simply being referred to as "Longoria."

True, there are those that have known me from before my transition that call me by my birthname and, usually, an awkward conversation follows. If nothing else, it is a reminder of who I have yet to come out to from my earlier life. Nevertheless, I embrace my name and use gender-neutral they/them pronouns to honor and be intentionally visible that I am a genderqueer person.

I have always known I was genderqueer, but due to societal and professional pressures, I felt I needed to hide my identity. Following the 2016 presidential election, I made the choice to be out and visible and demand my name and pronouns that honor who I am. My university, communities, colleagues, and friends have been accepting, although it is always a daily struggle to be visible as a person with a gender-variant identity. Anti-Queer sentiment persists, yet I believe if we are not visible then we cannot push on the systems we work in to be better, to make our communities better. Being out is a way, I believe, to make the inner-private public to help push on others for change.

In the highly binary, gendered Mexican American culture my gender identity is perceived as strange. The Spanish language itself has trouble describing me—through pronouns and gender—in a way that makes sense for its current grammar. Colleagues and friends still stumble over my name and pronouns, but they honor my self-determination when they do so.

At the same time, being multiracial among my cultural groups means I am often unique among them. Being Chinese Mexican from the Cantonese diaspora, I hold a distinct type of Mexican American identity different from typical experiences of being Mexican American. Being multiracial means I am fully Chinese American and fully Mexican American. I insist on using that language—having once used "half . . ." but found it inadequate. My intentionally visible presence in the cultural spaces I belong to effects a pedagogy of my inner being—of my body— that pushes on others to rethink and reform their practices of dominance and subordination.

I hold so much love for my cultures, but they are incredibly violent toward genderqueer people like me. Our communities have much work to do in confronting the ugly and the violent. In the backstage space I access, I still push on other BIPOCs by being visible, insisting on my name and pronouns, and insisting on my humanity and self-determination. Admittedly, there is patience and grace I must enact as I wait for my communities to make this space and embrace a future where people like me might not be an exception. Although I grow impatient, I believe when we confront domination we effect the greatest care for our communities by lovingly pushing on them to make space for people like ourselves and those that will come after us.

Recall that a core action for identity-sustaining pedagogy is to normalize pushback. This pushback is not always from others. It might be pushback from ourselves in our self-reflective and reflexive processes. It also might be from other BITOCs or BIPOCs, pushback shared in loving solidarity toward personal growth. We encourage you to embrace these moments of pushback. Tuck and Yang (2012) remind us to unsettle teaching practices toward true decolonization that honors Indigenous sovereignty and repatriation of land. We also might adapt this notion to embrace a healthy pursuit of our growth areas. Critical engagement demands some of the toughest work. This necessitates admitting that we are imperfect and participate in oppression ourselves, which sometimes can be difficult to admit. At times, we cannot fully practice empowering others because we might be caught up in intergroup conflicts. These we often keep among ourselves; yet they can be caustic to our collective liberation.

We might be quick to judge others or find ourselves engaged in internalized oppression. Note, we are not blaming a person for having developed internalized oppression. The ideologies of the dominant culture have socialized everyone into believing in the normalcy and rightfulness of their oppression. Calling out internalized oppression is not to call out some inherent personality flaw but rather is a siren call that something needs work. The blame should come if someone refuses to work on their own internalized racism.

The 2020 uprisings following the murder of George Floyd have shown our communities that it is a time of reckoning: to look at our closets and confront the ways we BIPOCs have perpetuated white supremacy and been complicit in anti-Blackness. Indeed, we all might need to confront our own privileges and anti-Blackness that run deep in many of our cultural communities and social circles in subtle, yet insidious, ways. We also must confront the settler moves to innocence that we enact in, for example, delivering empty land acknowledgments in our pedagogies, but not working toward Indigenous repatriation of land (Tuck & Yang, 2012). Intersectionality must be part of this critical gaze at our closets, and we must continue to advocate for the liberation of Queer BITOCs in our systems from discrimination and violence. There will need to be ways in the future for us to support Queer BITOCs in their own separate application of identity-sustaining pedagogy in a school system that historically has been slow to welcome and affirm all identities under its collective aegis.

At the same time, we must acknowledge those who continue to be absent from our collective table as teachers. Most BITOCs are citizens or hold residency status; some are formerly undocumented, yet for many undocumented aspiring educators, the path to employment does not exist. The school system continues to perpetuate assumptions that all students are or aspire to be citizens. Policies such as the Deferred Action for Childhood Arrivals, or DACA, are politically precarious and are prohibitive to some undocumented people. The undocumented community continues to be scapegoats for broader failures of national policies and practices. There continues to be a lack of undocumented representation among teaching faculty and school systems that leaves out per-spectives that necessarily would push us to better serve the schooling needs of the undocumented community.

As we implore you to consider how you can confront your own growth areas and build solidarity with other BITOCs, we acknowledge that you might feel pressure to engage in a defensive strategy commonly called "Oppression Olympics." In it, BIPOCs seemingly compete among one another for who should be listened to or whose oppression should be considered most pressing based on the cumulative amount of suffering. This can be horribly interruptive to collective liberation and we encourage you to find ways to avoid it.

The reality is that we can focus on and work toward confronting multiple justice issues without having to prioritize or engage in hierarchical thinking. This practice, often bitterly played out in inner-private spaces, typically pits BI-POC communities against one another; we hope that you find ways to lovingly push on other BITOCs (or yourself) when it arises. We all gain from the dis-mantling of oppressive systems—through actions and deeds—and we cannot continue to let such actions stunt our progress. Further, this cannot be a model we pass on to the next generation.

We believe it is important to pay attention to moments when you feel de-fensive about your positionality or privileges, or when you have been gifted with feedback for growth in your journey toward antiracism. It can be a vul-nerable and sometimes uncomfortable experience to have your shortcomings pointed out. We hope that you see these moments as growth and opportunities to become better in your pursuit of justice and liberation. *Without embracing this opportunity for personal and professional growth around the "inner job" of addressing our own oppression of others, we are in danger of blunting our human-ity and our collective liberation.*

 WONDER ALONE/WONDER TOGETHER

How are you reacting (thinking and feeling) to these issues of internalized oppression as well as oppression between minoritized groups? What im-plications emerge for you as you think about these issues?

On Caucusing

A way for us to push ourselves and our communities to confront our biases is to engage in caucusing. Some teacher education programs have found success in pushing candidates to frequently caucus with racial affinity groups—or a BITOC collective—to push on one another's thinking, build learning commu-nities, and practice solidarity (Beitlers et al., 2019; Varghese et al., 2019). Like-wise, a school or district may be the site of opportunities for teachers from a common heritage group to come together for support and solidarity. In these caucusing groups, students/teachers come together along racial lines to have private conversations that they might feel more comfortable engaging in with those who share a common heritage. For BITOC students/teachers, this can be an enriching space to build solidarity with other BITOCs.

These spaces are not always positive and comfortably transformative. It is common in these caucusing spaces for people to lay bare their own thinking and challenges that frequently exist only in our metaphorical closets. The heightened vulnerabilities can fill these spaces with emotional heaviness and temporary conflict. Caucusing demands a patient, kind, and firm facilitator to support these spaces, and, most important, these facilitators must belong to the caucusing group identity. This poses a problem for implementation in teacher preparation programs since there is already a paucity of faculty of color in many programs.

Programs that implement racial caucusing report that it is difficult to work through the quagmires of these organic processes. Nevertheless, they express hope that these spaces provide active venues for students to make visible questions, beliefs, and thinking about publicly sensitive issues that rarely are engaged with outside of these kinds of backstage spaces. If your teacher program or school/district does not engage with or provide opportunities for racial caucusing, we encourage you to push on and support your programs to create opportunities for these much-needed growth and solidarity spaces.

 WONDER ALONE/WONDER TOGETHER

Thinking about times when you have had an opportunity to engage in caucusing, what did you find helpful? How did the group navigate any particular tensions that might have arisen?

Cleaning Out Those Skeletons in the Closet

We hope the loving advice in this chapter has encouraged you to be mindful of the implications and costs of what we make public and what we choose to remain private, because it has bearing on your teaching practice and identity-sustaining pedagogy. We are making this explicit because we care deeply about you and your success in this profession. We also have included our *testimonios* to illustrate that we are on this journey alongside you. There is not an end goal in this work; there is only a call to embrace what we believe is necessary progress toward liberation from oppressive systems in schooling.

The work we carry out in these backstage or closet spaces is often not visible to others but can be the most powerful, for it engages with our most deeply held values and beliefs. It is important that we push on ourselves with a critical, self-reflexive practice that challenges our assumptions, beliefs, and values that ultimately serve anti-Blackness, antiracism, and anti-oppression.

The kitchen closet has cleaning supplies we must use regularly to make the space livable. Similarly, we must be ready and willing to clean up the messes in our communities. As Latinx people, for example, we must be willing to name and confront uses of "White presenting" or "White passing" as Whiteness and White dominance in our communities. We must confront homophobia, gender and sexual violence, language oppression, and documentation status privilege. These are only a few of the messes we, as Latinx BIPOCs, must clean up as part of this work. We must first name and then respond to and confront these.

To be clear, this is work we must do as members of our communities. We do not need nor should we expect outsiders that do not hold our identities to come in and facilitate or attempt do this work. Rather, we need to own this agency as a necessary process of cleaning our collective, metaphorical houses.

PREPROFESSIONAL ADVICE FOR PRESERVICE BITOCS

For those readers considering or on the early path toward entering a teacher preparation program, we offer some advice here. Choosing a teacher education program sometimes might be as simple as looking into your local or current undergraduate institution. If you live in a metropolitan area, you might have many different teacher education programs to consider. Above all, you will need to find out the admissions requirements for your desired program and pursue them passionately.

When evaluating programs to hone down your choices, you might want to find out whether they offer ample experiences in school settings and with youth, to peruse their stated commitments (and actions) to supporting BIPOCs, and to uncover their placement or employment rates of graduates. Some programs post their full course content on their websites; at other times, you might try to acquire a syllabus or dialogue with current students or recent graduates to get insight into the curriculum and their program experiences. In doing so, explore whether attending to equity issues is a theme that runs throughout the program or whether it is rarely raised/discussed. Short of access to the curriculum, consider the titles and descriptions of classes, as well as the diversity of the faculty in the program, as possible clues to what is important to the school. To prepare yourself for a teacher preparation program, you will want to make sure that you understand all of the licensure requirements for your state, which might include standardized exam requirements.

Programs often offer many different supports for recruitment and retention—do not hesitate to ask for these in your pursuit. Some colleges have recruitment and retention offices or staff that specifically work toward diversifying teaching programs, and these professionals can be excellent resources for providing an insider's knowledge of applying to, and navigating, a program. Program directors, admissions staff, or faculty in your targeted program also can be helpful resources; be sure to reach out to Black, Indigenous, and

Teachers of Color in the program. An introductory email is a good way to start.

A university education can be expensive, especially at private institutions, and it is important that you find out exactly how much the cost of attendance is for your target program, including tuition, fees, exams, and other expenses. While it is important to keep in mind that pursuing a preprofessional program like teacher certification or a degree program is an investment in your professional future, understanding the requisite financial burdens should be factored into your plans. Be sure to also explore any scholarship programs or opportunities—including special teacher preparation programs—that may be aimed specifically at increasing diversity in the teacher education program and in the profession.

Teachers are not just transmitters of knowledge and academic content. Youth work is at the core of teaching. It is imperative that before you apply to enter a teacher preparation program, you have gained sufficient experiences in schooling and in direct service with youth. Not only does this give you necessary experience to draw upon for success in your program, but it also is an important way to discern your future role. This might be accomplished through volunteering in a teacher's classroom for a few weeks or working in an after-school program that serves the target age you wish to work with as a teacher. As a teacher, you will spend most of your professional life with youth. You must determine early on whether this essential aspect of teaching is your cup of tea. We have encountered far too many teacher preparation students in our careers who have much interest and savvy in their desired content area—for example, they have a deep love for science or history or music—yet this does not translate to serving the needs of youth, especially BIPOC youth in schools.

As you advance in your teaching program, you might face a seemingly enormous decision of choosing a school setting for your student teaching or internship. Sometimes it can be strategic to choose a school or, at a minimum, a district that you desire working in professionally over the long term. Professional networks and building a general reputation can be helpful, but they are not make-or-break. As a BITOC, it is important for you to vet a placement to ensure that you will feel supported in your learning and growth as a novice teacher. You might ask yourself whether the school setting is supportive. We understand that choosing an internship site might feel like a high-stakes decision, but we believe that you can learn a great deal from a less-than-ideal placement. We do not mean for you to lower your expectations or to accept an environment where you will feel physically unsafe or that feels oppressive. Nevertheless, we insist that you indeed can learn from negative examples and

💬 WONDER ALONE/WONDER TOGETHER

What are some of the tensions you are experiencing or have experienced in your own teacher preparation program? Which of these were specifically related to who you are as a BITOC?

that imperfect placements can help you build your critical and reflective practice. Overall, we encourage you to avoid feeling pressure to find the perfect placement or mentors.

When to Push Back on Teacher Education Institutions

In our framing metaphor of the kitchen, there is also the possibility that we may cook up ideas and actions for change and reform. Is there course content in your program that is oppressive, indeed psychologically abusive, toward communities of color? Are there admissions policies that are clearly preventing BIPOC applicants from finding success? Are there no faculty of color teaching in your program? We know there will be times when you need to push back on your teacher preparation program. This can feel both frustrating and worrying. You might fear consequences to your advocacy, and these are valid concerns. Nevertheless, we have seen great changes effected by students collectively sharing grievances about their programs and working with faculty and staff to enact changes that aim to improve conditions for BIPOC students.

The first step to pushing for changes in your program is to make sure that you are following stated processes for grievances or feedback for your program. This often can be found in program handbooks or websites. We also encourage you to approach these processes with an orientation toward growth and justice. This does not mean that you are docile or subservient, or petty and cruel. Rather, it means that you approach this kind of necessary work as an opportunity to help bring about lasting change to improve learning and structural conditions for other BITOCs. We cannot stress this point enough, for often the changes you advocate for will not be seen immediately. This does not mean that they are not well worth the effort, but it can be frustrating to not see these results. Knowing that you have effected lasting change, we hope, will be a more fully realized way of accomplishing the identity-sustaining pedagogy action of empowering others. It might help to consider this as an opportunity to develop and apply your emerging skills at confronting institutional oppression.

You also might want, as you begin the process of pushing back, to consider opportunities for movement building with other BIPOC students in the program, as well as consider when/how to recruit White allies. There indeed is strength in numbers, and sometimes you are more likely, at a minimum, to be listened to if you are not alone. Finding faculty and staff allies supportive of your efforts can be helpful, too.

PURSUING YOUR FIRST TEACHING POSITION

Similarly, looking for a first job can feel stressful, and admittedly this choice has higher stakes. After graduating from your program and gaining initial certification, it is prudent to find a supportive professional community and school.

A helpful way to learn about schools is to gain insight from state demographic data. A lasting vestige of the No Child Left Behind policies of the early 2000s is that most state departments of education require schools to collect demographic data on students and teachers. These data, in turn, are reported publicly by the state. From the number of BISOCs to the number of students receiving free or reduced meal service, the data tell an important story about the school. Increasingly, states are publishing data about the diversity of the teaching force in districts and schools as well.

You also can gain insight on districts by finding the attendance boundary maps and seeing which communities are being served by the school you are interested in. You should couple this with the state data. Is there de facto re-segregation across the schools in the district? Additional research you might conduct includes looking up news and social media about the school and the community it serves. Key questions to answer from this research are: Is this the student population I want to work with? What opportunities for changes at the school do these data present? Will I be alone as a BITOC among the faculty?

When you interview for a position, we suggest that you embrace this as an opportunity to vet the school system as much as you are being vetted. We find Philip and Brown's (2020) principles for diversification of the education work-force an excellent place to start in crafting your questions. They recommend that you consider asking:

> What is the purpose of diversifying the teaching faculty at a school? . . . What are the current experiences of teachers of color in a school and/or district? . . . What will change by increasing the numbers of teachers of color? (pp. 4–5)

After you have conducted your research on the demographics of the school, district, and community, we encourage you to incorporate this into your vetting of the school. The bottom line is that, as a BITOC, there is a chance you will be sought after in the profession. This is not to say that you may not still encounter bias in the hiring process; you likely will. However, recognizing the many cultural and linguistic assets you can bring to teaching/learning, you will do well to responsibly use this as a way to embrace your agency in creating a professional setting that most fully supports your practice of identity-sustaining pedagogy.

In Chapter 7, we provide professional career advice beyond securing your first teaching position.

 WONDER ALONE/WONDER TOGETHER

What are your grandest hopes for yourself in terms of securing a teaching position? What are the most important factors you will be considering, as a BITOC, in the school where you hope to teach?

Advice for Pushing Back for Working BITOCs

One of the greatest expectations, although erroneous, that you will face as a BITOC is that somehow you inherently are able to magically reach BISOCs and serve their needs. You also might face assumptions that you are an expert at equity work simply by being a BITOC. Such assumptions can lead to you feeling tokenized in the profession. You also might feel hyper-visible while being highly sought after. Colleagues might come to you to lead diversity activities, to deal with BIPOC parents, or to reach "troublesome" students. On the flip side, you might feel hyper-invisible after having been passed over for an opportunity. About these situations, Philip and Brown (2020) write:

> [T]eachers of color are caught in a "double bind," trying to satisfy irreconcilable demands focused on extreme accountability on one hand and commitments for cultural relevance and justice on the other. Placing teachers of color in these precarious positions result in trauma and a lack of efficacy. (p. 13)

To confront this, we encourage you to develop your ability to say "no." We admit that this is a struggle, even for us. As BITOCs, we will be asked to do myriad tasks, and often these are good works to effect in schooling. Yet we cannot do it all, especially alone. Often, we will need to pass on opportunities to other great teachers. We encourage you to think about the "effect potential" when deciding whether to take on anything that you will be asked to do beyond your normal teaching responsibilities. Who will be affected? Is the time investment worth the ultimate effect?

We also understand that often this work is uncompensated financially. We do not encourage you to work for free; catalytic work that truly liberates others cannot be constant acts of charity, for this does not truly push on systems and institutions to support sustainable change. Yet we admit that sometimes the most effective equity work is uncompensated in its early stages, especially as it gains momentum. There are often situations in which we must attend to the needs of BISOCs without compensation because it is the right thing to do for their safety, well-being, and learning. In this way, when we advocate for the needs of a singular student, we advocate for change for all BISOCs, indeed for all students. You ultimately know your limits and we ask you to be mindful of these when navigating opportunities presented to you.

As a BITOC, you also can play a vital role in advocating for other BIPOCs and communities of color. One of the most transformative ways we can help serve our identity-sustaining pedagogy practices is to authentically include families and communities in our teaching practices. We must continue to create conditions in schooling where families and communities have input in our curriculum. This goes beyond guest speakers in our classes or one-time opportunities. In order to help our communities sustain their own identities, we ask you to consider how you might include authentic opportunities for them to have input in what is taught, who teaches in schools, and other key decisions in schooling.

Stepping Away and Stepping Out

As you advance in the profession, you often will face a decision about moving to a different school. This might be out of convenience. Perhaps you have purchased a new home or needed to travel to a different city to support a partner's professional move. We have provided you some guidance for finding and adapting to a new schooling context in these instances. Yet we hope that you finish well at the school you might be moving from. The community, youth, faculty, and staff will have been part of your experiences as a teacher—the good and the bad. They will have formed your professional narrative and helped you to sustain your own identities. We hope that you find ways to part that give you closure as you transition to the next school.

Sometimes, stepping away from the teaching profession altogether is the right thing to do. For these decisions, we hope you, after much deliberation, give yourself permission to do so. Students deserve educators who can support them fully and be present for and with them without reservation. If you cannot sustain this work, it is the better move to step out. You might find other ways to work with youth, families, or communities. You also might find ways to sustain your identities in another profession.

CONCLUDING REFLECTIONS

At the kitchen table, we are sometimes the audience to elders delivering their direction for family decisions. We might relate the hardships of the day in this place of privacy. Sometimes we will sit in silence here to process the joys of our lives or the hardships that might cross us. In the kitchen, we cook up food that nourishes our bodies and sustains us and those who journey with us. In this part of the house (and the closet), we get real with one another out of necessity and hope. We might have more to say, and we might have more we keep guarded. At the same time, we always have to be mindful of those things we keep hidden and think about ways in which we can fully understand the implications, for the health and uplift of our collective communities, of their remaining undiscussed.

➥ Make It Happen: Portfolio Activity—My Own Schooling Journey

To build on this chapter, we ask that you take this opportunity to challenge your thinking and critically engage with your portfolio materials. Begin by documenting a critical reflection of your own personal journey in education. What policies, procedures, or practices were evident in your own schooling that differently affected students from different social identity groups, such as tracking, high-stakes testing, within-school segregation, a Euro-centric curriculum, among other things? How, if at all, were your cultural and linguistic assets affirmed in schools? What were those pivotal moments for you as a learner? When did you begin to think of teaching as a possible career? What were the motivating forces for you to become a teacher?

Then build on and, considering most especially the issues that this chapter raises, take this opportunity to challenge your own thinking. What have you avoided including? Where do you need to grow? What attitudes and assumptions must you change? Rather than letting go, how might you confront these attitudes? What are responsible solutions to confronting your own biases and growth areas? Overall, this editing and these additions should help you find your edges—so that you might shape them toward a more critical end.

Think of an instance or event that did not turn out particularly satisfying for you. In a journal, briefly describe the most essential details of what occurred. Then create a T-bar graph. On the left side of the T, do a "reflection" of the event: What were some underlying causes, what were some unanticipated impacts, what missteps did you (and others) take, what would you do differently, and what were the overall lessons you have learned? On the right side of the T, engage in "reflexive" thinking: What assumptions were you making, what biases/stereotypes were in play, what typical ways of responding did you nearly automatically enact? as but a few examples. In the end, consider the value of this strategic approach to critical thinking.

≫⁺ Keep It Going!

- Read the poem "Perhaps the World Ends Here" by Joy Harjo.
- Watch the skit "Excedrin for Racial Tension Headaches" from the *Saturday Night Live* episode aired on October 4, 2004, hosted by Queen Latifah (https://www.youtube.com/watch?v=Wytk8AiRzAQ). In the skit, she shares a number of examples of microaggressions. Use this a starting point to identify and explore microaggressions you might confront. Additional information might be found on microaggressions.com.

CHAPTER 6

The Patio

Re/energizing Yourself in Community

Caring for myself is not self-indulgence, it is self-preservation, and that is an act of political warfare.

—Audre Lorde, *A Burst of Light* (1988, p. 131)

Having gone through (or around) the house, we emerge from the house onto the back patio. The patio is both a private and a public space. As a private space, the patio is still a place to relax and rejuvenate. It is a private space given that we might sit in solitude; we might think of the back patio as a place for quiet contemplation. We may go there to knit on a sunny day, to attend to plants and gardens, or to read a good book.

It is also a place for connecting with others; in this way, we think of the patio as an increasingly more public space. It is a public space because neighbors might see us and because people can bypass the house altogether and just meet in the back. But it is, most often, an intentional public space when we invite some of our closest friends, those who have come through the house, to join us there. We sit with a *camarada* of many years, sharing *consejos* and wisdom gleaned from life's experiences. We broaden this public sphere when we invite family and friends over for a barbecue, reconnect with friends about their week, or celebrate an important accomplishment: a graduation, a new job, a well-deserved promotion. In essence, we think of the patio as a private space for reflection and self-care *and* a public space to foster wisdom, joy, and celebrations.

In this chapter, we encourage you to find those places and those people who can help you to center self-care and joy in your work as Black, Indigenous, and Teachers of Color (BITOC), much as on the patio. We begin by stressing the importance of self-care and offer practical options for it, for building resistance, and for finding joy in teaching. We also focus on building those support networks and alliances across difference that will be central to your own efficacy as a BITOC. At the same time, we use this chapter to remind you that the experiences of BIPOCs in schooling are not just a narrative of oppression and marginalization; they are also a narrative of celebration, joy, and care for our communities.

Celebration, joy, and care include an acknowledgment of the necessary inner work we need to engage in to ensure that we are grounded for the work ahead of us as educators. They also acknowledge that the work on behalf of the social justice project is best done in meaningful interaction with others. We must not try to do this work alone. Rather, we need to build allies in this work. It behooves us to seek and foster allies across the racial, ethnic, social, and cultural continuum. Keeping in mind that this text is centered on you and your needs as a BITOC, we include ways you might find community and build allies. In thinking about these alliances, we offer suggestions for movement building, for activism, and for developing pathways to assist in our efforts to diversify the teaching profession.

As we have shared earlier, for those readers that identify as White allies, we have included our thoughts about the role you might play and some resources to assist you in Appendix B.

CAUTIONARY TALES:
FROM DAMAGE NARRATIVES TO DESIRE NARRATIVES

As we shared earlier in this text, the experience of BITOCs in schools has been one of marginalization in multiple ways. Given the history of BITOCs in the profession, including their placement in segregated schools and then their outright dismissal in desegregated schools, there is much to lament. Recall that once they have positions in schools, BITOCs are sometimes hyper-visible in addressing diversity-related challenges and, at other times, hyper-invisible when it comes time for professional opportunities (Souto-Manning & Cheruvu, 2016).

We do not wish to diminish the harsh realities of these experiences that BITOCs have had in the teaching profession. But we are mindful of and hear the caution that Eve Tuck (2009) offers around damage narratives. Tuck acknowledges that BIPOCs often use damage narratives when demanding reparations from Whites for injustices committed, but that these narratives also position us and our communities as "depleted, ruined and hopeless" (p. 409). At the same time, because they make us think of ourselves as broken, they problematically position Whites as those who can save us and our communities. Tuck (2009) asserts:

> These characterizations frame our communities as sites of disinvestment and dispossession; our communities become spaces in which under resourced health and economic infrastructures are endemic. They become spaces saturated in the fantasies of outsiders. (p. 412)

Tuck is clear that the problem with damage narratives is that they do not tell the more complicated, nuanced versions of the narrative, the ones that contain hope, longing, and wisdom, or, as she describes them, desire narratives. For Tuck, "desire-based frameworks defy the lure to serve as 'advertisements for power' by documenting not only the painful elements of social realities but also the wisdom and hope" (p. 416). Desire narratives are, as she says, "integral to our humanness" (p. 417).

And so it is, with this chapter, that we explore our pursuit of clarity around what are our innermost desires as well as those longings and that wisdom we seek in communion with others. It is our hope that, in doing so, you will find a way to sustain yourself and your allies into, through, and beyond your work in classrooms, schools, and the profession.

Above all, we cannot sustain ourselves in this work if we are not in good health and practicing a future oriented toward sustaining ourselves in this challenging but rewarding profession. In this chapter, we engage most directly in the identity-sustaining pedagogy core actions of normalizing pushback and empowering others.

You might be curious why we would invoke self-care as part of the process of normalizing pushback in carrying out identity-sustaining pedagogy, and we admit it is not self-evident. Yet we assert that it is important to care for our minds and bodies to soothe and heal the very real effects that facing pushback and resistance will have on you and your practice.

 WONDER ALONE/WONDER TOGETHER

In what ways, if at all, have you used damage narratives to seek action from others? What impact did it have? What would have been a desire narrative that you could have used in addition?

ENGAGING IN MEANINGFUL AND CRITICAL REFLECTION AND SELF-REFLEXIVITY

As part of your practice of resilience, it is important to maintain a consistent practice of critical reflection and self-reflexivity (see Bolton & Delderfield, 2018). *Reflection* asks you to consider what has occurred in a specific instance or event, what missteps may have occurred, what repair might need to be done, and what lessons can be learned. It becomes *critical reflection* when, in addition, you consider the role power and privilege may have played in the action that occurred. *Self-reflexivity*, at a different level, urges a deeper inner exploration around your thinking: your values, your assumptions, your attitudes, your habitual responding, your social positioning, among other things, that might explain both your behavior and also the deeper reasonings that lie underneath. More specifically, Sleeter and Delgado Bernal (2004) offer that *critical self-reflexivity* for equity and justice especially includes attention to voice (who speaks, who speaks for whom, who is not speaking, what is not spoken, as but a few examples), ideology (what theoretical and/or conceptual orientations are guiding individual or collective thinking), and culture (how do the cultural ways of living and being influence how people think, feel, and act).

As you can surmise, critical reflection and critical self-reflexivity are essential and overlapping: Our outer actions are a result of our inner thinking.

While engaging in critical reflection and critical self-reflexivity, we do not mean for you to beat yourself up over every misstep. Rather we ask that you engage in a practice of identity-sustaining pedagogy that embraces what we call the *pedagogy of the responsible misstep*. This means that you will expect to make missteps in your teaching practice. You will not always say the right thing to a student, enact a coherent lesson, or interact with a colleague or parent in the best way. You may even commit an oppressive action unintentionally. As Calabrese Barton and Tan (2020) point out, "Systematic injustices are made *invisible* through their regularities in practice. Teachers often unknowingly mete out injustices through quotidian teaching practices" (p. 433, emphasis in original). After all, you are human and operating in a less-than-perfect system.

This does not mean that you should be cavalier about your missteps. Rather, you should be responsible in attempting to minimize oppression and unintentional negative consequences of your pedagogical and professional actions. When you do make missteps, you should be responsible in admitting them and seeking amends.

Importantly, allow yourself grace through these missteps, with the confident knowledge that you will reflect upon them, admit your role in them, and then repair them as needed to reduce these gaffes in your pursuit of better practices. We believe that the best teaching happens tomorrow—that upon reflecting on the day's successes and mistakes, you engage in critical reflection in order to make the next day's lessons that much better. Great teaching and identity-sustaining pedagogy praxis are never wholly effected as something preplanned to perfection; rather, they are enacted as an iterative process toward constant betterment/improvement.

Regarding identity, critical reflexivity should include intentionally considering the ways and means that your identities have bearing on your teaching and missteps. Did you misunderstand a social cue from a student because of potential limitations around cultural differences? How did your own cultural worldview and repertoires of practice play into what occurred? Would sharing your full human self, perhaps by including a *testimonio* from your own experiences, have helped you better explain a concept to students or clarify your response to a situation?

We sustain our own identities by engaging in critical self-reflexivity upon the ways our identities might better serve our teaching practices. This affects both of the core actions of intentionally including identity in teaching and normalizing pushback. Yet, as mentioned, we know there will be missteps. We hope you have seen that there is nothing inherent in BITOCs that make them effective teachers; rather, our teaching practices are enriched by our social and cultural identities and experiences.

This critical self-reflexivity also includes pushing back on yourself for growth areas you recognize. We, BITOCs in the profession, are working to decolonize our own minds and to progress toward being critically prepared, culturally sustaining teachers. This includes asking ourselves: Have we engaged in essentialist thinking about a student's culture without recognizing nuance? Have we refused to correct our own gendered language? Have we engaged in saying the expected words to sound like we are engaging in social justice teaching without truly believing in the power of such words? All of these point to necessary reflexivity toward action.

We encourage you to examine deeply your own thinking. Read up on the experiences of other BIPOCs. Keep a private journal of ongoing growth areas and resources. It is vitally important that you not be self-satisfied with your own unexamined teaching practices. We acknowledge that it can be exhausting to constantly scrutinize your teaching practice and growth areas. In the next section we offer guidance on taking breaks and sustaining yourself through this difficult work.

We hope your efforts at critical self-reflexivity can be guided by the wisdom offered by feminist scholar Adrienne Rich (1979) as you seek out "criticism, recognizing that the most affirming thing anyone can do for you is demand that you push yourself further, show you the range of what you *can* do" (p. 234, emphasis in original). Rich demands that you claim your education as an "experience of *taking responsibility toward your-selves*[sic]" (p. 233, emphasis in original). Lamenting that often we think of ourselves as *receiving* an education, she asks us to think of our role in *demanding* an education. This is especially true given that much of what we receive in our education is antagonistic (indeed, oppressive) to our identity and integrity.

 WONDER ALONE/WONDER TOGETHER

As you ponder the role of critical self-reflexivity, what strategies will provide you the greatest possible personal and professional growth? How will this impact the way you think about yourself?

SUSTAINING OURSELVES THROUGH SELF-CARE

The term *self-care* is fraught with notions of commercialism. Its popular applications bring up images of soaking in a luxurious bubble bath surrounded by scented candles and calming music. Rather, we advocate for a deeper practice of self-care. By all means, please do treat yourself to massages or products that are safe for your budget and well-being. As with critical self-reflexivity, we directly engage the identity-sustaining pedagogy core action of normalizing pushback. As we have stated earlier, teaching for equity and justice as a BITOC is deeply challenging work, and it will influence each of us differently. At the same time, how we find ways to engage in self-care will look different for different people. Knowing how you experience the stress of this work and what brings you joy, peace, hope, and rejuvenation is a big part of knowing yourself.

It is necessary to find rest and relaxation and seek refuge from the most difficult aspects of teaching and critical reflection and critical self-reflexivity. This is not an excuse to put off difficult tasks—in fact, avoiding challenging tasks can often make things worse. Rather, it is to acknowledge that with a deeply transformational practice, we must engage in periodic retreat from it. In normalizing pushback as a core action of identity-sustaining pedagogy, we must prepare and maintain our bodies, our minds, and our spirits to do this work.

We do not give you medical advice, for only you and a trained, qualified medical and/or mental health professional can determine what works best for you. Rather, we hope this section serves as a reminder that you indeed must attend to the needs of your body. Physical and mental burnout, as a result of the weight of professional stressors, abounds in the teaching profession; we believe that this is especially true for BITOCs. We suggest you attend to the needs of your body, to your own mental health, and to the health of your interpersonal relationships and family needs.

Our bodies often suffer subtle and invisible effects through teaching. Do you find yourself sitting throughout your teaching day without getting adequate physical activity for fitness? Do you not eat healthy foods during teaching hours because you can conveniently find only unhealthy foods? In the hustle and bustle of everyday teaching, it can be too easy to not schedule visits with medical professionals and to avoid habits that maintain a healthy body. How can we be present for others—especially BISOCs—if we are not able to healthily do so?

Some teachers conduct walking meetings or challenge one another to achieve daily step counts to encourage physical activity. Flu shot clinics and wellness checks such as blood pressure screenings often are offered by employers. Human resource departments within school districts also have wellness resources, employee assistance, and health incentive programs available. We invite you to explore what a healthy journey looks like for you.[1]

Mental health can be a difficult topic for people to talk about, given cultural differences. Without doubt, stress, anxiety, and depression are commonplace in schooling and among school professionals. Some BITOCs might experience cultural taboos around these topics, and we acknowledge this. Nevertheless, we cannot deny that BITOCs experience mental health challenges in the teaching profession, perhaps as a result of their being marginalized in the profession in ways we have described earlier. We believe it is imperative that you consider your mental health needs and options as part of your identity-sustaining pedagogy as a teacher. Again, you might consider those support systems available to you through your employer. Mental health professionals also are trained to help us with these issues if challenges persist.

Too often our interpersonal, romantic, and familial relationships suffer from our commitments to teaching. In fact, 85% of teachers reported work–life imbalance affecting their ability to teach (Carver-Thomas & Darling-Hammond, 2017). It is important to continually check in with those we count on for support. We care for ourselves by attending to these relationships, which may include scheduling dedicated time for loved ones in our day and, once together, sharing the joys and challenges of our professional lives.

We acknowledge that identity-sustaining pedagogy can be affected by attitudes about health. While our greatest hope is that you find a healthy balance—or, at a minimum, commit to finding it—between your teaching and self-care, we know that what it means to be healthy is defined in multiple ways and sometimes is culturally defined. Adhering to our cultural norms around health and wellness is indeed an opportunity to sustain our identities. Above all, we hope that you ultimately find sustainable ways to maintain your physical health, mental well-being, and relationships so that you can keep teaching and enacting identity-sustaining pedagogy for as long as you choose to do so.

In addition, consider some of the following suggestions from the Learning for Justice webinar on educator self-care:

- Physical activity—stretching, running, walking, yoga, Pilates, capoeira, dancing, hydrating, eating healthy
- Social/communal activity—connecting with friends, writing letters, activism/organizing, book clubs
- Artistic activity—creating art, making music, creative writing, poetry, vision board
- Spiritual/reflective activity—meditation, journaling, reading, or apps like Liberate or Calm

 WONDER ALONE/WONDER TOGETHER

When looking at these approaches to self-care, which ones do you already employ with positive results? Which of these are you likely to want to delve into more deeply?

BUILDING ALLIES

We do not walk this journey of teaching alone as BITOCs. The tasks are too big and the challenges too deep to try to go it alone. More pointedly, there simply are not enough BITOCs in the profession for us to hope to enact meaningful social justice work on our own. Working with White educators is a given. We must ask ourselves how we can help White teachers put themselves into, draw upon, or push on their own experiences to inform their teaching. In building allies, we must encourage fostering critical allyship rather than merely celebrating diversity. This often means asking one another deeper, vulnerable, and critical questions. We know that this is extra emotional labor on your part;

however, it is connected to our collective futurity in a pathway for encouraging more BITOCs into the profession and our continued practice of identity-sustaining pedagogy.

Sometimes we gain allies when we speak truth to power (see the RFK Center Resource in the toolshed, Appendix A). There will be times when we must take the opportunity to invite those with power and privilege to embrace allyship. In pushing on our White allies—calling out and calling in problematic practices (Ross, 2019)—we both interrupt oppression and offer a path toward a collective future together. This sometimes can be as subtle as insisting on our identities. Sometimes this must be a very direct naming of oppression.

You might find yourself needing to confront a White colleague, professor, or administrator. These moments will come and, at times, will be filled with uncomfortable pushback on all parties. We encourage you to consider the costs of speaking truth to power in these moments, but we ask you to err on the side of calculating risk, for the stakes of our collective futures demand that we take up these moments for our futures when they are most prudent and seemingly effective. It does none of us any good if you have not thought through the risks of speaking truth to power and face consequences that exclude you from the teaching profession.

One thing you can do is to model what allyship looks like in your daily life. It could be that you challenge someone's use of language that is demeaning to others. It could be that you tell a peer that their "ethnic joke" is neither funny nor appropriate. It could be that you console a person who was the victim of someone else's hate speech. It could be that you raise questions about the influence of policies and practices being discussed on students from marginalized communities. In essence, it is important that you act in ways you want your allies to enact, as you model the kinds of active engagement in equity and justice that are in demand.

We are also encouraged, by Sleeter and Delgado Bernal (2004), to consider those ways in which we model our pedagogical practices, including understanding the reciprocal relationship between teachers and students (and teaching and learning), enacting "empowering pedagogical practices within the classroom" (p. 242), and widening our understandings around what counts as language and literacy in the classroom, especially when we value and emphasize students' lived experiences in our classrooms and schools.

💬 WONDER ALONE/WONDER TOGETHER

Where do you think you are most likely to find allies? In what ways do you hope they will support you? How will you support them?

Los Vecinos:
Connecting With Other BITOCs and Social Justice Organizations

As we hope you hear loud and clear, we do not walk this teaching path alone, for there are other BITOCs in the profession. Our own ability to sustain ourselves as professionals as well as to sustain our identities is dependent upon having BITOC peers in our schools, districts, and professions. These are our professional neighbors—our *vecinos*—who are close to us in the work of equity and justice. Building networks among other BITOCs with similar identities and building solidarity with other groups are not simply "feel-good" exercises; they are vital. We need to cultivate, support, and sustain those neighbors (peers, administrators, service staff, as but a few examples) who are doing work that is complementary to our identity-sustaining pedagogy work in schooling.

We encourage you to explore and sustain those individuals and organizations that are most close to home for you. It could be members of the diversity council within the school. It could be a district's efforts to sponsor an after-school support program for teachers and staff of color. It could be joining with a local community organization that brings professionals of color together to advance community uplift.

We also might benefit from thinking about those neighbors who are more distant: those support networks and professional organizations that are statewide or national in scope. Some of these will be focused generally on supporting any and all teachers in their work to enact a culturally centering or multicultural education. Some of these are focused specifically on supporting teachers who are engaged in anti-oppressive work. And a few (but growing) number of these are focused specifically on supporting BITOCs into, through, and beyond the profession. Because we believe in the power of these, the bulk of our resources in the toolshed (Appendix A) focus on those most germane to supporting you as a BITOC.

 WONDER ALONE/WONDER TOGETHER

What organizations/groups in your own community might support your work as a BITOC? What organizations/groups exist on your campus that have been helpful to you?

Caring for Our Communities

To enact the action of empowering others, we must engage families and communities meaningfully in this work. The teaching profession is in service to families and communities, for we are working to sustain their lives, their values, and their knowledges. Additionally, we are sustaining our communities through cultural renewal. We believe that your practice of identity-sustaining pedagogy sustains the livelihood of our communities.

An additional way for us to care for our communities through identity-sustaining pedagogy is to engage in intergenerational dialogues. In many ways this book was born out of and written in an intergenerational dialogue, with Francisco being a senior scholar and Longoria at the beginning of their career as a professor. In identity-sustaining pedagogy, sometimes we reflect upon or invoke ancestors in sustaining our identities. So many of our cultural traditions hold up the wisdom and privilege of elders. We believe it is necessary to truly value the contributions and wisdom of elders. This is not an uncritical practice, for we must acknowledge that their experiences may have been under different circumstances and may have enacted practices that were less than truly liberatory. Yet we intentionally must fold in the wisdom of elders, for it is their experiences that form the legacy of our own identity-sustaining pedagogy. We hope that you find ways to learn about and include the wisdom of elders in your own practice.

At the same time, we know that it is the new generation of BITOCs who hold the promise for moving schooling forward to that ideal of education as the great equalizer. We recognize that it is those students, teachers, and scholars who are re/visioning and renewing the traditions of our elders in ways that speak to the contemporary issues that our communities are most deeply engaged in addressing. It is the hope, the passion, the energy, and the vision of what is possible that will move us toward true equity and justice. We hope that this call serves as an invitation to you, as new BITOCs, to ask new questions, create a vision of greater progressive possibilities, and set the stage for educational and professional renewal.

We also want to hold up the promise of many communities, working together, that is the essence of movement building. We must work toward movement building that sustains our collective work in the multiple communities in which BITOCs find themselves. We recognize that in these unprecedented times during the COVID-19 pandemic we might feel very isolated from one another and the movements that are effecting change.

We should be equally inspired by the multiple opportunities to engage with movement building. Pre-pandemic, we were witness to student and parent advocacy groups around the United States who stood up for gun reform as a result of the multiple gun violence incidents that have been plaguing schools. We were inspired by young people around the world who stood up for actions to address the very real challenges associated with climate change. Even during the COVID-19 pandemic, we have been amazed at the energy and passion, the anger and the frustration, as yet another Black mother's son was murdered on the street, which has reignited the Black Lives Matter movement. We agree with Fuentes and Pérez (2016) that these movements, in the collective, are "grounded in racial and social justice. Communities across the United States and the world are rising up to assert their right to self-determination and to live with dignity" (p. 7).

WONDER ALONE/WONDER TOGETHER

As you think about the ways you can support the vitality and vibrancy of your cultural community, what do you imagine you can do as a BITOC? Why will doing this be important to you and the ways you want to engage teaching/learning?

We have included several resources in the toolshed for you to check out that might serve as a catalyst for movement building within your identities.

RECOGNIZING AND EMBRACING JOY

An ongoing practice of self-care also should include embracing joy in our gaze and praxis. We hope that you see this as retreating from the constant narratives that seek to pathologize our experiences of otherness. It is important for us to pay attention to the ways that we talk about our cultures and identities. Do we highlight trauma more than other experiences? Do we find ourselves seeking out the negative aspects of our experiences of marginalization and oppression?

It is vitally important for us to seek that which is joyous in our experiences. It can be tempting in the social media milieu to perpetuate only narratives that center on experiences of marginalization and injustices. While these are important for our collective understanding, they cannot be the only experiences that define our identities. Do we not also experience joy and success? We must connect our lived experiences to joy, achievement, and success in order to offer powerful counter narratives to erroneous perceptions of our communities. To be clear, we are not advocating for joy to be the only narrative shared about our communities. Rather, we are saying that the collective survival of our identities through identity-sustaining pedagogy hinges on our awareness, orientation toward, and communication of the joyous aspects of our experiences as BITOCs. If the core of our identities is defined only by experiences of trauma and marginalization, are we working toward and perpetuating narratives that are ultimately harmful for our communities?

✍ *Testimonio*: Joy as Low Blood Pressure Critical Praxis—Longoria

In any given week, my BIPOC colleague-friends regularly will receive a GIF or meme from me commenting on a shared experience or the happenings of the week. These are always meant to elicit laughter amid what undoubtedly are intense days for them. Rather than get angry at adversity or the stresses of this work, I am in continual pursuit of finding joy and humor since it cannot be all doom and gloom. My colleague-friend Giselle Alcantar Soto calls this "low blood pressure critical praxis." As a hypertensive, it must be the only way I proceed in my professional life.

In graduate school, I recall having a deep conversation with my colleague-friend Winston Benjamin about the need for more humor in social justice—that laughter should necessarily be part of this work. Of course we had scholarly and deeply philosophical conversations. But most important, we laughed. In spite of the pressures of our graduate assistant work or the pressing needs of our dissertation-writing timelines, our conversations and collaborations with each other and colleagues always included laughter. This joy and laughter nourished me and helped me finish my degree.

We do not trivialize our work when laughter ensues. I have felt colleagues perceive it as such and I think the dominant culture expects us not to see laughter as professionally necessary. But I think laughter and joy are our reminders of our humanity in being a BITOC in education. Have you ever had that deep belly laugh about something only you and other colleagues understand and share? Our laughter and joy builds solidarity among us. We cannot bond only through our collective oppression and its effects. I hope this *testimonio,* at minimum, finds you lost in the memory of a deep laugh you last had and from it a manifestation of joy. That's the *testimonio.*

ON *CHISME*

On the patio, we might engage in *chisme,* which sometimes is referred to erroneously as simply and only gossip. We borrow this term from our Latinx cultures and especially highlight its positive form. At first glance, we might think negatively about all kinds of gossip. However, *chisme* can be important for getting the inside word on the systems we serve in—the systemic contexts and insider knowledge we are often not privy to as BITOCs. We might call this facilitative gossip or *chisme.* Building networks with other educators, particularly those typically outside of our social networks, is important for gaining *chisme.* It is also vital to develop an ear for it, too. A healthy curiosity about the goings-on of your school and district will help build your ear toward finding out crucial information. Much *chisme* comes your way by being an avid participant in your school system, and we encourage you to build this into your teaching practice.

We do not imply here that you should be nosy and pry into the business of every single person within your school system. We also understand that as we navigate school systems as BITOCs, we sometimes can be hesitant to exchange information with others and sometimes *chisme* is monodirectional. In the latter situation, *chisme* is not reciprocal—or helpful for all parties—and functions more as destructive gossip. We might call this debilitative gossip and not *chisme.*

Nevertheless, we acknowledge that there can be an insidious element to *chisme* that destroys communities. There sometimes can be a transactional nature to gossip that you feel pressures you to give up personal or guarded information you would rather keep to yourself—at least until you know more about who in the system is a trustworthy confidante and whom you might need to be cautious around. Debilitative gossip, hearsay, and cliques also can be unproductive practices that can place you in sensitive or professionally precarious situations. When shared with the intent to harm others, debilitative gossip can become a truly harmful practice that can malign your own professional reputation and inhibit your ability to advocate for changes in your schooling contexts.

For all these reasons, we encourage you to practice caution and think through the implications of your sharing of and participating in *chisme*. Ultimately, we believe that *chisme* has the potential to help break down cultural dominance and insider–outsider barriers, and can help build social networks when engaged in as a responsible professional practice.

 WONDER ALONE/WONDER TOGETHER

What role do you envision *chisme* playing in your professional experiences and your ability to navigate your work as a BITOC? How will you know when it's not helpful but rather counter to who you are as a BITOC?

TEACHER EDUCATION PROGRAMS HAVE A ROLE, TOO

We must continue to push our teacher education programs to work toward effecting meaningful change in recruiting, retaining, and supporting BIPOC teacher candidates. Engaging in advocacy in the teaching program where you find yourself is an excellent way to begin to learn those strategies that will make meaningful change happen. As a student you have many opportunities to insist on sustaining your identity in this profession. We include here some issues you might consider in advocating for and effecting change in teacher education programs to better support identity-sustaining pedagogy and empower other BITOCs in this work.

Recruitment and retention is a pressing problem for teacher education programs that want to ensure more BITOCs in the profession. Encouraging and cultivating BIPOCs to pursue the teaching profession is crucial. This includes pathways that help potential applicants take the requisite courses and gain sufficient experience with youth to be competitive applicants for teacher preparation programs.

Providing a pathway seems necessary but often is unidentified in discussions about recruitment and retention. However, there are deeper actions that might supplement such efforts. As teacher educators, we both feel a responsibility to ensure that our own practices and those of our colleagues work toward empowering BITOCs to enact identity-sustaining pedagogy. You, too, as a student in a teacher preparation program or a BITOC in the profession have agency and power to help effect changes to our programs.

One issue we must consider is whether our teacher preparation programs are ready to support and retain BITOCs. This is a difficult lens to shine on our programs, but a necessary one to truly help BITOCs effect identity-sustaining pedagogy. Are admissions practices culturally biased and in what way do they fail to account for the rich identities and strengths BIPOCs bring to their applications? Are program design and coursework geared toward White students and not designed for the unique needs of BITOCs and their application of curricular learning? Are university supervisors and supervising teachers trained in culturally responsive practices? Have BIPOC communities been invited to have input on program and curricular design and/or application processes? Resources or efforts to recruit BITOCs into our programs seem moot if they are not worthy of the brilliance of BITOCs.

We encourage you to advocate for collaboration with BIPOC communities, program and curricular redesign, and admissions practices that aim to boost the success and retention of BITOCs. Forming student advisory committees for your teacher preparation program, serving on application review committees, getting involved in student governance, and engaging with professional teacher organizations are a few ways to effect advocacy for change.

CONCLUDING REFLECTIONS

The patio is one of those places that help us to find ourselves as individuals and as members of a broader community. It is the place where we can chill, rest, and rejuvenate. It is also the place to welcome others, whether it is to share stories, swap *chismes*, or uncover wisdom. It is a place to just be in community. It is a place where we can celebrate joyfully those important accomplishments and milestones in our lives and the lives of those around us. We hope you will always find your personal patio along your professional pathways.

While the patio is a place of refuge, we cannot spend all of our time here. Self-care and rejuvenation can be only a place to re-up, not a constant state of being. At times the patio gets rained upon or needs repair, and in our everyday lives this can translate to the times we cannot find time to seek refuge from the din of our work lives. A balance must be achieved to find meaningful ways to sustain our identities and our health in this profession. We hope this chapter has helped you to think more deeply about ways that you can reenergize yourself in this work.

➥ Make It Happen: Portfolio Activity—Developing a Sustainability Plan

To add to your portfolio, we ask that you continue addressing your areas for growth from the previous activity. This work, however, should not exclude necessary self-care and solidarity building. Make a log of your self-care practices, if any, and set goals for how you might improve this necessary practice. Think also about what will sustain you in this important work. Where will you find nourishment: personally, culturally, socially?

Additionally, reflect on how you realistically might share your portfolio work with others to build solidarity. How can you intentionally share *testimonios* with others? How might you initiate caucusing? What resources might you draw upon to connect with other BITOCs in your community?

Having considered this, is there a *testimonio* that best captures your schooling experience and that highlights why it is important for you to be a teacher? What would that *testimonio* look/sound like?

⟫⟶ Keep It Going!

- Read the essay "A Burst of Light" by Audre Lorde.
- Read the poem "If We Hold Hands" by Cecilia Rodriguez Milanes.
- Watch the motion picture *The 40-Year-Old Version* by director Radha Blank.

CHAPTER 7

The Rooftop

Visioning and Action Planning for Sustainable Futures

> The idea that hope alone will transform the world, and action undertaken in that kind of naïveté, is an excellent route to hopelessness, pessimism, and fatalism. But the attempt to do without hope, in the struggle to improve the world, as if that struggle could be reduced to calculated acts alone, or a purely scientific approach, is a frivolous illusion.
>
> —Freire and Freire (2002, p. 8)

Perhaps the last place you might consider inspecting when thinking of your house/home is the rooftop. If you did, you would inspect it to see what materials it was made from: wood, ceramics, asphalt, slate, metal, as but a few examples. You would want to know the quality of those materials, including how they will withstand the weather. You also would look to see whether the roof was flat or pitched (and perhaps to what degree). You might even consider looking to see where you would have the easiest access in case you needed to clean or repair the roof. In effect, we typically imagine the roof as that part of the house that protects you and your home from the elements: wind, sun, rain, among other things.

Beyond this very basic description of what you might view on a roof, we also might think about what we can view from a roof. Given the appropriate roofing materials and the right pitch, the roof might be a place where we can sunbathe. It can be a place to get a broader overview of the immediate area and local community. It can be a place to watch a fireworks display in a different part of town. And it can be a place to watch a meteor storm or simply to peer deep into the vastness of the stars in the night sky. Perhaps it provides a place for contemplation; in doing so, you might even begin to imagine an infinite array of possibilities and futures as yet unknown.

In our minds, a powerful image of the rooftop comes from children's book author and illustrator Carmen Lomas Garza. Her painting,[1] titled "Camas para Sueños," shows two young people atop the roof of a house, pointing at and admiring the moon while contemplating their future. Inside the house, a caregiver is making up the bed; the roof and the bed are two places for dreaming.

It is this image of the roof to which we now turn. We want you to imagine sitting on the roof, thinking about the longer trajectory of your career within the teaching profession. We want you to imagine yourself as part of a larger community. We want you to imagine what kind of education and schooling the future holds in store. We want you to be and remain hopeful. And we want you to be thinking about what you might plan to do to move toward those possibilities and futures. Like the physical structure and makeup of the roof, we believe these are central to protecting you from the elements and weathering any storms that you may encounter in the profession.

In this chapter, we ask you to look toward the future and think of radical possibilities. We must be mindful of our collective futurity, or the futures that we all effect together as Black, Indigenous, and Teachers of Color (BITOC). This includes the futures that we imagine and the futures that we are working toward—including missteps or different paths we unintentionally take along the way. This will require you to imagine new ways of thinking about yourself and your roles as a BITOC in schools. It will include being clear about what those visions of possibilities are, what theories of change might best support them, and how to maintain hope even as you remain attentive to the challenges that you may be experiencing. We end by asking you to develop a specific action plan for yourself in relation to your movement into and through the profession. In short, we ask you to think about visioning *and* action planning.

 WONDER ALONE/WONDER TOGETHER

What are your grandest hopes for yourself as a teacher? What are you hoping a career in education will be like for you?

BRINGING IT ALL TOGETHER

As you have read in these pages, the challenges facing Black, Indigenous, and Teachers of Color are difficult and complicated. Unfortunately, there are no easy, short-term, or quick-fix answers to address these pervasive challenges if we are to attain genuine educational equity. Likewise, while acknowledging the incredible assets BITOCs bring to the teaching profession that can mitigate some of these challenges, we also recognize the challenges to diversifying the teaching profession along every step of the pathway and career trajectory.

One thing we are certain of: Waiting for others and institutions to change, for others to become critically conscious, for others to do something, is not a productive theory of change. We need to take it upon ourselves, in meaningful collaboration with others (people, communities, professional organizations, as a few examples), to advance the vision of equity and justice that inspired you to be a teacher in the first place. We remind you that we have collected some resources, located in the toolshed (Appendix A), and encourage you to consider that many of our favorite books and articles in our references can support you in this work. We know this is an initial list and hope it takes you on a wonderful scholarly journey as you build your own professional library.

ENVISIONING FUTURITIES

We borrow from Queer studies the notion of *futurity*—a tethering of our current realities to the futures we imagine and seek to effect (Muñoz, 2009). As we imagine these futurities, we do not simply consider them in the abstract. Rather, we must seek ways to work toward effecting a world and conditions that will sustain our identities. We have futurities about our identities, and we have futurities about our schools. Engaging with futurities is an active process and not simply a matter of imagination.

We first might ask ourselves: What is the future of our identities? Are our identities bound to this historical moment or to a U.S.-only context? Are there ways in which we imagine our identities might change over time, especially grow in critical and anti-oppressive ways? How do I imagine my role in education in 10 years? These questions encompass our individual futures.

We also might ask ourselves: What is the future of schooling? How specifically do we imagine schooling must change to make space for us to sustain our identities? What systemic changes are necessary to ensure a more just school system? Finally, we might ask ourselves: How should we go about effecting changes and reforms to make the futures we imagine? The future of all BITOCs, as well as our futures in schooling, represent collective futures. Movement building is part and parcel of what it means to engage in collective futurities.

In effecting these changes, we simultaneously must imagine both individual and collective futures. We hope that you consider ways that the two positively inform each other and that you are cautious about barriers that inhibit progress. Continually engaging in thinking about these barriers, as well as productive actions, should inform your work as a BITOC. We offer in the next section some theories of change to help you in this process.

💬 WONDER ALONE/WONDER TOGETHER

What are your grandest hopes for education and our nation's schools? What would schools look like if you and your family/community could organize them?

THEORIES OF CHANGE

When thinking of looking up and looking out, to envision futurities marked by equity and justice, we need to also ask ourselves, What is our theory of change? Recognizing that change is a constant, we can ask how change happens. For this, we listen carefully to the description offered by Native scholar Eve Tuck who, in 2009, wrote:

> Theories of change are implicit in all social science research, and maybe all research. The implicit theory of change will have implications for the way in which a project unfolds, what we see as the start or end of a project, who is our audience, who is our "us," how we think things are known, and how others can or need to be convinced. A theory of change helps to operationalize the ethical stance of the project, what are considered data, what constitutes evidence, how a finding is identified, and what is made public and kept private or sacred. (p. 413)

We agree fully with Tuck (2014) about the need to be clear about our theory of change. For example, Tuck (2014) asks whether we believe that social justice–oriented scholarship will create the kind of changes we need, or might change occur more productively if we spend collective energy organizing? That is, given the vision of justice that we have for ourselves, our schools, our community, and our nation, what approaches might we actively take to create change consistent with that vision? With respect to schooling, this requires that we have ideological and political clarity in how we think education might be renewed in ways that move us beyond "the methods fetish" (Bartolome, 1994).

An initial question that we need to ask when pursuing a social justice orientation, regarding our theories of change, is, What needs to change first: Ourselves as individuals, our institutions, the broader cultural milieu, or the underlying ideological (axiological, ontological, and epistemological) orientations? We know that each of these is important.

We also recognize that you may be early on in your teaching preparation experience and have little influence over institutions, societal culture, and ideologies. Thus, it may be more productive, at this point, to do the individual change work. It is necessary to identify and interrogate your own positionalities and ideologies regarding power and privilege around difference and oppression. Recall that none of us is immune from oppressive ideologies, and they are sometimes so powerful that we have internalized this oppression. By doing this early work, when you have the opportunity, you can bring this into every aspect of your work within the classroom and within the school.

Once you are in school settings, you can decide which approach to institutional change makes the most sense given the particular time and place where you find yourself, recognizing that each of the following approaches has advantages and disadvantages (Senger & Mayer, 2019). An *incremental approach* focuses mostly on individual change you can effect with your peers and colleagues. It might include making some small system changes (such as requiring that all search committees have at least one BITOC on them) or creating an initiative that fills a much-needed gap (such as an after-school heritage-language club). The *antagonism approach* seeks to create change by creating, naming, and maintaining conflict via confrontation and obstruction. In this approach, you would continue to raise questions about why the test scores of Black, Indigenous, and Students of Color are well below those of White students; you would raise these often and with everyone who could effect change. The *agonism approach* (a term borrowed from pharmacology) works within the system around a creative tension and cognitive dissonance. Rather than serving an antagonist role, you would work with others who are open to new ways of understanding school issues and to pursuing previously unconsidered solutions.

This often leads to the *radical reimagining approach.* In this approach, you generate radically different ideas; from there you might develop a prototype or pilot a program as an opportunity to experiment and learn/improve. The key in this approach is to generate new knowledge toward reconfiguring how the innovation functions and is structured. It requires us to be transgressive (that is, to pull/stretch boundaries), to be imaginative, and to be counter hegemonic.

 WONDER ALONE/WONDER TOGETHER

As you read about these four different approaches to thinking about change in schools, which approach speaks to you best? Why? What are some ways you would think, feel, and act that are consistent with that approach?

If you happen to be involved in anti-oppressive work, Kleinrock (2020) offers some important questions to ask (and ponder) when considering your own engagement with these activities:

- Why (and why now) is anti-oppressive work a priority?
- How can you ensure that involvement in activities is not optional or a one-and-done?
- How will BIPOCs be centered in this work?
- How will BIPOCs be supported in this work?
- How will this contribute to long-term change?

In enacting your theory of change, you also might consider Reid's (2002) questions: "Is your spirit clear? Do you have a good heart? What other baggage do you carry? Are you useful to us? Can you fix our generator? Can you actually do anything?" (p. 16).

CAREER DEVELOPMENT: A PURPOSEFUL TRAJECTORY

In the past, individuals coming into the teaching profession would envision that they might teach at one school, in one content area, and even perhaps in one grade level over the full and complete span of their professional lives. Schools and school districts often offer (indeed, require) continuing education units as part of the professional development of their teachers; these might consist of short courses, seminars, conferences, and other learning opportunities deemed worthy. Some individuals would pursue, or be asked/groomed to take on, an administrative role such as vice-principal or principal.

On a more individual level, there are opportunities to get advanced certification through the National Board Exam, for example. In addition, you may decide to pursue advanced degrees, a master's degree and then a doctorate, in education. Beyond providing an opportunity to extend the depth and breadth of your understanding about teaching, learning, schooling, and education, these advanced degrees often pay off by placing teachers on a different (higher) rung of the salary ladder.

Because of the cultural and linguistic assets that you bring to teaching as a BITOC, you can seek (and sometimes are actively sought out) to engage in other activities that serve the interests of the school and the district, especially in those settings where who you are and what you bring are valued. We share some of these activities here so that you can begin to imagine ways in which you can make a (perhaps more) significant difference in the quality of the school where you work. We share these also because we believe that these activities likely will allow you to extend, revitalize, and rejuvenate your teaching.

Some of these roles occur within your current assignment as a classroom teacher. One such role is in *curriculum development*. Curriculum development occurs informally and frequently in discussions between teachers at the same grade level or in the same content area. More formally, teachers may be asked to engage in curriculum development at either the school or district level (and often during the summer) to renew an existing unit of instruction or develop a new one; as we write, many schools or districts are writing new curriculum around antiracist education and ethnic studies. Helping to develop and shape curriculum is a great way to ensure that culturally centering education is encouraged and supported across the school and/or district.

Most of you have completed student teaching in a teacher's classroom; that teacher served the role of *mentor teacher*. Mentor teachers often are assigned to new teachers as well to ensure that their induction into the school is positive and productive. You often will have an opportunity to serve in the mentor role capacity after you have been teaching for several (typically, at least 3) years. Serving as a mentor teacher provides you an opportunity to support and ensure that a new generation of individuals, especially BITOCs, get off to a great start as a teacher. It allows you to begin to share the wisdom that you have gleaned as a BITOC with them in ways that will sustain these new teachers throughout their professional careers.

Related to the role of mentor teachers, seasoned teachers who are particularly apt at teaching are asked to serve as a *lead teacher* or teacher on special assignment. In this role, a teacher may be asked to coach another teacher or a group of teachers as they move through their own curriculum development or the implementation of a new content-specific program, or to assist in a team or school that is struggling. Again, these become opportunities for you to positively effect change at a much higher level than a single classroom.

Almost every school has a number of committees where teachers are asked for their participation. *School-level and district-level committees* are yet another place to actively participate in professional activities. These committees may have a short-term focus, such as how the school will enact antiracist activities or the professional development activities for the coming year. Or they may have a long-term focus, such as serving with the Parent Teacher Student Association or helping to develop the school's improvement plan for the next 5 years. Even in these examples, you can see possible opportunities for moving the school toward greater equity, inclusion, and diversity.

We also want to be certain you know about the possibilities of your involvement as a *union member and in union-based activities*. The union is concerned primarily with the salary and working conditions of teachers. Unions ensure another opportunity for teachers to exert their voice. Importantly for this text, we appreciate that unions are also keen to support teachers, as their members, in exemplary teaching, including teaching for equity and justice. As we describe in the toolshed, the two largest national teacher unions—the American Federation of Teachers and the National Education Association—have wonderful resources for teaching for diversity and for considering ways to diversify the teaching profession.

We end this discussion with an acknowledgment that some of these roles may take you outside of the full-time teaching assignment. And, of course, there are those roles that take you out of your "traditional" teaching assignment altogether (vice-principal, principal, or district-level administrator). We certainly need BITOCs to step into these significant roles, when the opportunity presents itself. For now, however, we ask you to think about yourself as a teacher leader who takes an activist stance: an activist teacher leader.

WONDER ALONE/WONDER TOGETHER

As you think about these various roles you might play someday in a school setting, are there some that are intriguing to you? Why? What about roles that you would not want to hold?

ACTIVIST TEACHER LEADERS

One of the primary "theories of change" that you are operating under—although you may not have thought about it as such—centers around the value of education and, by extension, the power of teaching. That is, you most likely believe that a quality education can open greater life opportunities for students, can enhance the vitality of communities, and can serve the greatest public interests of the nation and world. We stand with you in this regard.

But we also know that you, as a BITOC, have an even greater level of commitment to ensuring that schools do right by students, parents/caregivers, and communities that historically have been marginalized. This requires that you take a more active stance as a teacher; that is, that you see yourself as an activist teacher leader. Ann Lopez (in press) defines it this way:

Activist teacher leadership is bottom-up action by teachers who engage in a process of examining their practice and schoolwide policies, bringing about positive outcomes for students, and activist teacher leadership is socially just. Activist teacher leadership calls for not only critical conversation and dialogue, but critical action.

Activist teacher leaders exert their leadership in three ways: at the classroom level, at the school level, and at the community level. At the *classroom level*, activist teacher leaders work to facilitate the intellectual, social, emotional, and cultural growth of their students. This level asks teachers to strive to be exemplary in their craft of helping students to learn meaningful content, develop critical thinking skills, exhibit caring for others, and develop those competencies around crossing multiple cultural/linguistic borders. At the *school level*, activist teacher leaders serve to help foster a climate of continual learning and improvement around shared and inclusively developed schoolwide goals, positive professional relationships, and collective responsibility for every aspect of the schooling experience. At the *community level*, activist teacher leaders employ their knowledge of culture and language within the local communities to engage in collaborative problem solving around school-based issues as well as to pursue ways to bring schools more meaningfully into the life of communities.

While there are many characteristics of activist teacher leaders, we believe the following are especially central for BITOCs:

1. Re/committing to equity and social justice—We believe that you need to keep this at the center/core of your approach to teaching and leading.
2. Re/claiming our role as curriculum developers—We believe that you need to see yourself as a curriculum maker, not just a curriculum consumer.

3. Finding spaces within curriculum and instruction for disruption of the status quo—We believe you need to pursue those opportunities to create and enact alternative approaches to teaching and learning.
4. Having a group of critical friends—We believe you need to find those collaborators, critical friends, and mentors to support you on this important journey (as described in Chapter 6).
5. Forging safe places for dialogue and support—We believe you need to be sustained in this work by finding those spaces and places for visioning, addressing challenges, and feeling safe.

In short, what we most need for BITOC activist teacher leaders is context-specific, tactical diversity, inclusion, and equity work in our schools.

 WONDER ALONE/WONDER TOGETHER

What have you learned thus far, prior to reading this chapter, about leadership? About yourself as a leader? How does what you have read here extend or refute your initial understandings of yourself as a teacher leader?

Musings on Leadership

We know there will be opportunities for you to take a leadership role in a school setting. In particular, given the paucity of BITOCs in schools, your colleagues may seek to garner your input and active participation in school-level efforts even, at times, to the point of tokenization. For your part, you might be keenly interested in getting off to a positive start as a classroom teacher. We urge you, especially early on, to not feel pressured to fill these leadership roles until you feel ready for the challenge, recognizing that there likely will be leadership opportunities later in your career.

You might begin in a variety of small (but important) ways, such as leading a small group of teachers on a specific project, and engage in multiple of these prior to considering leading in a broader way—later in your career—such as serving a school as principal. We offer a few of our own thoughts given our experiences with leadership over the years.

- *Keep big purposes in mind.* When we think about leadership, we ask: Toward what vision and for what purpose? It is the answers to these questions that will serve as grounding for you, especially on those days and at those moments when you wonder why you took on the leadership role in the first place. Recognizing that the role is bigger than you, given your big purposes, will help you to navigate any challenges you may encounter. While the end goals are important, never forget that so are the means to achieve them.

- **Be prepared to uncover oppression.** Leading often includes seeing all the insidious ways that bias and oppression have manifested themselves in our schools. They might show themselves in the language someone uses that exemplifies a deficit ideology. They might show themselves in a policy that has a differential negative impact on one group of students and/or favors another. They might show themselves in an underlying, unquestioned, and unfair belief about people broadly or schools specifically.
- **Partner with like-minded colleagues.** Find those individuals who share your vision and passion for leading; this is your support network. Do not forget that sometimes those who are most important to you in this work may not agree with you. Think about their disagreement as an offer of love in a critical way.
- **Bring your full cultural self to this work.** As we have been suggesting in this book, we urge you to bring your full self to this work. It also means that you should not accept anything that violates the integrity of your identity or that is dehumanizing.
- **Keep the conversation going.** Think of conversation—consistent, sustained, focused, collaborative, and open to critical reflection—as the strategy that will allow action to occur. If you keep bringing something up, at some point people are going to have to deal with that issue in a way that they and you can find mutually agreeable.

While there is so much more to thinking about leadership, we hope that you take to heart what we offer here: the importance of a vision of the possible, action toward its realization, and persistence in its attainment. We also ask: Where will you find wisdom, hope, humor, and longing?

ACTION PLANNING

This chapter has been leading up to helping you develop an action plan. An extended version of this plan is provided in Appendix D: An Action-Planning Worksheet: Crafting Your Story. A central idea is that a vision for yourself and your career is necessary but not sufficient. You need a plan of action to move that vision forward. For us, that plan of action includes having a set of intentions, skills, and dispositions.

For now, we want to highlight three parts of that action plan. First, we ask what *intentions* you want to pursue. What are those broad goals that motivate you and are driving you into the profession? What are those things you most want to accomplish in your work as a teacher, colleague, and educational professional? When you think of people describing you as a BITOC, what would you hope they would say that exemplified what you accomplished? Having a clear set of intentions is essential since these serve as the building blocks for enacting your vision for yourself as a BITOC. Narrow those down to two to three intentions.

The second part of your action plan is around your *assets* (including skill set). What is within your current skill set, both personally and professionally? What personal and professional skills do you still need to develop? What combination of both personal and professional skills is necessary for the specific intentions you have identified? It is important to recognize that you already have important skills, talents, and abilities. Valuing the opportunity to sharpen those skills and develop new ones is part of your own personal and professional revitalization.

The third part of the action plan, and perhaps the most important, asks about your most central *dispositions*—your overall temperament. In this, we ask what dispositions do you want to be most associated with in the work of teaching? What would you want students, parents, or colleagues to say about the kind of person and the kind of teacher you are? How would those dispositions be of service to you? Are the actions you propose authentic to and sustaining your identities? How can you ensure that these dispositions are part of who you are and how you show up (engage with others in the everyday)? We urge you to be true to yourself when it comes to thinking about dispositional elements, and we urge you to think about how these play out differently in your role as a BITOC.

TELLING YOUR STORY

We believe that there is power in sharing stories, your own and those of your students. Storytelling plays a significant role in many of our communities. These stories sometimes are written but more often are shared orally, including in narrative form but also in poetry, song, or dance, as a few examples. We think and dream in narratives, in stories.

For us, storytelling has several important dimensions. At one level, it provides an example of who we are as BIPOCs—what we have referred to as our positionalities—and how our real experiences have shaped our identity. As we have been suggesting throughout this text, how and what we teach, as well as what we value, emerge from our identities and our biographies.

At another level, we often share these stories to disrupt, challenge, and call into question dominant narratives that are oppressive or to highlight our community's funds of knowledge or cultural capital. That is, they serve as a counter narrative to the master narrative. Recall our discussion of *testimonios* as a type of counter narrative, as described in the Introduction. While challenging majoritarian narratives, these counter narratives are designed purposefully to create an emotional response on the part of those listening as well as to elicit an urgency to respond.

We share two other key parts to storytelling. First is the importance of multivocality, of the recognition that there are many kinds of stories—and ways of telling those stories—even for those from the same social-cultural identity group. The differences are explained by the fact that there are many different ways of being and of being fully human; thus, we need to affirm these different ways of storying. Second, our stories gain their power from sharing, and we recognize that others share our stories, too. The emotions and experiences expressed in these testimonies, these *testimonios*, have been experienced more broadly by others, too (albeit differently).

We ask you to consider the following questions about the stories you most value and hold near:

- What are the stories of your own schooling as a minoritized student?
- What stories have yet to be told about schooling?
- Whose stories must be told about schooling?
- How do we hear those stories, especially of people who experience marginalization or whose identities are marked by intersectionality?
- What stories do you tell about your own coming to critical consciousness?
- How might you use storytelling in your teaching?
- Where might storytelling fit in with liberation pedagogy, multicultural education, and/or culturally centered teaching?
- What story will you want to create about teaching, teaching well, and teaching for equity and diversity?

In the end, sharing who we are and where we stand via our *testimonios* is an act of our own identity-sustaining work. It humanizes, serves an instructive role, complicates simplistic visions, demonstrates that culture matters, and shows how resistance occurs both in the light and in the shadows. We know we continue to need stories that provide inspiration and hope. We hope that you can find meaningful ways to share your authentic stories in your instruction and in schooling.

 WONDER ALONE/WONDER TOGETHER

What stories do you, as a BITOC, wish to tell about becoming a teacher? What stories are you hoping to tell as you move through the profession?

ON HOPE

One of the most essential dispositional elements of teaching for BITOCs is maintaining your sense of hope. There are many reasons to despair, as you have read in these pages, given the history and conditions of schooling as well as its influence on learning for students from marginalized communities—let alone the challenges of teaching within school systems not meant to support us as BI-TOCs. But as you also have read, there is an essential role you can play in making a change; in fact, making a difference in the educational experiences and lives of others might be one of the reasons you are pursuing a career in teaching.

As we share above, we know you are developing a vision for doing school better and are planning for what that might look like. In addition, you may want to teach to connect with others, to grow and help students to grow, to serve others, and to give back as a visible way to thank the people, families, and communities that supported you. As you do this, we know that you also are carrying the hope of others—your family, your friends, and your community—with you as you embark on your teaching career.

✍ *Testimonio*: **You Have No Choice—Francisco**

I had been teaching for 13 years and was offered an opportunity to pursue my doctoral degree. I was uncertain that teaching at the university level was something I wanted to do and about whether or not I could effect change at that level via academic and scholarly pursuits. I also was uncertain about my own academic potential and stepping away from my teacher's salary for a graduate-level stipend. Given that no one in my family ever had even gone to college, let alone to graduate school, I was also a little afraid of what it all would entail and had no one to speak with about it.

My youngest sister was graduating from high school and we had an extended family celebration. I recall telling one of my tías about my dilemma and uncertainties. I thought for certain she would understand and encourage me to forgo graduate school. After all, she had only earned her high school diploma.

But she surprised me by saying, "You have no choice." I understood immediately she was telling me I had to pursue my doctoral degree.

"Look around at your *primos y primas,* our *vecinos,* and our *amigos,*" she continued. "They need to know from you who we [as Latinx people] can become."

In small ways, I resented that she put this responsibility on me. But in so many other ways, I have heard the spirit of those words. They have guided me in countless ways: in opportunities I would pursue, in ways I would conduct myself, and in my own responsibilities to the Latinx community.

What is important is that the young people whom you will serve, need to be inspired about their potential and the opportunities to create their futures—under whatever conditions they might find themselves. We feel that inspiration and hope are as important as whatever academic content students might learn from you or as whatever engaging teaching activity you might employ. We imagine that those teachers, family members, and community activists who inspired you planted those important seeds of hope into you.

We are mindful that inspiring hope in others has many different dimensions. We have found Jeff Duncan-Andrade's (2009) framework around hope instructive. To begin, Duncan-Andrade identifies three *enemies of hope. Hokey hope* occurs when people urge you to have hope with no accompanying support or action on their part. *Mythical hope* happens when people identify someone from your community who has been successful, despite barriers in their way; in this way, it suggests that a person's own success relies entirely on them so as not to discuss (let alone dismantle) those barriers that are in the way. *Dream deferred* is the third enemy of hope; it transpires when a person suggests that things will get better in the future.

For Duncan-Andrade (2009), there are also three *enemies of hopelessness. Material hope* is found when people provide tangible and genuine support for others—resources or networks of support—to help them along their way. *Socratic hope* is found when people help others to understand dehumanizing societal conditions and factors, recognizing that understanding and dismantling these conditions "may pave the path to justice" (p. 188). *Audacious hope* can be found in those teachers who stand in solidarity with students, who share in their suffering, and who are willing to make personal sacrifices to support the collective struggle.

What each of the forms of *enemies of hope* have in common is an unwillingness to name and discuss real barriers to success, let alone to begin to dismantle those barriers. The onus for success falls entirely on a person's belief in themself. While that belief is important, it doesn't lead to transformative change. What each of the *enemies of hopelessness* have in common is a willingness to support others (tangibly and concretely), to help shed light on the conditions negatively influencing them, and to stand with them to dismantle those barriers in solidarity with them and with others.

We hope you too will add to your plan of action how you can be a hope monger (Kohl, 1994) in working with young people, their families, and their communities. We are reminded about the importance of hope by Kingsolver (2010), who writes:

The arc of history is longer than human vision. It bends. We abolished slavery, we granted universal suffrage. We have done hard things before. And every time it took a terrible fight between people who could not imagine changing the rules, and those who said, "We already did. We have made the world new." The hardest part will be to convince yourself of the possibilities and hang on. If you run out of hope at the end of the day, rise in the morning and put it on again with your shoes. (p. 456)

WONDER ALONE/WONDER TOGETHER

What are your hopes for your students? For their families? For their communities? What are the grandest hopes you have for yourself? How do you imagine you can move from hope to action?

OUR UNFINISHEDNESS

We end by coming back to an idea we very briefly touched on at the end of Chapter 1. It has to do with the Freirean notion of "unfinishedness." Writing in *Pedagogy of Freedom*, Freire (2000) notes that not only are we unfinished as human beings, we are also conscious of our unfinishedness. He writes that "this unfinishedness is essential to our human condition" (p. 52). Precisely because we are unfinished, we can be active agents in the world, forging those ways in which we can write the story we want to tell.

More directly to your role as a teacher, we know that our understandings of what it means to be a BITOC are evolving, including what it means to teach with a critically conscious framework; we are unfinished. Because of our unfinishedness, we have to continually both pursue critical reflexive work as well as engage in dialogue with others. That is, as Philip and Zavala (2016) assert, "Dialogue cannot exist without humility and an acknowledgement of our own ignorance and limitations" (p. 664).

In recognizing our own humanity, and our unfinishedness therein, we also recognize that others are also unfinished. We are unfinished together. It will be important to offer grace to those others—our students, their caregivers, our colleagues—who are also on the journey of self-reflexivity and dialogue in their pursuit of learning about equity and justice.

Toward this end, we remind you of the toolshed that we have in Appendix A to help you and those with whom you journey to continue to learn, to continue to grow, to continue to inspire, and to continue to teach.

WONDER ALONE/WONDER TOGETHER

What are some areas of your own personal unfinishedness? What are some areas of your professional unfinishedness? What might you do to move away from the unfinishedness that you've just described?

CONCLUDING REFLECTIONS

We return to our initial description of the roof. We described the roof as that part of your house that protects you from the elements. But we also described it as the place to envision the community, to dream, to plan, to find purpose, and to hope. We see these as connected. That is, seeing yourself as part of a broader professional and cultural community, having a dream of possibilities and futurities, understanding the long-range options for yourself to have a purpose-driven career, developing a plan for yourself as a BITOC, and maintaining a radical sense of hopefulness will protect you and help you weather whatever professional storms you may encounter.

We hope we have not understated how important your presence in the profession is and will be for our students, their families, and the communities you serve.

We have been waiting for you.
In solidarity and hope,

⮞⁺ Make It Happen: Portfolio Activity: Develop an Action Plan

As a final step for your portfolio, we ask that you build on the action plan encouraged in this chapter (see Appendix D). Above all, we implore you to truly make identity-sustaining pedagogies happen. We have asked you to constantly reflect, and now we encourage you to act. What is your 5- and 10-year plan? What is your plan for sustaining yourself and other BITOCs in the profession? What is your plan for supporting those who need to step out of the profession?

We also encourage you to consider writing a letter to your future students. What is it that you want them to know about you? What are your expectations and hopes for them? How do you intend to be a source of hope and inspiration for them?

Finally, we ask that you do not let this portfolio sit on a shelf or as an unopened file on a computer desktop. Revisit and revise it from time to time. Our great hope is that you make this your own living, supplemental text to sustain yourself in this profession.

⮞⁺ Keep It Going!

- Read the poem "Something to Read" by Marvin Carter.
- Watch the Key and Peele parody skit "TeachingCenter" in which they wondered what it would be like if we treated teachers as we do professional athletes. How would education be different? What would have to happen to make this radical imaginary a reality? Find the skit at https://www.youtube.com/watch?v=dkHqPFbxmOU

Postscript (PS)

As we began to write this text, we described the house in disarray. Unfortunately, the chaos has continued to occur. As we were writing this, Jacob Blake, a Black man, was shot seven times in the back by police in Kenosha, Wisconsin, as he walked to his car. In the protests that followed, a teenage vigilante and follower of the police and White supremacists, armed with a rifle, shot two protesters. Retreating behind police lines with rifle in tow, he was not even hassled until the full magnitude of what he had done came to be understood.

An unarmed Black man shot by police seven times in the back, a White teen carrying a rifle untouched by the police. These contrasting atrocities have made a terrible crescendo in a chaotic fugue of racial reckoning amid the COVID-19 pandemic of 2020.

If that were not enough, rather than calling for greater police accountability, including better training around the continuing role of racism in our society and in our public servants, the Trump administration, through Executive Order 13950 (2020), moved to ban any diversity training that aimed to address White privilege or used a Critical Race Theory framework (recall, from Chapter 2, that this framework centers racism as endemic to our society). These trainings were described as "divisive, anti-American propaganda" (Vought, 2020, p.1). The lasting effects of the Trump era presidency are yet to be fully understood and addressed.

In the current moment in which we write, as well as in the years to come, we are reminded that our schools, our communities, and our nation are not utopian spaces; they are often messy, filled with varying degrees of tension and conflict. There may be times when you even feel like an outsider in your own country, given the vision of equity and justice that lies at your center. In a similar way, there will be moments in schools when—as a result of school policies or practices, the continuation of microaggressions, or the outright oppression you see occurring in classrooms—you will feel like an outsider in schools.

As we have written here, we ask you to lean into this, to work to find "homeness" in the spaces where you find yourself. That sense of home might be crafted in the space of your own classroom with your own students. You might find that sense of home at the school level or even in your role in the teaching profession. We believe that this sense of homeness occurs when you sustain your identities, and those of your students, in all that you do.

We ask that you do your best to keep unwanted guests—bigotry, oppression, and hegemony—out of your house; and when present, that you do your best to quickly show them to the door as unwelcomed in those spaces where you find yourself. Classrooms, schools, and communities are your home, too. We must maintain these as a healthy home also, given its necessity for our collective well-being.

We share a final *testimonio* here to help you, beloved reader, be reminded of what it means to own your belonging, your sense of home, as a BITOC.

✍ *Testimonio*: This Is Your House—Francisco

I had just begun my first teaching position at a university as an assistant professor. I had moved to a new state where I knew very few people. I began to develop professional relationships with a few of my colleagues in the college and university.

Early on, a proposal I submitted was accepted at a statewide bilingual education conference where I would be presenting, as a professor with a real university position, for the first time.

Arriving at the conference, I was both anxious and excited. I was so relieved to see one of my new professional colleagues from the college, a White professor, near the front door of the convention center. I felt it would be good to have an initial connection with at least one person at the conference.

This colleague clearly saw me with direct eye contact—and then promptly hid behind a pillar!

I was deflated. He was hiding from me.

For a moment, I felt like going around the pillar to confront him but thought the better of it.

I went into the conference center and promptly saw a Chicana colleague, who embraced my presence. I immediately told her what had happened. She took me by the arm deeper into the convention center and said, "This is your house. This is where you belong."

She promptly took me to meet some of the key leaders of the association and one of the keynote speakers. It was, as she said, where I belonged.

What we ask you to do is to claim these spaces, to create this home. *And we ask it because this is your house, and this is where you belong.*

The Toolshed

The toolshed is a place where you find those instruments that help you accomplish important goals you have for yourself. The right tool enables you to do things you could not do otherwise or makes a task easier with better results. As in any toolshed, there might be a range of tools for accomplishing lots of different goals. Most often, however, you choose specific tools that will help you accomplish a particular goal.

The toolshed of the teaching profession is no different. A wide range of professional organizations, conferences, readings, videos, listservs, and so on, are available to help you accomplish a wide range of goals around curriculum, instruction, assessment, classroom organization, school improvement, teaching as a profession, and so on.

What we focus on here are those specific tools, those specific organizations, that provide professional support and resources outside of the mainstream teacher professional organizations you may encounter as a BITOC. To be sure, many of these mainstream organizations also are committed to equity and diversity in education. Consider, as but two examples, the leading teacher unions. Both the American Federation of Teachers and the National Education Association, while centered on supporting teacher working conditions and teacher salaries, also are deeply committed to ensuring that their members are prepared to offer the kind of culturally and linguistically diverse, high-quality instruction students deserve.

The focus in this appendix is on those organizations, resources, and professional development opportunities that are dynamic, producing and making available to educators the most contemporary of resources that also have a distinct focus on equity, diversity, and social justice. Note that many of these can fit into multiple categories; for example, the National Association for Multicultural Education (NAME) is a professional organization that has both an academic and a practical teacher focus, as well as hosting an annual conference.

A few other notes. First, for books and articles we recommend, look in our reference list for a wide range of printed and electronic materials that you might find helpful to your work. These are important tools, too, to add to the professional toolshed. Second, we want to encourage you to explore each of these organizations for a greater depth of understanding related to their work and how it might support you. What we provide here is a general description, most often taken from their mission/vision or goals statements. We signify this by putting their own description in quote marks.

We do not include ethnic-specific organizations (such as the NAACP) or general diversity materials (such as the *New York Times'* Race Related materials) that do not have a specific focus on education, although we know these are highly valuable to you in ways that will help you sustain your personal and professional identities. We also do not include state or local organizations (such as Educators Network for Social Justice in Milwaukee) but strongly encourage you to seek out these "closer to home" networks. We also do not include movies, podcasts, or other forms of contemporary media, even though we know that these, too, can be extremely helpful to you. And we do not include organizations whose primary focus is higher education, although they can be very helpful, too.

We know you will regard this as an initial and not comprehensive list of tools. As you continue to grow and learn, we encourage you to continue adding to your professional toolshed.

Professional/Academic/Scholarly Organizations

- *Abolitionist Teaching Network*—The Abolitionist Teaching Network aims to confront injustice in schools via bringing together a range of individuals committed to taking "action for educational freedom." Available at https://abolitionistteachingnetwork.org/. Includes an Educator (Agitators) Page at https://abolitionistteachingnetwork.org/resources-for-agitators
- *Engaging Schools (formerly Educators for Social Responsibility)*— Engaging Schools seeks to "create a schoolwide community of learning that integrates academic, social, and emotional development . . . [as well as] resources with practical strategies that are grounded in the values of equity, community, and democracy." Available at https://engagingschools.org/
- *Equity Alliance at Arizona State University*—The Equity Alliance seeks "to promote access, participation and positive outcomes for all students by engaging educational stakeholders, reframing and advancing the discourse on educational equity and transforming public education, locally, nationally and internationally." While it has a broad focus on equity and justice, it has a strong emphasis on inclusion of students who are disabled. Available at https://issuu.com/equityallianceatasu
- *National Education Policy Center (NEPC)*—The NEPC provides access to "high-quality, peer-reviewed research to inform education policy discussions . . . based on sound evidence." It should be a go-to resource for looking for the best scholarly and academic evidence (i.e., research) around school policy concerns with an equity and justice focus. Available at https://nepc.colorado.edu/
- *Regional Educational Laboratories (REL)*—Begun in 1965, the 10 RELs use "research and evidence, enhance education programs, and ultimately,

improve student performance. Each REL facilitates several research—practice partnerships . . . to address high-leverage issues in education." Search by region or by topic (e.g., American Indian/Indigenous, English learners, etc.). Available at https://ies.ed.gov/ncee/edlabs/

- **Robert Kennedy Human Rights Center**—The Robert Kennedy Human Rights Center is committed to (among other things) protecting human rights, inspiring young leaders, and teaching human rights via their Speaking Truth to Power project (described below). Available at https://rfkhumanrights.org/
- **Schools of Opportunity**—The Schools of Opportunity project recognizes high schools that have demonstrated an extraordinary commitment to equity and excellence by expanding opportunities for all students to succeed. Based on the principles of the book *Closing the Opportunity Gap*, Schools of Opportunity provides profiles of schools that have been successful in closing the opportunity gap for all learners. Available at http://schoolsofopportunity.org/
- **Southern Poverty Law Center (SPLC)**—The SPLC takes a three-pronged approach to equity and justice: fighting hate via tracking hate groups and crimes, teaching tolerance in schools (see Learning for Justice, below), and seeking justice via court cases and public policies. Available at https://www.splcenter.org/
- **WestEd**—WestEd is a "research, development, and service agency . . . to promote excellence, achieve equity, and improve learning for children, youth, and adults." Includes many professional development opportunities. Available at https://www.wested.org/

Teaching for Diversity Resources

- **Anti-Defamation League (ADL)**—While their mission statement expresses a commitment "to stop the defamation of the Jewish people, and to secure justice and fair treatment to all," the ADL has a strong emphasis on identifying and countering hate groups, as well as promoting respectful schools and communities. Available at https://www.adl.org/. Includes resources for educators at https://www.adl.org/education-and-resources/resources-for-educators-parents-families
- **ED Change**—EdChange provides "resources, workshops, and projects that contribute to progressive change in ourselves, our schools, and our society," with the aim of promoting equity and justice. Available at http://www.edchange.org/
- **Education Civil Rights Alliance**—The Education Civil Rights Alliance is a diverse and experienced group of organizers, educator organizations, community groups, professional associations, civil rights organizations, and government agencies that are committed to protecting the civil rights of marginalized students. Available at https://edrights.org/. Includes an Educators' Page at https://edrights.org/educators-page/

- *Human Rights Campaign*—This is a network dedicated and committed to supporting the LGBTQ+ community to "live their truth without fear and with equality under the law." Includes initiatives on behalf of voting, racial justice, pro-equality policy and litigation, and education around LGBTQ+ issues. Available at https://www.hrc.org/. Includes an Educators' Page via https://www.hrc.org/resources
- *Learning for Justice (formerly Teaching Tolerance)*—A project of the SPLC, Learning for Justice "provides free resources to educators . . . to supplement the curriculum, to inform their practices, and to create civil and inclusive school communities where children are respected, valued and welcome participants." Includes a magazine, webinars, a lesson plan generator rooted in standards for equity and justice, and posters, as a few examples—all for free. Available at https://www.learningforjustice.org/
- *National Association for Multicultural Education*—NAME is a national and international organization that is committed to issues of equity, inclusion, diversity, and justice in schooling. Along with publications and teaching resources, they host a conference annually. Available at https://nameorg. org/. Includes multicultural learning resources at: https://nameorg.org/ learn/
- *Rethinking Schools*—Rethinking Schools is a "leading grassroots organization for social and racial justice in education." Their primary means of doing so is via the quarterly production of *Rethinking Schools* magazine, as well as curriculum guides and other teacher-directed professional materials. Available at https://rethinkingschools.org/
- *Speaking Truth to Power*—The teaching resource–specific project of the Robert Kennedy Human Rights Center, Speaking Truth to Power shares "stories of human rights defenders around the world [and] provides compelling content for a set of flexible, standards-aligned digital resources, designed to educate, engage and inspire the next generation of human rights defenders." Available at https://www.speaktruthtopowerinschool. com/speak-truth-power

Teacher and Teaching Organizations/Conferences and Collectives

- *Badass Teachers Association*—The Badass Teachers Association strives to "reject racially and socially oppressive profit-driven education reform" via advocacy on racial, social, and economic justice matters, including pushing against privatization and standardization in education. Each state has its own member association. Available at https://www.badassteacher.org/
- *Education for Liberation Network*—The Education for Liberation Network is a "national coalition of teachers, community activists, researchers, youth and parents who believe a good education should teach people— particularly low-income youth and youth of color—how to understand and challenge the injustices their communities face. . . . The network provides a space for members to share knowledge and work together to create tools

for liberatory education." Available at https://www.edliberation.org/

- **Educators for Antiracism**—This is a collective of educators oriented toward practice that works toward antiracism. The group offers videos from their virtual conference, curricular resources, and opportunities for collaboration. Available at https://www.edantiracism.com
- **Free Minds, Free People**—Free Minds, Free People hosts a "national conference that brings together teachers, young people, researchers, parents and community-based activists/educators . . . to build a movement to develop and promote education as a tool for liberation. . . . The conference is a space in which these groups can learn from and teach each other, sharing knowledge, experience and strategies." Available at https://fmfp.org/
- **Institute for Teachers of Color Committed to Racial Justice (ITOC)**—ITOC is a "three-day professional development to facilitate the growth, success, and retention of teachers of Color in K–12 public schools serving students of Color, with on-going community and continued site-based support." Available at http://www.instituteforteachersofcolor.org/
- **Teacher Activists Groups (TAG)**—TAG is a "national coalition of grassroots teacher organizing groups" that aim to engage in "political education and relationship building in order to work for educational justice both nationally and in . . . local communities." Available at https://teacheractivists.org/
- **Teachers for Social Justice (T4SJ)**—T4SJ "is a grassroots non-profit teacher support and development organization" whose aim is to promote "self-transformation, leadership, and community building to educators in order to affect [sic] meaningful change in the classroom, school, community and society." Includes local networks in various cities and regions. Available at https://t4sj.org/

A Note to White Readers

Dear White Reader:

As we mentioned in the Introduction, this book is written intentionally centering the identities and needs of Black, Indigenous, and Teachers of Color. We imagine some readers are White and, for multiple reasons, might have chosen (or been required) to read this book. While this text is intended for BITOCs, we speak here directly to you, as our allies in this work.

A concern White students have stated in our classes—especially having begun to develop a critical consciousness about hegemony and white superiority—is whether they should even be pursuing their teaching license. We appreciate this stated concern as it reflects a level of both deep understanding and sensitivity regarding what Black, Indigenous, and Students of Color most need from their teachers, as well as the many positive assets BITOCs bring to the profession and to communities of color. It shows an anxiety and struggle to find their place in the teaching profession, which problematically has centered Whiteness in just about every aspect of schooling.

If, as a reader, this speaks to some of your own anxieties, we ask that you keep in mind a few key ideas. The lack of diversity is both a historical legacy and a contemporary trajectory. We shared (in Chapter 1) that the lack of presence of BITOCs has historical roots, given the termination of nearly 40,000 Black teachers when schools were integrated after the *Brown v. Board of Education* court case (Epps, 2002). This lack of presence of BITOCs, in the current moment, is also structural. It has to do with everything from the quality of schools in many poor, ethnically diverse communities to the practices in teacher education, including, for example, admissions policies and testing requirements. It continues into the teaching profession itself, where we see barriers for BITOCs with respect to recruitment/hiring, induction, professional development, and mentoring programs, as a few examples, many of which we describe in this text.

Given the myriad of challenges facing our best efforts to diversify the teaching workforce, we will not change the face of the teaching profession overnight. In the meantime, we will need to rely on you as decolonized, critically prepared, culturally sustaining White teachers to become the best possible teachers for minoritized youth. We need you to be a strong advocate alongside BITOCs for greater teacher diversity, to call out practices that have a negative influence on their recruitment and retention, and to support as allies those BITOCs who are hired on your school staff.

A central role of this critical consciousness for you as a White teacher is understanding the social and cultural experiences that serve as the important assets BITOCs bring to teaching and to the profession. You could consider pursuing, to the degree possible, common social and cultural experiences for yourself. These might include living in another country for an extended period of time, going to school in another country, living in an ethnic community, learning a language/vernacular spoken by students in the school, or immersing yourself in the presence of BIPOCs, as a few examples. Importantly, in doing any of these, you need to engage in critical reflection and critical self-reflexivity regarding what those experiences mean.

Two examples might be helpful for you. Consider Irizzary and Raible's (2011) description of exemplary teachers of Latinx youth. These teachers, including White teachers, worked to learn the language of their students and immersed themselves in the Latinx community. Similarly, Kasun (2018) not only learned Spanish, but upon returning home from Mexico, where she lived for a time, immersed herself in the Latinx community in personal and professional ways, choosing, for example, to work in a highly diverse school setting. Most interesting was her deep dive into the scholarship around Chicana feminism to help guide her in these important commitments, as well as her sense-making about those experiences.

Critical consciousness also begins with listening to the voices of BITOCs around what is most helpful to them that White allies can provide. Brazas and McGeehan (2020) describe some of these, including managing the White fragility (DiAngelo, 2018) that you or other White educators might be experiencing, ensuring that work is divided fairly throughout the school staff, educating yourself about critical issues of oppression and privilege so that you can teach about them authentically, and using your power and taking action when inequities are evident.

Finally, consider White ally and activist organizations and collectives. If you do not know where to begin, consider starting with these: Building Anti-Racist White Educators (www.barwe215.org), Showing Up for Racial Justice (https://www.showingupforracialjustice.org/), and the White Nonsense Roundup (https://whitenonsenseroundup.com/).

In solidarity,
Francisco and Longoria

Other Goals for Culturally Centering Education

Forbes (1969)	Bigelow et al. (2007)
• Knowledge essential for the nation's development • Personality traits valued by community • Skills for living harmoniously with nature and others and understanding the unity of life • Add "beauty" to the world	• Grounded in the lives of your students • Critical • Multicultural, antiracist, pro-justice • Participatory, experiential • Hopeful, joyful, kind, visionary • Activist • Academically rigorous • Culturally sensitive
Davidman & Davidman (1994)	**Cipolle (2010)**
• Focus on educational equity • Empower students/caregivers • Promote intergroup harmony • Expand the cultural knowledge base • Develop a multicultural perspective • Value cultural diversity • Respond affirmatively to linguistic diversity	• Developing a deeper awareness of self • Developing a deeper awareness and broader perspective of others • Developing a deeper awareness and broader perspective of social issues • Seeing one's potential to make change

Source: Rios & French (2016).

An Action Planning Worksheet
Crafting Your Story

DIRECTIONS: Use this action planning worksheet to think more purposefully and intentionally about what you hope to accomplish as a Black, Indigenous, and Teacher of Color. One way to think about this is that you are creating an outline of the story you want to tell about yourself—yourself as a teacher, and yourself as a BITOC. We encourage you to keep these visible in your workspace, classroom, or somewhere meaningful and likely to remind you of your goals.

Use the prompts below to brainstorm your initial thoughts/reactions.

Intentions—What Goals You Want to Accomplish

- What are the most central reasons why you want to become a teacher?
  - » What is motivating you in this work?
  - » What will sustain you in this work?
- What are the two or three things/intentions you most want to accomplish as a BITOC?
- What will success look like if you are meeting your intentions?
- What is your vision for how you would like to see your career unfold?
- When you think of people describing you as a BITOC, what do you hope they would say that exemplified what you accomplished?
- In the spirit of normalizing pushback, what are some barriers to achieving these goals that you need to address?

Given your answer to these, list two or three key Intentions you want to accomplish:

1. _____
   _____
2. _____
   _____
3. _____
   _____

Assets—What You Already Bring

- What do you feel are your greatest overall strengths as a (an emerging) BITOC?
- What cultural/identity skills or skill sets do you already have?
- What networks/partnerships/support systems stand behind you (think family, friends, community connections, organizations to which you belong, and so on)?

Given your answer to these, list two or three key Assets you are bringing into the profession:

1. _____
   _____
2. _____
   _____
3. _____
   _____

Dispositions—What Kind of Person You Want to Be

- What are those dispositions that you want to be most associated with how you came to the profession and your day-to-day work?
- What would you want students, parents, or colleagues to say about the kind of person and the kind of teacher you are?
- How would those dispositions be of service to you?
- Are the intentions you propose authentic to and sustaining your identities?
- How can you ensure that these dispositions are part of who you are and how you show up?

Given your answer to these, list two or three key Dispositions you hope others see that best exemplify you:

1. _____
   _____
2. _____
   _____
3. _____
   _____

Wonderings—What You Need to Know and Be Able to Do

- What questions do you most need answered as a BITOC?
- What skills do you feel like you most need to cultivate?
- What combination of both personal and professional knowledge and skills are necessary for the specific intentions you have identified for yourself?

Given your answer to these, list two or three key Learnings you need to pursue:

1. _____
   _____
2. _____
   _____
3. _____
   _____

Acting—What You Expect You Will Do

- How will you enact activities connected with your own self-care?
  _____
  _____

- How will you act to foster hope in yourself and others?
  _____
  _____

- How will you address conflicts that might occur in the school setting?
  _____
  _____

- How will you disrupt oppression when you see it occurring?
  _____
  _____

- How will you uncover and affirm students' and families' funds of knowledge and cultural capital?
  _____
  _____

- How will you revitalize and sustain your own cultural/racial identities?
  _____
  _____

Notes

Introduction

1. We recognize that Spanish, like English, is also a colonizing language.

Chapter 1

1. For more details around these issues of inequity, see Nieto and Bode (2018); Gay (2018).

2. It is important to note that we recognize that the notion of what constitutes formal education is contestable. Native communities in the United States have engaged in formal schooling—although unlike what most experience today—since time immemorial (W. Au et al., 2016).

3. It should be noted that there were differing opinions within the Black community about whether it was better to send their children to White schools, a topic we will address later in this chapter.

4. It is important to note that while this was the primary experience, because immigrants congregated among others of their respective social-cultural identity group, and because schools were locally controlled, many of these new immigrants attended schools that provided dual-language instruction (German and English, for example).

5. We use Hispanic/Latino here only because the statistics we draw from federal government statistics use this terminology for these data sets.

Chapter 2

1. We wish to acknowledge that there is an entire academic discipline focused on cross-cultural communication that explores these differences, their meanings, and their implications for interacting, which you can explore as interest allows.

Chapter 3

1. For a more in-depth discussion of the history of and important scholars in multicultural education, see J. A. Banks (2004, 2013); Spring (2017).

2. We acknowledge the limitation of this list (and those we share in the coming pages) in that there were many other, less well-known scholars and activists who also were working around many of these same aims: naming white supremacy, confronting

oppression, challenging deficit/pathological ideologies, and engaging in community uplift. Indeed, all those collective instances of resistance to oppression of marginalized
communities serve as the forerunners of ethnic studies and, later on, multicultural education.

3. We strongly encourage you to review this definition to understand more fully
each of the dimensions contained in it.

Chapter 4

1. For an extended timeline overview of the teaching profession, see Public Broad-
casting Service's *Only a Teacher.* Available at https://www.pbs.org/onlyateacher/about.
html

2. See Kleinfeld (1975) for a more in-depth description of teachers as warm de-
manders.

Chapter 6

1. We found the *Value of Educator Self-Care* webinar from Learning for Justice to be
insightful in this regard (https://www.learningforjustice.org/professional-development/
webinars/the-value-of-educator-selfcare); see also WEST-ED's webinar, *Strategies for
Districts to Support Self-Care for Educators During the COVID-19 Pandemic* (https://
www.wested.org/resources/self-care-for-educators-during-the-covid-19-pandemic/).

Chapter 7

1. The image and description of the painting, in the collection of the Smithsonian
American Art Museum, are available at https://americanart.si.edu/artwork/camas-pa-
ra-suenos-34978

References

Achinstein, B., & Aguirre, J. (2008). Cultural match or culturally suspect: How new Teachers of Color negotiate sociocultural challenges in the classroom. *Teachers College Record, 110*(8), 1505–1540.

Achinstein, B., Ogawa, R., Sexton, D., & Freitas, C. (2010). Retaining Teachers of Color: A pressing problem and a potential strategy for "hard-to-staff" schools. *Review of Educational Research, 80*(1), 71–107.

Affolter, T. L. (2019). *Through the fog: Towards inclusive anti-racist teaching.* Information Age.

Alexander, M. (2020). *The new Jim Crow: Mass incarceration in the age of colorblindness.* New Press.

An, S. (2017), Teaching race through AsianCrit-informed counterstories of school segregation. *Social Studies Research and Practice, 12*(2), 210–231.

Anderson, J. D. (1988). *The education of Blacks in the South, 1860–1935.* University of North Carolina Press.

Andrews, E. (2019). *What is a 'climate refugee' and how many are there?* https://grist.org/article/climate-refugee-number-definition/

Anzaldúa, G. (1990). Haciendo caras, una entrada. In G. Anzaldúa (Ed.), *Making face, making soul: Creative and critical perspectives by feminists of color* (pp. xv–xxviii). Aunt Lute Books.

Aronson, B., & Laughter, J. (2016). The theory and practice of culturally relevant education: A synthesis of research across content areas. *Review of Educational Research, 86*(1), 163–206.

Au, K. H. P., & Jordan, C. (1981). Teaching reading to Hawaiian children: Finding a culturally appropriate solution. In H. T. Trueba, G. P. Guthrie, & K. Au (Eds.), *Culture and the bilingual classroom: Studies in classroom ethnography* (pp. 139–152). Newbury House.

Au, K. H. P., & Kawakami, A. J. (1985). Research currents: Talk story and learning to read. *Language Arts, 62*(4), 406–411.

Au, W., Brown, A. L., & Calderón, D. (2016). *Reclaiming the multicultural roots of U.S. curriculum: Communities of color and official knowledge in education.* Teachers College Press.

Baldwin, J. (1962). A letter to my nephew. *The Progressive, 1.* https://progressive.org/magazine/letter-nephew/

Baldwin, J. (1963). A talk to teachers. *Child Development and Learning,* 7–12.

Baldwin, J. (1965). White man's guilt. *Ebony, 20,* 47–48.

Banks, C. A. M. (2005). *Improving multicultural education: Lessons from the intergroup education movement.* Teachers College Press.

Banks, J. A. (1981). *Multiethnic education: Theory and practice*. Allyn & Bacon.

Banks, J. A. (2004). Multicultural education: Historical development, dimensions, and practice. In J. A. Banks & C. A. M. Banks (Eds.), *Handbook of research on multicultural education* (2nd ed., pp. 3–29). Jossey-Bass.

Banks, J. A. (2008). *Teaching strategies for ethnic studies* (8th ed.). Pearson.

Banks, J. A. (2013). The construction and historical development of multicultural education, 1962—2012. *Theory into Practice, 52*, 73–82.

Banks, J. A. (2017). Diversity and citizenship education in multicultural nations. In Y-K Cha, J. Gundara, S-H Ham, & M. Lee (Eds.), *Multicultural education in glocal perspectives: Policy and institutionalization* (pp. 73–90). Springer.

Bartolome, L. (1994). Beyond the methods fetish: Toward a humanizing pedagogy. *Harvard Educational Review, 64*(2), 173–195.

Beitlers, A., Gourd, T. Y., Krichevsky, B., Newton, M., Shank, R., & Stahl, S. D. (2019). *Recognizing positionality, power, and privilege: Institutionalizing identity caucusing in a secondary teacher education program* [Paper presentation]. American Educational Research Association Annual Conference, Toronto, ON, Canada.

Belenky, M. F., Clinchy, B. M., Goldberger, N. R., & Tarule, J. M. (1986). *Women's ways of knowing* (Vol. 15). Basic Books.

Berliner, D. C. (2006). Our impoverished view of educational research. *Teachers College Record, 108*(6), 949–995.

Berliner, D. C., & Biddle, B. (1995). *The manufactured crisis: Myths, fraud and the attack on America's public schools*. Harper Collins.

Bigelow, B., Christensen, L., Karp, S., Miner, B., & Peterson, B. (2007). *Rethinking our classrooms: Vol 1*. Rethinking Schools.

Bolton, G., & Delderfield, R. (2018). *Reflective practice: Writing and professional development*. Sage.

Bourdieu, P., & Passeron, J. (1977). *Reproduction in education, society and culture*. Sage.

Bowling, N. (2016, January 24). *The conversation I'm tired of not having*. https://www.natebowling.com/a-teachers-evolving-mind/2016/1/24/the-conversation-im-tired-of-not-having

Brayboy, B. M. J. (2005). Toward a tribal critical race theory in education. *The Urban Review, 37*(5), 425–446.

Brayboy, B. M. J., & McCarty, T. L. (2010). Indigenous knowledges and social justice pedagogy. In T. K. Chapman & N. Hobbel (Eds.), *Social justice pedagogy across the curriculum: The practice of freedom* (pp. 184–200). Routledge.

Brazas, C., & McGeehan, C. (2020, Spring). What White colleagues need to understand. *Learning for Justice, 64*. https://www.learningforjustice.org/magazine/spring-2020/what-white-colleagues-need-to-understand

Calabrese Barton, A., & Tan, E. (2020). Beyond equity as inclusion: A framework of "rightful presence" for guiding justice-oriented studies in teaching and learning. *Educational Researcher, 49*(6), 433–440.

Cardenas, B., & Cardenas, J. (1972). The theory of incompatibilities. *Today's Education*, pp. 42–45.

Carter, P., & Darling-Hammond, L. (2016). Teaching diverse learners. In D. H. Gitomer & C. A. Bell (Eds.), *Handbook of research on teaching* (pp. 593–638). American Educational Research Association.

Carter, P. L., & Welner, K. G. (Eds.). (2013). *Closing the opportunity gap: What America must do to give every child an even chance*. Oxford University Press.

Carver-Thomas, D. & Darling-Hammond, L.(2017). Teacher turnover: Why it matters and what we can do about it. The Learning Policy Institute. https://learningpolicy-institute.org/product/teacher-turnover-report

Cazden, C., & Leggett, E. (1981). Culturally responsive education: Recommendations for achieving Lau remedies II. In H. T. Trueba, G. P. Guthrie, & K. Au (Eds.), *Culture and the bilingual classroom: Studies in classroom ethnography* (pp. 69–86). Newbury House.

Centers for Disease Control and Prevention. (2020, July 23). *The importance of reopening America's schools this fall.* https://www.cdc.gov/coronavirus/2019-ncov/community-ty/schools-childcare/reopening-schools.html

Chamberlin, M., & Thompson, P. (1998). *Narrative and genre.* Routledge.

Chang, R. S. (1993). Toward an Asian American legal scholarship: Critical race theory, poststructuralism, and narrative space. *California Law Review, 19,* 1243–1323.

Cherng, H. Y. S., & Halpin, P. F. (2016). The importance of minority teachers: Student perceptions of minority versus White teachers. *Educational Researcher, 45*(7), 407–420.

Cipolle, S. B. (2010). *Service-learning and social justice: Engaging students in social change.* Rowman & Littlefield.

Clark, C. (2012). School-to-prison pipeline. In J. A. Banks (Ed.), *Encyclopedia of diversity in education* (pp. 1894–1897). Sage.

Clark, K. B. (1963). *Prejudice and your child.* Beacon Press.

Clark, S. P., & Brown, C. (1986). *Ready from within: Septima Clark and the civil rights movement, a first person narrative.* Wild Trees Press.

Coates, T. N. (2015). The Black family in the age of mass incarceration. *The Atlantic, 316*(3). https://www.theatlantic.com/magazine/archive/2015/10/the-black-family-in-the-age-of-mass-incarceration/403246/

Collins, C. (2018, May). What is white privilege, really? *Learning for Justice.* https://www.learningforjustice.org/magazine/fall-2018/what-is-white-privilege-really

Collins, P. H. (2002). *Black feminist thought: Knowledge, consciousness, and the politics of empowerment.* Routledge.

Cook-Lynn, E. (2007, Spring). Scandal. *Wicazo Sa Review, 2*(1), 85–89.

Costello, M., & Dillard, C. (2019). *Hate at school.* Southern Poverty Law Center.

Crenshaw, K. (1991). Mapping the margins: Intersectionality, identity politics, and violence against women of color. *Stanford Law Review, 43,* 1241–1299.

Cruz, C. (2012). Making curriculum from scratch: *Testimonio* in an urban classroom. *Equity & Excellence in Education, 45*(3), 460–471.

Cruz, C. (2015). When does resistance begin? In G. Q. Conchas (Ed.), *Cracks in the schoolyard—Confronting Latino educational inequality* (pp. 131–143). Teachers College Press.

Cuauhtin, R. T. (2019a). Ethnic studies pedagogy as CxRxPx. In R. T. Cuauhtin, M. Zavala, C. E. Sleeter, & W. Au (Eds.), *Rethinking ethnic studies* (pp. 26–32). Rethinking Schools.

Cuauhtin, R. T. (2019b). Teaching John Bell's 4 I's of oppression. In R. T. Cuauhtin, M. Zavala, C. E. Sleeter, & W. Au (Eds.), *Rethinking ethnic studies* (pp. 216–217). Rethinking Schools.

Cuauhtin, R. T. (2019c). We have community cultural wealth! In R. T. Cuauhtin, M. Zavala, C. E. Sleeter, & W. Au (Eds.), *Rethinking ethnic studies* (pp. 244–251). Rethinking Schools.

Cuauhtin, R. T., Zavala, M., Sleeter, C. E., & Au, W. (Eds.). (2019). *Rethinking ethnic studies.* Rethinking Schools.

Cummins, J. (2009). Pedagogies of choice: Challenging coercive relations of power in classrooms and communities. *International Journal of Bilingual Education and Bilingualism, 12*(3), 261–271.

Cummins, J., & Early, M. (Eds.). (2011). *Identity texts: The collaborative creation of power in multilingual schools.* Rubicon Press/Pearson.

Cummins, J., Hu, S., Markus, P., & Montero, M. K. (2015). Identity texts and academic achievement: Connecting the dots. *TESOL Quarterly, 49*(3), 555–581.

Daniels, C. L. (2008). From liberal pluralism to critical multiculturalism: The need for a paradigm shift in multicultural education for social work practice in the United States. *Journal of Progressive Human Services, 19*(1), 19–38.

Davidman, L., & Davidman, P. T. (1994). *Teaching with a multicultural perspective: A practical guide.* Longman.

de Brey, C., Musu, L., McFarland, J., Wilkinson-Flicker, S., Diliberti, M., Zhang, A., Branstetter, C., & Wang, X. (2019). *Status and trends in the education of racial and ethnic groups 2018* (NCES 2019-038). U.S. Department of Education, National Center for Education Statistics. https://nces.ed.gov/pubs2019/2019038.pdf

de Oliveira Andreotti, V., Stein, S., Ahenakew, C., & Hunt, D. (2015). Mapping interpretations of decolonization in the context of higher education. *Decolonization: Indigeneity, Education & Society, 4*(1), 21–40.

Dee, T. (2004). Teachers, race, and student achievement in a randomized experiment. *Review of Economics and Statistics, 86*(1), 195–210.

Delgado Bernal, D. (2001). Learning and living pedagogies of the home: The mestiza consciousness of Chicana students. *Qualitative Studies in Education, 14*(5), 623–639.

Delpit, L. (2014a). Ebonics and culturally responsive instruction. In W. Au (Ed.), *Rethinking multicultural education* (pp. 167–174). Rethinking Schools.

Delpit, L. (2014b). Multiplication is for White people. In W. Au (Ed.), *Rethinking multicultural education,* (pp. 17–24). Rethinking Schools.

Deyhle, D., & Swisher, K. (1997). Research in American Indian and Alaska Native education: From assimilation to self-determination. *Review of Research in Education, 22*(1), 113–194.

DiAngelo, R. (2018). *White fragility: Why it's so hard for White people to talk about racism.* Beacon Press.

Dilworth, M. E. (2018). *Millennial Teachers of Color.* Harvard Education Press.

Dilworth, M. E., & Brown, A. L. (2008). Teachers of Color: Quality and effective teachers one way or another. In V. Richardson (Ed.), *Handbook of research on teacher education* (pp. 424–467). American Educational Research Association.

Dixon, D., Griffin, A., & Teoh, M. (2019). *If you listen, we will stay: Why Teachers of Color leave and how to disrupt teacher turnover.* The Education Trust.

Donato, R., & Hanson, J. (2019). Mexican-American resistance to school segregation. *Phi Delta Kappan, 100*(5), 39–42.

Du Bois, W. E. B. (1903). *The souls of Black folk.* A.C. McClurg.

Dumas, M. J. (2010). What is this 'Black' in Black education? Imagining a cultural politics without guarantees. In Z. Leonardo (Ed.), *Handbook of cultural politics and education* (pp. 403–422). Sense.

Dumas, M. J. (2014). 'Losing an arm': Schooling as a site of Black suffering. *Race Ethnicity and Education, 17*(1), 1–29.

Dumas, M. J. (2016). Against the dark: Antiblackness in education policy and discourse. *Theory Into Practice, 55*(1), 11–19.

Dumas, M. J. (2018). Beginning and ending with Black suffering: A meditation on and against racial justice in education. In E. Tuck & K. W. Yang (Eds.), *Toward what justice? Describing diverse dreams of justice in education* (pp. 29–46). Routledge.

Duncan-Andrade, J. (2009). Note to educators: Hope required when growing roses in concrete. *Harvard Educational Review, 79*(2), 181–194.

Dunn, R., Griggs, S. A., Olson, J., Beasley, M., & Gorman, B. S. (1995). A meta-analytic validation of the Dunn and Dunn model of learning-style preferences. *The Journal of Educational Research, 88*(6), 353–362.

Epps, E. (2002). Race and school desegregation: Contemporary legal and educational issues. *Urban Education Journal, 1*(1), 388–393.

Erevelles, N. (2018). Toward justice as ontology: Disability and the question of (in)difference. In E. Tuck & K. W. Yang (Eds.), *Toward what justice? Describing diverse dreams of justice in education* (pp. 77–110). Routledge.

Executive Order No. 13950. (2020). https://www.federalregister.gov/documents/2020/09/28/2020-21534/combating-race-and-sex-stereotyping

Farahmandpur, R., & McLaren, P. (1999). Critical multiculturalism and the globalization of capital: Some implications for a politics of resistance. *Journal of Curriculum Theorizing, 15*(4), 27–46.

Farinde, A. A., LeBlanc, J. K., & Otten, A. S. (2015). Pathways to teaching: An examination of Black females' pursuits of careers as K–12 teachers. *Educational Research Quarterly, 38*(3), 32.

Flores, G. M. (2017). *Latina teachers: Creating careers and guarding culture.* New York University Press.

Forbes, J. D. (1969). *The education of the culturally different: A multi-cultural approach.* Far West Laboratory for Educational Research and Development.

Foster, M. (1997). *Black teachers on teaching.* New Press.

Frankenberg, E., Ee, J., Ayscue, J. B., & Orfield, G. (2019). *Harming our common future: America's segregated schools 65 years after Brown.* https://www.civilrightsproject.ucla.edu/research/k-12-education/integration-and-diversity/harming-our-common-future-americas-segregated-schools-65-years-after-brown/Brown-65-050919v4-final.pdf

Frankenberg, E., & Orfield, G. (Eds.). (2007). *Lessons in integration: Realizing the promise of racial diversity in American schools.* University of Virginia Press.

Freire, P. (1996). *Pedagogy of the oppressed* (Rev. ed.). Continuum. (Original work published 1970)

Freire, P. (2000). *Pedagogy of freedom: Ethics, democracy, and civic courage.* Rowman & Littlefield.

Freire, P., & Freire, A. M. (2002). *Pedagogy of hope: Reliving pedagogy of the oppressed.* Continuum.

Fuentes, E. H., & Pérez, M. A. (2016). Our stories are our sanctuary: Testimony as a sacred of belonging. *Association of Mexican American Educators Journal, 10*(2), 6–15.

Galeano, E. (2007). In defence of the word. *Index on Censorship, 6*(4), 15–20.

Galeano, E. (2013). *Children of the days: A calendar of human history.* Bold Type Books.

Galván, R. (2006). Campesina epistemologies and pedagogies of the spirit: Examining women's sobrevivencia. In D. Delgado Bernal, C. A. Elenes, F. E. Godinez, & S. Villenas (Eds.), *Chicana/Latina education in everyday life: Feminista perspectives on pedagogy and epistemology* (pp. 161–179). State University of New York Press.

Gardner, H. (2011). *Frames of mind: The theory of multiple intelligences.* Hachette.

Gaspar de Alba, A. (1997). *Chicano art: Inside/outside the master's house.* University of Texas Press.

Gay, G. (2000). *Culturally responsive teaching: Theory, research, and practice.* Teachers College Press.

Gay, G. (2003). Introduction: Planting seeds to harvest fruits. In G. Gay (Ed.), *Becoming multicultural educators: Personal journey toward professional agency* (pp. 1–16). Jossey-Bass.

Gay, G. (2010). *Culturally responsive teaching: Theory, research, and practice* (2nd ed.). Teachers College Press.

Gay, G. (2018). *Culturally responsive teaching: Theory, research, and practice* (3rd ed.). Teachers College Press.

Geiger, A. W. (2018). *America's public school teachers are far less racially and ethnically diverse than their students.* Pew Research Center. https://www.pewresearch.org/fact-tank/2018/08/27/americas-public-school-teachers-are-far-less-racially-and-ethnically-diverse-than-their-students/

Gershenson, S., Hart, C., Hyman, J., Lindsay, C., & Papageorge, N. W. (2018). *The long-run impacts of same-race teachers* (No. w25254). National Bureau of Economic Research.

Gist, C., & Bristol, T. (Eds.). (in press). *Handbook of research on Teachers of Color and Indigenous teachers.* American Educational Research Association.

Gordon, J. A. (2000). *The color of teaching.* RoutledgeFalmer.

Gorski, P. (2008). Peddling poverty for profit: A synthesis of criticisms of Ruby Payne's framework. *Equity and Excellence in Education, 41*(1), 130–148.

Gorski, P. C. (2013). *Reaching and teaching students in poverty.* Teachers College Press.

Gramlich, J. (2019). *19 striking facts from 2019.* https://www.pewresearch.org/fact-tank/2019/12/13/19-striking-findings-from-2019/

Grande, S. (2004). *Red pedagogy: Native American social and political thought.* Rowman & Littlefield.

Grande, S. (2014). Save the forest and think like a mountain. In L. Reynolds (Eds.), *Imagine it better: Visions of what school might be* (pp. 14–20). Heinemann.

Grande, S., & Anderson, L. (2017). Un-settling multicultural erasures. *Multicultural Perspectives, 19*(3), 139–142.

Grant, C. A., & Portero, A. (2011). Preface. In C. A. Grant & A. Portero (Eds.), *Intercultural and multicultural education* (pp. xi–xii). Routledge.

Gutiérrez, K. D., & Rogoff, B. (2003). Cultural ways of learning: Individual traits or repertoires of practice. *Educational Researcher, 32*(5), 19–25.

Hamann, E. T., Wortham, S., & Murillo, E. G., Jr. (Eds.). (2015). *Revisiting Education in the new Latino diaspora.* Information Age.

Hammond, Z. (2015). *Culturally responsive teaching and the brain: Promoting authentic engagement and rigor among culturally and linguistically diverse students.* Corwin Press.

Harding, S. (Ed.). (1993). *The "racial" economy of science: Toward a democratic future.* Indiana University Press.

Harding, S. (2007). Feminist standpoints. In S. N. Hesse-Biber (Ed.), *Handbook of feminist research: Theory and praxis* (pp. 45–70). Sage.

Haynes Writer, J. (2010). Broadening the meaning of citizenship education: Native Americans and tribal nationhood. *Action in Teacher Education, 32*(2), 70–81.

Herrnstein, R. J., & Murray, C. (1995). *The bell curve: Intelligence and class structure in American life*. Simon & Schuster.

Hopkins, J. P. (2020). *Indian education for all: Decolonizing Indigenous education in public schools*. Teachers College Press.

Irizarry, J. G., & Raible, J. (2011) Beginning with *el barrio*: Learning from exemplary teachers of Latino students. *Journal of Latinos and Education, 10*(3), 186–203.

Irvine, J. J. (1988). An analysis of the problem of disappearing Black educators. *The Elementary School Journal, 88*(5), 503–513.

Irvine, J. J. (2003). *Educating teachers for diversity: Seeing with a cultural eye*. Teachers College Press.

Jay, M. (2003). Critical race theory, multicultural education, and the hidden curriculum of hegemony. *Multicultural Perspectives, 5*(4), 3–9.

Jung, C. G. (1981). *The archetypes and the collective unconscious* (No. 20). Princeton University Press.

Kasun, G. S. (2018). Chicana feminism as a bridge: The struggle of a White woman seeking an alternative to the eclipsing embodiment of whiteness. *Journal of Curriculum Theorizing, 32*(3), 115–113.

Kendi, I. X. (2017). *Stamped from the beginning: The definitive history of racist ideas in America*. Random House.

Kendi, I. X. (2019). *How to be an antiracist*. One World/Ballantine.

Kingsolver, B. (2010). How to be hopeful. In K. D. Moore & M. P. Nelson (Eds.), *Moral ground: Ethical action for a planet in peril* (pp. 452–457). Trinity University Press.

Kirk, G., & Okazawa-Rey, M. (2004). *Women's lives: Multicultural perspectives* (3rd ed.). McGraw-Hill.

Kleinfeld, J. (1975). Effective teachers of Eskimo and Indian students. *School Review, 83*, 301–344.

Kleinrock, E. (2020, June 30). Anti-racist work in schools: Are you in it for the long haul? *Learning for Justice.* https://www.learningforjustice.org/magazine/antiracist-work-in-schools-are-you-in-it-for-the-long-haul

Klopfenstein, K. (2005). Beyond test scores: The impact of Black teacher role models on rigorous math taking. *Contemporary Economic Policy, 23*(3), 416–428.

Kohl, H. (1994). *I won't learn from you*. New Press.

Kohli, R. (2009). Critical race reflections: Valuing the experiences of Teachers of Color in teacher education. *Race Ethnicity and Education, 12*(2), 235–251.

Kohli, R. (2014). Unpacking internalized racism: Teachers of color striving for racially just classrooms. *Race Ethnicity and Education, 17*(3), 367–387.

Kohli, R. (2016). Behind school doors: The impact of hostile racial climates on urban Teachers of Color. *Urban Education, 53*(3), 307–333.

Kohli, R., & Pizarro, M. (2016). Fighting to educate our own: Teachers of Color, relational accountability, and the struggle for racial justice. *Equity & Excellence in Education, 49*(1), 72–84. https://doi.org/10.1080/10665684.2015.1121457

Kozol, J. (2012). *Savage inequalities: Children in America's schools*. Broadway Books.

Kumashiro, K. K. (2000). Toward a theory of anti-oppressive education. *Review of Educational Research, 70*(1), 25–53.

Kumashiro, K. K. (2002). *Troubling education: Queer activism and antioppressive pedagogy*. Psychology Press.

Ladson-Billings, G. (1994). *The dreamkeepers: Successful teachers of African American children*. Wiley.

Ladson-Billings, G. (1995). Toward a theory of culturally relevant pedagogy. *American Educational Research Journal, 32*(3), 465–491.

Ladson-Billings, G. (1998). Just what is critical race theory and what's it doing in a nice field like education? *International Journal of Qualitative Studies in Education, 11*(1), 7–24.

Ladson-Billings, G. (2004a). Landing on the wrong note: The price we paid for *Brown. Educational Researcher, 33*(7), 3–13.

Ladson-Billings, G. (2004b). New directions in multicultural education. In J. A. Banks & C. A. M. Banks (Eds.), *Handbook of research on multicultural education* (2nd ed., pp. 50–65). Jossey-Bass.

Ladson-Billings, G. (2005). *Beyond the big house: African American educators on teacher education.* Teachers College Press.

Ladson-Billings, G. (2006). From the achievement gap to the education debt: Understanding achievement in U.S. schools. *Educational Researcher, 35*(7), 3–12.

Ladson-Billings, G. (2014). Culturally relevant pedagogy 2.0: Aka the remix. *Harvard Educational Review, 84*(1), 74–84.

Ladson-Billings, G., & Tate IV, W. F. (1995). Toward a critical race theory of education. *Teachers College Record, 97*(1), 47–68.

Ladson-Billings, G., & Tate, IV, W. F. (2016). Toward a critical race theory of education. In A. D. Dixson, C. K. Rousseau Anderson, & J. K. Donnor (Eds.), *Critical race theory in education: All God's children got a song* (2nd ed., pp. 21–41). Routledge.

Lake, R. (Medicine Grizzlybear). (2000, September 1). An Indian father's plea. *Education Week.* https://www.edweek.org/tm/articles/2000/09/01/02indian.02.html

Laura, C. T. (2018). Against prisons and the pipeline to them. In E. Tuck & K. W. Yang (Eds.), *Toward what justice? Describing diverse dreams of justice in education* (pp. 19–28). Routledge.

Lec, S. J. (1969). *More unkempt thoughts.* Funk & Wagnalls.

Lee, T. S., & McCarty, T. L. (2017). Upholding Indigenous education sovereignty through critical culturally sustaining/revitalizing pedagogy. In D. Paris & S. Alim (Eds.), *Culturally sustaining pedagogies: Teaching and learning for justice in a changing world* (pp. 61–82). Teachers College Press.

Lomawaima, K. (2004). Educating Native Americans. In J. A. Banks & C. A. M. Banks (Eds.), *Handbook of research on multicultural education* (2nd ed., pp. 441–461). Jossey-Bass.

Lomawaima, K. T., & McCarty, T. L. (2002). When tribal sovereignty challenges democracy: American Indian education and the democratic ideal. *American Educational Research Journal, 39*(2), 79–305.

Lopez, A. E. (in press). Teacher leadership and activism: A conceptual critical re-imagining. In A. E. Lopez & E. L. Olan (Eds.), *Re-imagining transformative leadership in teacher education.* Information Age.

Lorde, A. (1984). *Sister outsider.* The Crossing Press.

Lorde, A. (1988). *A burst of light.* Firebrand.

Lortie, D. (1975). *Schoolteacher: A sociological study.* University of Chicago Press.

Loutzenheiser, L. W. (2010). Can we learn queerly? Normativity and social justice pedagogies. In T. K. Chapman & N. Hobbel (Eds.), *Social justice pedagogy across the curriculum: The practice of freedom* (pp. 137–159). Routledge.

Lunenberg, M., Korthagen, F., & Swennen, A. (2007). The teacher educator as a role model. *Teaching and Teacher Education, 23*(5), 586–601.

Mabee, C. (1979). *Black education in New York State: From colonial to modern times.* Syracuse University Press.

Macedo, D. (2000). The colonialism of the English only movement. *Educational Researcher, 29*(3), 15–24.

Mann, H. (1848). Report No. 12 of the Massachusetts school board. https://usa.usembassy.de/etexts/democrac/16.htm

McCarthy, C. (1988). Rethinking liberal and radical perspectives on racial inequality in schooling: Making the case for nonsynchrony. *Harvard Educational Review, 58*(3), 265–280.

McIntosh, P. (2007). White privilege: Unpacking the invisible knapsack. In P. S. Rothenberg & C. Hsu Accomando (Eds.), *Race, class, and gender in the United States: An integrated study* (11th ed., pp. 177–182). Worth.

McLaren, P., & Farahmandpur, R. (2002). Breaking signifying chains: A Marxist position on postmodernism. *Marxism against postmodernism in educational theory*, 35–66.

Meier, K. J., Stewart, J., & England, R. E. (1989). *Race, class, and education: The politics of second-generation discrimination.* University of Wisconsin Press.

Milner, H. R., IV. (2006). The promise of Black teachers' success with Black students. *Educational Foundations, 20*, 89–104.

Mohatt, G., & Erickson, F. (1981). Cultural differences in teaching styles in an Odawa school: A sociolinguistic approach. In H. T. Trueba, G. P. Guthrie, & K. Au (Eds.), *Culture and the bilingual classroom: Studies in classroom ethnography* (pp. 105–119). Newbury House.

Moll, L. C., Amanti, C., Neff, D., & Gonzalez, N. (1992). Funds of knowledge for teaching: Using a qualitative approach to connect homes and classrooms, *Theory Into Practice, 31*(2), 132–141.

Montecinos, C. (2004). Paradoxes in multicultural teacher education research: Students of color positioned as objects while ignored as subject. *International Journal of Qualitative Studies in Education, 27*, 167–181.

Muñiz, J. (2019). *Culturally responsive teaching: A 50-state survey of teaching standards.* New America. https://www.newamerica.org/education-policy/reports/culturally-responsive-teaching/

Muñoz, J. (2009). *Cruising utopia: The then and there of queer futurity.* New York University Press.

Musu-Gillette, L., de Brey, C., McFarland, J., Hussar, W., Sonnenberg, W., & Wilkinson-Flicker, S. (2017). *Status and trends in the education of racial and ethnic groups 2017* (NCES 2017-051). U.S. Department of Education, National Center for Education Statistics. https://nces.ed.gov/pubs2017/2017051.pdf

National Education Policy Center. (n.d.). *How to close the opportunity gap: Key policy recommendations.* https://edpolicy.stanford.edu/sites/default/files/Opp%20Gap%20Policy%20Recommendations.pdf

National Museum of American History. (n.d.). *Separate is not equal: Brown v. Board of Education.* https://americanhistory.si.edu/brown/history/2-battleground/pursuit-equality-1.html

Neem, J. (2020, July 31). Does the COVID pandemic spell the end of public schools? *USA Today.* https://www.usatoday.com/story/opinion/2020/07/31/covid-19-and-public-schooling-threat-public-education-column/5521151002/

Neto, S., Iza, D. F. V., & da Silva, M. F. G. (2017). Learning of teaching in the professional socialization in physical education. *Motriz: Revista de Educacão Física, 23*(2). https://

www.scielo.br/scielo.php?script=sci_arttext&pid=S1980-65742017000200308&l-ng=en&tlng=en

Nieto, S. (2006). Solidarity, courage and heart: What teacher educators can learn from a new generation of teachers. *Intercultural Education, 17*(5), 457–473.

Nieto, S., & Bode, P. (2007). *Affirming diversity: The sociopolitical context of multicultural education* (5th ed.). Pearson.

Nieto, S., & Bode, P. (2018). *Affirming diversity: The sociopolitical context of multicultural education* (7th ed.). Pearson.

Oluo, I. (2019). *So you want to talk about race.* Hachette UK.

Osler, A., & Starkey, H. (2017). *Teacher education and human rights.* Routledge.

Paris, D. (2012). Culturally sustaining pedagogy: A needed change in stance, terminology, and practice. *Educational Researcher, 41*(3), 93–97.

Paris, D., & Alim, H. S. (Eds.). (2017). *Culturally sustaining pedagogies: Teaching and learning for justice in a changing world.* Teachers College Press.

Parker, L., & Hood, S. (1995). Minority students vs. majority faculty and administrators in teacher education: Perspectives on the clash of cultures. *The Urban Review, 27*(2), 159–174.

Payne, R. K. (2005). *A framework for understanding poverty.* Aha! Process

Pennycook, A. (2006). *Global Englishes and transcultural flows.* Routledge.

Pérez Huber, L. (2009). Disrupting apartheid of knowledge: *Testimonio* as methodology in Latina/o critical race research in education. *International Journal of Qualitative Studies in Education, 22*(6), 639–654.

Pérez Huber, L., Malagón, M. C., Ramirez, B. R., Camargo Gonzalez, L., Jimenez, A., & Vélez, V. (2015). *Still falling through the cracks.* UCLA Chicano Studies Research Center. https://www.chicano.ucla.edu/files/RR19.pdf

Petchauer, E., & Mawhinney, L. (Eds.). (2017). *Teacher education across minority-serving institutions: Programs, policies, and social justice.* Rutgers University Press.

Philip, T. M., & Brown, A. L. (2020). *We all want more Teachers of Color, right? Concerns about the emergent consensus.* National Education Policy Center. http://nepc.colorado.edu/publication/diversity

Philip, T. M., & Zavala, M. (2016). The possibilities of being "critical": Discourses that limit options for educators of color. *Urban Education, 51*(6), 659–682.

Picca, L. H., & Thompson-Miller, R. (2020). Backstage racism: Implications for teaching. In J. A. Banks & C. A. M. Banks (Eds.), *Multicultural education: Issues and perspectives* (10th ed., pp. 158–173). Wiley.

Portelli, J., & Campbell-Stephens, R. (2009). *Leading for equity: The investing in diversity approach.* EdPhil Books.

Pratt, R. H. (1892). The advantages of mingling Indians with Whites. In I. C. Barrows (Ed.), *Proceedings of the National Conference on Charities and Correction, 19th annual session* (pp. 45–59). Ellis.

Quiñones, S. (2016). (Re)braiding to tell: Using trenzas as a metaphorical–analytical tool in qualitative research. *International Journal of Qualitative Studies in Education, 29*(3), 338–358.

Quiocho, A., & Rios, F. (2000). The power of their presence: Minority group teachers and schooling. *Review of Educational Research, 70*(4), 485–528.

Ramírez, P. C., Ross, L., & Jimenez-Silva, M. (2016). The intersectionality of border pedagogy and Latino/a youth: Enacting border pedagogy in multiple spaces. *The High School Journal, 99*(4), 302–321.

Reeves, F. (1983). *British racial discourse: A study of British political discourse about race and race-related matters.* Cambridge University Press.

Reid, L. (2002) Issues in Indigenous research, *BiiteN,* 11, 16.

Rich, A. (1979). *On lies, secrets, and silence: Selected prose 1966–1978.* W.W. Norton.

Rios, F. (2018). The legacy and trajectories of multicultural education: Recognition, refusal, and movement building in troubling times. *Multicultural Education Review, 10*(3), 165–183.

Rios, F., & French, K. (2016). *Cultivating critical principles of practice from culturally responsive practices* [Paper presentation]. Eastern Oregon University, La Grande, OR, United States.

Rios, F., & Marcus, S. (2011). Multicultural education as a human right: Framing multicultural education for citizenship in a global age. *Multicultural Education Review, 3*(2), 1–36.

Rogers, J., Franke, M., Yun, J. E., Ishimoto, M., Diera, C., Geller, R., Berryman, A., & Brenes, T. (2017). *Teaching and learning in the age of Trump: Increasing stress and hostility in America's high schools.* UCLA's Institute for Democracy, Education, and Access. https://idea.gseis.ucla.edu/publications/teaching-and-learning-in-age-of-trump

Ross, L. J. (2019, Spring). Speaking up without tearing down. *Learning for Justice.* https://www.learningforjustice.org/magazine/spring-2019/speaking-up-without-tearing-down

Salinas, C., Vickery, A. E., & Franquiz, M. (2016). Advancing border pedagogies: Understandings of citizenship through comparisons of home to school contexts. *The High School Journal, 99*(4), 322–336.

San Miguel, G., Jr., & Valencia, R. R. (1998). From the Treaty of Guadalupe Hidalgo to Hopwood: The educational plight and struggle of Mexican Americans in the southwest. *Harvard Educational Review, 68*(3), 353–412.

Santiago, M. (2019). A framework for an interdisciplinary understanding of Mexican American school segregation. *Multicultural Education Review, 11*(2), 69–78.

Schott Foundation. (2016). *Lifting all children up.* http://schottfoundation.org/infographic/lifting-all-children

Scott, D. M. (1997). *Contempt and pity: Social policy and the image of the damaged Black psyche, 1880–1996.* University of North Carolina Press.

Senger, L. G., & Mayer, A. (2019). SJEC annual report. https://wp.wwu.edu/sjec/strategy/

Sensoy, Ö., & DiAngelo, R. (2017). *Is everyone really equal? An introduction to key concepts in social justice education* (2nd ed.). Teachers College Press.

Shannon-Baker, P. (2018). A multicultural education praxis: Integrating past and present, living theories, and practice. *International Journal of Multicultural Education, 20*(1), 48–66.

Sleeter, C. E. (2001). Preparing teachers for culturally diverse schools: Research and the overwhelming presence of whiteness. *Journal of Teacher Education, 52*(2), 94–106.

Sleeter, C. E. (2020). Critical family history: An introduction. *Genealogy, 4*(2), 64. https://doi.org10.3390/genealogy4020064

Sleeter, C., & Delgado Bernal, D. (2004). Critical pedagogy, critical race theory, and antiracist education: Implications for multicultural education. In J. A. Banks & C. A. M. Banks (Eds.), *Handbook of research on multicultural education* (2nd ed., pp. 240–258). Jossey-Bass.

Sleeter, C. E., & Grant, C. A. (2007). *Making choices for multicultural education* (5th ed.). Wiley/Jossey-Bass Education.

Sleeter, C. E., & Zavala, M. (2020). *Transformative ethnic studies in schools: Curriculum, pedagogy, and research.* Teachers College Press.

Smitherman, G., & Smitherman-Donaldson, G. (1986). *Talkin and testifyin: The language of Black America* (Vol. 51). Wayne State University Press.

Solórzano, D. G., & Delgado Bernal, D. (2001). Examining transformational resistance through a critical race and LatCrit theory framework: Chicana and Chicano students in an urban context. *Urban Education, 36*(3), 308–342.

Solórzano, D. G., & Pérez Huber, L. (2020). *Racial microaggressions.* Teachers College Press.

Solórzano, D., & Yosso, T. (2000). Toward a critical race theory of Chicana and Chicano education. In C. Martinez, Z. Leonardo, & C. Tejada (Eds.), *Charting new terrains of Chicana(o)/Latina(o) education* (pp. 35–65). Hampton Press.

Souto-Manning, M., & Cheruvu, R. (2016). Challenging and appropriating discourses of power: Listening to and learning from early career early childhood Teachers of Color. *Equity & Excellence in Education, 49*(1), 9–26.

Spring, J. (2016). *Deculturalization and the struggle for equality.* Routledge.

Spring, J. (2017). *The intersection of cultures: Multicultural education in the United States and the global economy* (4th ed.). Erlbaum.

Stoskopf, A. (1999). The forgotten history of eugenics. *Rethinking Schools, 13*(3), 12–13.

Suárez-Orozco, C., & Suárez-Orozco, M. M. (2009). *Children of immigration.* Harvard University Press.

Sue, D. W. (2010). *Microaggressions in everyday life: Race, gender, and sexual orientation.* Wiley.

Sullivan, D., & Tifft, L. (Eds.). (2008). *Handbook of restorative justice.* Routledge.

Tatum, B. D. (1997). *"Why are all the Black kids sitting together in the cafeteria?"* Basic Books/Hachette.

Taylor, D. (2014). *Toxic communities: Environmental racism, industrial pollution, and residential mobility.* New York University Press.

Teitelman, I. (2015, December 21). On the history of teaching and the value of "women's work". *The Toast.* https://the-toast.net/2015/12/21/history-teaching-womens-work/

Tintiangco-Cubales, A., Kohli, R., Sacramento, J., Henning, N., Agarwal-Rangnath, R., & Sleeter, C. (2015). Toward an ethnic studies pedagogy: Implications for K–12 schools from the research. *The Urban Review, 47*(1), 104–125.

Trump, D. J. [@realDonaldTrump]. (2020, September 5). *Trump orders purge of 'critical race theory' from federal agencies . . . this is a sickness that cannot be allowed to continue* [Tweet]. Twitter. https://twitter.com/realdonaldtrump/status/1302212909808971776?lang=en

Tuck, E. (2009). Suspending damage: A letter to communities. *Harvard Educational Review, 79*(3), 409–428.

Tuck, E. (2014). *Respect & risk: Chasing the benefits of research in Indigenous communities.* YouTube https://www.youtube.com/watch?v=V1nOlwrXG-k

Tuck, E., & Yang, K. W. (2012). Decolonization is not a metaphor. *Decolonization: Indigeneity, Education & Society, 1*(1), 1–40.

Tuck, E., & Yang, K. W. (Eds.). (2018). *Toward what justice? Describing diverse dreams of justice in education.* Routledge.

Ullicci, K., & Battey, D. (2011). Exposing color blindness/grounding color consciousness: Challenges for teacher education. *Urban Education, 46*, 1195–1225.

U.S. Commission on Civil Rights. (2019). *Beyond suspensions.* https://www.usccr.gov/

pubs/2019/07-23-Beyond-Suspensions.pdf

U.S. Department of Commerce, Census Bureau. (2012). *Decennial census of population, (5-percent sample), 1980 to 2010.* https://www.census.gov/newsroom/cspan/1940census/CSPAN_19404.pdf

U.S. Department of Commerce, Census Bureau. (2018). *2018 American community survey 1-year estimates.* https://data.census.gov/cedsci/table?q=ACSDP1Y2018.DP05%20United%20States&g=0100000US&tid=ACSDP1Y2018.DP05&hidePreview=true

U.S. Department of Education, National Center for Education Statistics. (2019). *Spotlight A: Characteristics of public school teachers by race/ethnicity.* https://nces.ed.gov/programs/raceindicators/spotlight_a.asp

U.S. Department of Education, Office of Planning, Evaluation and Policy Development, Policy and Program Studies Service. (2016). *The state of racial diversity in the educator workforce.* http://www2.ed.gov/rschstat/eval/highered/racial-diversity/state-racial-diversity-workforce.pdf

Valencia, R. R. (2002) "Mexican Americans don't value education!" On the basis of the myth, mythmaking, and debunking. *Journal of Latinos and Education, 1*(2), 81–103.

Valenzuela, A. (2010). *Subtractive schooling: U.S.-Mexican youth and the politics of caring.* State University of New York Press.

Vargas, J. A. (2018). *Dear America: Notes of an undocumented citizen.* HarperCollins.

Varghese, M., Daniels, J. R., & Park, C. C. (2019). Structuring disruption within university-based teacher education programs: Possibilities and challenges of race-based caucuses. *Teachers College Record, 121*(4), n4.

Villegas, A. M., & Davis, D. E. (2008). Preparing teachers of color to confront racial/ethnic disparities in educational outcomes. In M. Cochran-Smith, S. Feiman-Nemser, & D. J. McIntyre (Eds.), *Handbook of research on teacher education: Enduring questions in changing contexts* (3rd ed., pp. 583–605).

Villegas, A. M., & Irvine, J. J. (2010). Diversifying the teaching force: An examination of major arguments. *The Urban Review, 42*(3), 175–192.

Villenas, S. (1996). The colonizer/colonized Chicana ethnographer: Identity, marginalization, and co-optation in the field. *Harvard Educational Review, 66*(4), 711–732.

Vought, L. (2020). *Memorandum for the heads of executive departments and agencies (Re: Training in the federal government).* Executive Office of the President. Available at: https://www.whitehouse.gov/wp-content/uploads/2020/09/M-20-34.pdf

Walcott, R. (2018). Against social justice and the limits of diversity: Or Black people and freedom. In E. Tuck & K. W. Yang (Eds.), *Toward what justice? Describing diverse dreams of justice in education* (pp. 85–99). Routledge.

Walia, H. (2018, May 2). *Racism, austerity, and precarity: Canada's role in shaping anti-migrant policies.* World Issues Forum, Western Washington University. https://vimeo.com/267833008

Walker, V. S. (2000). Valued segregated schools for African American children in the south, 1935–1969: A review of common themes and characteristics. *Review of Educational Research, 70*(3), 253–285.

Weiner, L. (2000). Research in the 90s: Implications for teacher preparation. *Review of Educational Research, 70*(3), 369–406.

Whiteplume, B., & Rios, F. (2010). Tooté American Indian teachers? Challenges, assets and decolonizing practices. *Journal of Teacher Recruitment and Retention, 1*(1), 30–44.

Williams, D. R., Lawrence. J. A., & Davis, B. A. (2019) Racism and health: Evidence and needed research. *Annual Review of Public Health, 40,* 105–125.

Yosso, T. J. (2002). Toward a critical race curriculum. *Equity & Excellence in Education, 35*(2), 93–107.

Yosso, T. J. (2005). Whose culture has capital? A critical race theory discussion of community cultural wealth. *Race Ethnicity and Education, 8*(1), 69–91.

Yosso, T. J. (2013). *Critical race counterstories along the Chicana/Chicano educational pipeline.* Routledge.

Zamudio, M., Aragón, C., Alvarez, L., & Rios, F. (2009). Immigrant rights protests in the rural west. *Latino Studies, 7*(1), 109–111.

Zamudio, M., Russell, C., Rios, F., & Bridgeman, J. L. (2011). *Critical race theory matters: Education and ideology.* Routledge.

Zeichner, K. (2009). *Teacher education and the struggle for social justice.* Routledge.

Index

About the Authors

Francisco Rios, PhD, is a professor of secondary education at Woodring College of Education, Western Washington University (WWU). He served as dean of the College from 2011–2017. His research interests include teachers of color, Latinxs in education, and preservice teacher education with a multicultural focus. Francisco was senior associate editor of *Multicultural Perspectives*. He served as president of the National Association for Multicultural Education from 2014–2016.

A Longoria, PhD, is an assistant professor of secondary education at Woodring College of Education, Western Washington University (WWU).